Demystifying Causal Inference

Vikram Dayal · Anand Murugesan

Demystifying Causal Inference

Public Policy Applications with R

Vikram Dayal
Indian Economic Service Section
Institute of Economic Growth
Delhi, India

Anand Murugesan
Central European University
Vienna, Austria

ISBN 978-981-99-3907-7   ISBN 978-981-99-3905-3 (eBook)
https://doi.org/10.1007/978-981-99-3905-3

© The Editor(s) (if applicable) and The Author(s), under exclusive license to Springer Nature Singapore Pte Ltd. 2023

This work is subject to copyright. All rights are solely and exclusively licensed by the Publisher, whether the whole or part of the material is concerned, specifically the rights of translation, reprinting, reuse of illustrations, recitation, broadcasting, reproduction on microfilms or in any other physical way, and transmission or information storage and retrieval, electronic adaptation, computer software, or by similar or dissimilar methodology now known or hereafter developed.

The use of general descriptive names, registered names, trademarks, service marks, etc. in this publication does not imply, even in the absence of a specific statement, that such names are exempt from the relevant protective laws and regulations and therefore free for general use.

The publisher, the authors, and the editors are safe to assume that the advice and information in this book are believed to be true and accurate at the date of publication. Neither the publisher nor the authors or the editors give a warranty, expressed or implied, with respect to the material contained herein or for any errors or omissions that may have been made. The publisher remains neutral with regard to jurisdictional claims in published maps and institutional affiliations.

This Springer imprint is published by the registered company Springer Nature Singapore Pte Ltd.
The registered company address is: 152 Beach Road, #21-01/04 Gateway East, Singapore 189721, Singapore

To Ma and Papa, Varsha and Ranu,
(Vikram Dayal)

To Amma, Appa, Tiziana and Chandru,
(Anand Murugesan)

For understanding and encouragement.

Acknowledgements

Anand remembers a prominent wall-hanging poster in his childhood home that remains burned in his memory. A platinum blonde toddler bore a beaming smile, and in each of his outstretched hands, he was held by two adults helping him walk. It read, "WE ALL NEED A HELPING HAND."

In writing this book, we have surely had many helping hands.

We are grateful to our students who have amplified our curiosity for the topic by asking insightful questions.

We are thankful to Springer in general and Nupoor Singh in particular, who encouraged and supported us from the start.

We thank Marton Vegh for his outstanding research assistance and for initiating the empirical results replication process in R. We are sure he will develop into an exceptional analyst and wish him the best of luck.

We thank Dana Andersen, Edoardo Cefalà, Tiziana Centofanti, Oindrila De, Alexis Diamond, Subhasish Dugar, Simon Hess, Erich Kirchler, Charles Louis-Sidois, Rahul M, Ariel Ortiz-Bobea, Matteo Gamalerio, Ivan Maryanchyk, and SabaWaseem, whom we reached out to for comments.

Vikram would like to acknowledge the Institute of Economic Growth, where he works, for providing an atmosphere conducive to reflection and exploration.

Lastly, Anand would like to thank the Central European University for their generous research support and for granting a sabbatical that helped write this book, as well as the Institute of Advanced Studies Vienna for hosting him as a fellow at the inspiring Strozzi palace during the writing process.

We are both deeply grateful for the opportunities that allowed us to create this work.

Contents

1 John Snow and Causal Inference 1
   1.1 Grey Skies and Cholera Deaths in London 1
   1.2 Curious Dr. Snow's Early Investigations 2
       1.2.1 Unpacking the Mode of Communication
             of Cholera 3
       1.2.2 Snow's Clinical Work on the Pathology of Cholera 5
       1.2.3 Mechanisms and Conditions of Cholera
             Transmission 6
   1.3 Cholera, a Waterborne Disease 6
   1.4 The Interesting but Inconclusive Broad Street Pump
      Incident 8
   1.5 The Grand Experiment in London 9
       1.5.1 Snow's Shoe-Leather Work for Identifying
             the Causal Links 11
   1.6 Snow's Quasi-experimental Design 12
       1.6.1 Treatment Intensity and Comparative Cases 14
   1.7 Archimedean Lever: Instrumental Variables 15
   1.8 Potential Outcomes 16
   1.9 The Chapters Ahead 16
      References 17

2 RStudio and R 19
   2.1 Introduction 19
   2.2 RStudio 19
   2.3 Use Projects and a Script 19
   2.4 Typical R Code 20
       2.4.1 Making a Vector 20
       2.4.2 Installing and Loading Packages 21
       2.4.3 Data 21
       2.4.4 Graphs 21
       2.4.5 Regression 22
   2.5 Bare Bones Example of Working with R 22

	2.6	Resources	30
		2.6.1 For Better Understanding	30
		2.6.2 For Exploring Further	30
		References	31
3	**Regression and Simulation**		33
	3.1	Introduction	33
	3.2	Sampling Distribution and Simulation	33
	3.3	Mean and Regression	34
		3.3.1 Estimating the Mean is the Same as Regressing on a Constant	34
		3.3.2 Sampling Distribution of the Mean	36
	3.4	Bivariate Regression	40
		3.4.1 Bivariate Regression and Conditional Means	40
		3.4.2 Sampling Distribution of the Regression Coefficient in a Bivariate Regression	42
		3.4.3 Estimating a Difference is the Same as Regressing on an Indicator Variable	43
	3.5	The P Value Function: A Tool for Inference	45
	3.6	Systematic and Random Error	51
	3.7	Resources	53
		3.7.1 For Better Understanding	53
		3.7.2 For Going Further	53
		References	54
4	**Potential Outcomes**		55
	4.1	Introduction	55
	4.2	Basic Ideas	55
	4.3	Basic Identity of Causal Inference	57
	4.4	Rubin Doctor Example	57
	4.5	Assumptions for Causal Inference Using Potential Outcomes	59
	4.6	Manski Bounds: Recidivism	60
	4.7	R Code (Corresponding to Section 4.4)	61
	4.8	Resources	63
		4.8.1 For Better Understanding	63
		4.8.2 For Going Further	63
		References	64
5	**Causal Graphs**		65
	5.1	Introduction	65
	5.2	Concepts and Examples	65
		5.2.1 Causal Graphs for Two Variables	66
		5.2.2 Causal Graphs for Three Variables	68
		5.2.3 Causal Graphs with ggdag Package	71

		5.2.4	Assumptions for Causal Inference Using Causal Graphs	72
		5.2.5	Electoral Systems	73
		5.2.6	Collider Bias in Public Health	73
	5.3	R code		75
		5.3.1	Causal Graphs for two Variables (Corresponding to Section 5.2.1)	75
		5.3.2	Causal Graphs for Three Variables (Corresponding to section 5.2.2)	76
		5.3.3	ggadag use (Corresponding to section 5.2.3)	78
		5.3.4	Electoral Systems (Corresponding to section 5.2.5)	78
	5.4	Resources		79
		5.4.1	For Better Understanding	79
		5.4.2	For Going Further	79
		References		80
6	**Experiments**			81
	6.1	Introduction		81
	6.2	Examples and Concepts		82
		6.2.1	Anchoring Affects Judgments	82
		6.2.2	Women as Policymakers	84
		6.2.3	Small Class Size and Student Learning Outcomes	88
		6.2.4	Simulate to Understand	92
	6.3	R Code		96
		6.3.1	Anchoring Affects Judgments	96
		6.3.2	Women as Policymakers	99
		6.3.3	Small Class Size and Student Learning Outcomes	101
		6.3.4	Simulate to Understand	105
	6.4	Resources		107
		6.4.1	For Better Understanding	107
		6.4.2	For Going Further	107
		References		108
7	**Matching**			109
	7.1	Introduction		109
	7.2	Concepts and Examples		110
		7.2.1	Lalonde's Study	110
		7.2.2	Simple Numerical Example	111
		7.2.3	Generating Apples to Apples	113
		7.2.4	Exact Matching	115
		7.2.5	Coarsened Exact Matching	116
		7.2.6	Decentralized Forest Management	116
		7.2.7	Propensity Score Matching	118
		7.2.8	Mahalanobis Distance Matching	120
		7.2.9	Genetic Matching	120
		7.2.10	Model Dependence and Cherry-Picking	123

	7.3	R Code	124
		7.3.1 Lalonde's Data	124
		7.3.2 Decentralized Forest Management	127
		7.3.3 Your Turn, Compensation for Injury	130
	7.4	Resources	132
		7.4.1 For Better Understanding	132
		7.4.2 For Exploring Further	132
		References	133
8	**Instrumental Variables**		135
	8.1	Introduction	135
	8.2	Concepts and Examples	136
		8.2.1 A Basic Example with an Encouragement Design	136
		8.2.2 Prologue to Leveraging Instrumental Variables	140
		8.2.3 Colonial Origins of Economic Development	142
		8.2.4 Globalization, Voter Preferences, and Brexit	147
		8.2.5 Wrights' Lever Solves the 'Chicken and Egg Problem'	150
		8.2.6 Taxes and Consumption of Cigarettes	152
		8.2.7 Overidentification Test is only Indicative of IV Validity	155
	8.3	R Code	158
		8.3.1 A Basic Example with an Encouragement Design	158
		8.3.2 Colonial Origins of Economic Development	160
		8.3.3 Globalization, Voter Preferences, and Brexit	161
		8.3.4 Taxes on Consumption of Cigarettes	162
		8.3.5 Overidentification is Only Indicative of IV Validity	164
	8.4	Resources	165
		8.4.1 For Better Understanding	165
		8.4.2 For Going Further	166
		References	168
9	**Regression Discontinuity Design**		169
	9.1	Introduction	169
	9.2	Concepts and Examples	170
		9.2.1 Minimum Legal Drinking Age and Fatalities in the US	170
		9.2.2 Term Limits and Politician Performance in Brazil	173
		9.2.3 Rural Roads and Economic Development in India	176
	9.3	R Code	179
		9.3.1 Minimum Legal Drinking Age and Fatalities in the US	179
		9.3.2 Term Limits and Politician Performance in Brazil	181
		9.3.3 Rural Roads and Economic Development in India	184
		9.3.4 Simple Example with Simulation	185

	9.4	Resources	191
		9.4.1 For Better Understanding	191
		9.4.2 For Going Further	191
		References	192
10	**Panel Data and Fixed Effects**		**193**
	10.1	Introduction	193
	10.2	Concepts and Examples	194
		10.2.1 Schooling and Wages	194
		10.2.2 Alcohol Policies and Traffic Fatalities	198
		10.2.3 Causal Graphs for Panel Data	202
		10.2.4 Income and Democracy	209
	10.3	R Code	212
		10.3.1 Schooling and Wages	212
		10.3.2 Alcohol Policies and Traffic Fatalities	214
		10.3.3 Causal Graphs for Panel Data	217
		10.3.4 Income and Democracy	221
	10.4	Resources	223
		10.4.1 For Better Understanding	223
		10.4.2 For Going Further	223
		References	226
11	**Difference-in-Differences**		**227**
	11.1	Introduction	227
	11.2	Concepts and Examples	228
		11.2.1 Worker Injury Benefits and Time Out of Work	228
		11.2.2 Great Depression Policies to Avoid Banking Collapse	231
		11.2.3 Snow's Prototype DID Design	234
		11.2.4 Assumptions and DID Validity	235
		11.2.5 Informative Bounds on the Effect of Right-to-Carry Gun Laws	237
		11.2.6 The Synthetic Control Method	240
	11.3	R Code	243
		11.3.1 Worker Injury Benefits and Time Out of Work	243
		11.3.2 Great Depression Policies to Avoid Banking Collapse	244
		11.3.3 Informative Bounds on the Effect of Right-to-Carry Gun Laws	246
		11.3.4 Economic Costs of German Reunification	247
	11.4	Resources	251
		11.4.1 For Understanding Better	251
		11.4.2 For Going Further	251
		References	253

12 Integrating and Generalizing Causal Estimates 255
- 12.1 Introduction 255
- 12.2 Concepts and Examples 256
  - 12.2.1 Statistical Approach 256
  - 12.2.2 Analyses Guided by the Potential Outcomes Framework 258
  - 12.2.3 Analyses Guided by Causal Graphs 263
- 12.3 R Code 266
  - 12.3.1 Statistical Approach 266
  - 12.3.2 Analyses Guided by the Potential Outcomes Framework 276
  - 12.3.3 Analyses Guided by Causal Graphs 287
- 12.4 Resources 291
  - 12.4.1 For Better Understanding 291
  - 12.4.2 For Going Further 291
  - References 293

About the Authors

Vikram Dayal is a Professor at the Institute of Economic Growth, Delhi. He has been using the R software in teaching quantitative economics to diverse audiences and is the author of two popular Springer publications titled *An Introduction to R for Quantitative Economics: Graphing, Simulating and Computing*, and *Quantitative Economics with R: A Data Science Approach*. He has published research on a range of environmental and developmental issues, from outdoor and indoor air pollution in Goa, India, to tigers and Prosopis juliflora in Ranthambore National Park. He studied economics in India and the USA and received his doctoral degree from the Delhi School of Economics, University of Delhi.

Anand Murugesan is an Associate Professor at the Central European University in Vienna. He combines insights from economics and related disciplines with causal inference tools, including lab and lab-in-the-field experiments, and observational data, to study social problems. He holds a Ph.D. from the University of Maryland College Park and studied at the Jawaharlal Nehru University in New Delhi.

John Snow and Causal Inference

1.1 Grey Skies and Cholera Deaths in London

In the early months of 2020, the world was caught off guard as the COVID-19 pandemic spread rapidly. Epidemiologists and medical experts scrambled to understand its cause and mode of transmission. The pressing question was: what was driving the outbreaks, and how was the virus transmitted? Initially, health policy officials advised the public to focus on handwashing and avoid close contact. They assumed that the contagion spread through physical proximity and contact, much like the common cold. However, thanks to the accumulation of knowledge, advanced statistical methods, and technological advancements, experts swiftly identified the true vector of transmission: airborne aerosols carrying the coronavirus. Within a matter of weeks, wearing face masks became mandatory worldwide, reflecting the importance of rapidly identifying the cause for effective policy responses.

In stark contrast to the swift identification of COVID-19's mode of transmission, several historical episodes were different. Even as late as the nineteenth century, there were long lags between disease outbreaks and the identification of their causes. Early records of Asiatic Cholera spread in the Madras Province of India, date back to 1769. Yet, it was not until the devastating cholera outbreak of 1831–32 in London, where the mortality rose to 38 per 10,000 inhabitants, that policymakers finally took note of the disease (Snow 1849). London was visibly plagued by unsanitary conditions, overflowing sewage, smog-filled air, and foul odors. The prevailing belief in the 1830s, the Miasma theory, attributed the spread of Cholera to polluted air. It took several decades for the true understanding of cholera's spread to emerge, thanks to the heroic efforts and tireless investigations of an extraordinary doctor in England—Doctor John Snow.

Snow's suspicion about the airborne spread of cholera likely arose from observing patients during the 1831 cholera outbreak in England. The prevailing belief then was that cholera was transmitted through the air. This belief had implications for hygiene practices, prevention strategies, and quarantine policies. Remarkably, Snow was just a 16-year-old medical apprentice working in Newcastle-Upon-Tyne at the time (Ramsay 2006). However, before the cholera outbreak in London in 1849, Snow had established himself as a highly respected medical doctor. He had gained recognition for investigating the safety and effectiveness of using chloroform (or ether) as an anesthetic.

1.2 Curious Dr. Snow's Early Investigations

In 1849, Snow's attention was again drawn to cholera when he saw clustered fatalities occurring in different parts of Europe, including his hometown London. He observed that cholera patients primarily suffered from acute intestinal problems rather than issues affecting the lungs or other organs. This led Snow to question the prevailing belief that cholera spread through airborne particles. He followed his intuition and considered the possibility that contaminated water might be the primary cause of the disease.

Motivated by his suspicions, Snow conducted a thorough investigation over several months in 1849. He compiled his findings in a concise 31-page pamphlet. In this 1849 monograph, Snow boldly challenged the prevailing Miasma theory by presenting compelling case studies and many pieces of evidence. He articulated his skepticism, "It used to be generally assumed that if Cholera were a catching or communicable disease, it must spread by effluvia given off from the patient into the surrounding air and inhaled by others into the lungs. This assumption led to very conflicting opinions respecting the disease".

While promising, Snow's 1849 monograph on cholera did not provide definitive evidence to establish that contaminated water was the cause of the cholera spread. Snow faced the daunting task of refuting arguments in favor of the Miasma theory. Additionally, the theory suggested that these airborne particles could indirectly contribute to cholera outbreaks by contaminating water sources. We can visualize this argument underlying the Miasma theory through a graph (Fig. 1.1).

Pearl and Mackenzie (2018) provide an illuminating account of the science of cause and effect, employing causal graphs as their preferred analytical tool. In our book, we also use causal graphs to depict the relationships between variables (see Chap. 5). Figure 1.1, adapted from Pearl and Mackenzie (2018), represents the pivotal causal inference issue in Snow's investigation. It highlights how the Miasma theory challenged Snow's causal claim that water quality was the cause of cholera. Miasma, in theory, can affect cholera directly, but also indirectly by affecting water quality.

Fig. 1.1 Causal graph for cholera, adapted from Pearl and Mackenzie (2018)

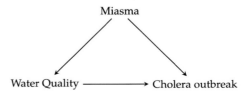

1.2 Curious Dr. Snow's Early Investigations

While Miasma threw a spanner in the investigations of Snow, his resolve to find a lever to refute the Miasma theory and establish water contamination as the true cause of cholera will become clear in the rest of this chapter. Snow methodically changed the discourse on the spread of cholera over a decade, beginning with his 1849 monograph, "On the mode of communication of cholera".

Snow's second edition of the monograph, published in 1855, is a remarkable tour de force exemplifying a skilled researcher's use of scientific methods, data, and grit in drawing inferences. It underscores the notion that causal inference is more than data and methods. In the monograph, Snow integrates various forms of evidence to pin down cause and effect. Through case-by-case detective work, clinical observations on the disease's pathology, microscopic examination of water quality, rigorous data collection efforts, ingenious mapping techniques, innovative methods, and compelling narratives, Snow shows that contaminated water was the primary cause of the spread of cholera.

Snow analyzed data from various sources, including a large-scale natural experiment in London. His innovative method of identifying cause and effect is a precursor to the difference-in-differences method in causal inference. In Chap. 11, we delve into the difference-in-differences method, and in Chap. 10, we explore the related topic of panel data. Using early versions of these methods, among others, Snow tested his hypothesis that contaminated water was responsible for cholera deaths.

Snow compared the incidence of cholera between the treated group (with access to relatively clean water) and the control group (without such access). He ensured that the control and treated groups were similar in all aspects except for the exposure, adhering to the principle of comparing 'apples-to-apples'. In Chap. 6, we discuss experiments that use random assignment to achieve such similarity, and in Chap. 7, we discuss matching methods that establish similarity between the treatment and control groups based on observed characteristics.

Snow's sleuth work in identifying the killer has been celebrated in both popular books and academic writings (Tufte 1997; Coleman 2019; Pearl and Mackenzie 2018). In the upcoming sections of this chapter, we delve into the different approaches employed by Snow in his investigation, highlighting his contributions as an early master of causal inference.

1.2.1 Unpacking the Mode of Communication of Cholera

Snow begins his 1849 monograph with a brief historical account of Cholera and its spread. He highlights a cholera outbreak in the former Madras Presidency in 1814, where one battalion 'mysteriously' suffered a severe attack while another was left unscathed, which we will return to at the end of this chapter. With his usual clarity and flair, Snow writes about the nature of cholera spread: "[cholera]...travels along the great tracks of human intercourse, never going faster than people travel, and generally much more slowly. In extending to a fresh island or continent, it always appears first at a sea-port. It never attacks the crews of ships going from a country free from Cholera, to one where the disease is prevailing, till they have entered a port, or had intercourse (meaning contact) with the shore. Its exact progress from town to town cannot always be traced but it has never appeared except where there has been ample opportunity for it to be conveyed by human intercourse".

Dr. Snow discusses several cases to support this initial argument that cholera spreads from person to person. One such case is that of Mr. John Barnes, who contracted Cholera and passed it on to his wife, as well as two others who visited him. Mr. Barnes's sister had died of cholera two weeks before Mr. Barnes. The sister had no children, so her clothes were shipped to Mr. Barnes in a closed box. Mr. Barnes fell ill the day after opening the box. Furthermore, Barnes's mother had visited her ailing daughter before her death and later became ill. She was placed next to her bedridden husband while their other daughter cared for them. Tragically, all three succumbed to cholera within two days.

Snow connects the dots in these case studies to provide evidence for person-to-person transmission. He meticulously includes specific information such as dates, individuals involved and their interactions, locations, and modes of travel. These precise details serve to tighten the nuts and bolts of the causal links in his argument. For example, mentioning that "clothes were shipped in a closed box" helps determine if the contagion was contained before the healthy person's exposure to possible contamination. Additionally, the inclusion of dates and hours of the attack and death further reinforces the connections between cause and effect. Here is another gripping narrative from Dr. Snow:

> Mrs. Kneeshaw was attacked with Cholera on Monday, 9 September, and her son William on the 10th. He died on Saturday the 15th; she lived three weeks; they lived at Pocklington. On Sunday, 16 September, Mr. and Mrs. Flint, Mr. and Mrs. Giles Kneeshaw, and two children, went to Pocklington to see Mrs. Kneeshaw. Mrs. Flint was her daughter. They all returned the same day, except Mr. M. G. Kneeshaw, who stayed at Pocklington, until Monday, 24 September, when he returned to York. At three o'clock on the same day, he was attacked with Cholera, and died on Tuesday, 25 September, at three o'clock in the morning. There had been no cholera in York for some time. On Thursday, 27 September, Mrs. Flint was attacked but recovered. On Saturday, 29 September, her sister, Mrs. Stead, came from Pocklington to York, to attend to her was attacked on Monday, 1 October, and died on 6 October.

After documenting numerous interconnected stories that indicated person-to-person transmission of cholera, Dr. Snow reaches a preliminary conclusion in the 1849 monograph. He posits that Cholera spreads from one person to another, stating,

> It would be easy, by going through the medical journals and works which have been published on Cholera to quote as many cases as similar to the above as would fill a large volume. But the above instances are quite sufficient to show that Cholera can be communicated from the sick to the healthy for it is quite impossible that even a tenth part of these cases of consecutive illness could have followed each other by mere coincidence, without being connected as cause and effect.

Despite Snow's efforts in his 1849 monograph, the belief that cholera was transmitted through the air remained unchanged. However, when a new cholera epidemic struck London in 1854, Snow was determined to tackle the causal question of cholera

1.2 Curious Dr. Snow's Early Investigations

spread with renewed vigor. In the preface to the second edition of his work, Snow expresses his hope "that my present labours will receive the same kind consideration from the Medical Profession which has been accorded to my former endeavours to ascertain the causes of cholera".

1.2.2 Snow's Clinical Work on the Pathology of Cholera

Dr. Snow's second edition of the cholera monograph, published in 1855, begins by delving into the pathology of the disease. Drawing upon his medical expertise and firsthand experience in treating cholera patients, Snow astutely observes that cholera primarily affected the alimentary canal, rather than the lungs of his patients. This suggests that the causative agent was ingested rather than inhaled. The lungs would have been affected if the contamination had been airborne.

Furthermore, Snow examines clinical evidence, specifically focusing on the significant differences in the fecal samples of cholera patients compared to other patients, indicating that the cholera agent was ingested as either food or drink. In contrast, Snow finds no notable changes in the blood toxicity or cardiac operations of cholera patients, further supporting the hypothesis that cholera is transmitted through the water rather than through the air.

In the language of causal inference, Snow's approach (in the previous paragraph) can be recognized as identifying the treatment mechanism by carefully examining the effects and non-effects of the treatment, in this case, of contaminated water. By studying the specific outcomes that the treatment should affect, such as diseases of the alimentary canal, and the placebo outcomes that the treatment should not affect, such as lung diseases, Snow deduces the mechanism of the effect. In his clinical examination, Snow concludes that, "the morbid material producing cholera must be introduced into the alimentary canal—must, in fact, be swallowed accidentally."

It is important to note that the bacteriological theory of disease had not yet been established by 1855, and the limitations of microscopes prevented him from directly observing the bacteria, vibrio cholerae, as we now know it. However, these limitations did not hinder Snow from noting that "the structure of the cholera poison cannot be recognised by the microscope, for the matter of smallpox and of chancre (a type of ulcer) can only be recognised by their effects, and not by their physical properties". Snow keenly observes that the incubation period or reproduction of cholera "progeny" is significantly shorter than in "most other epidemic or communicable diseases,...between twenty-four to forty-eight hours..." This quick reproduction he argues is the reason for rapid cholera spread.

Although the existence of bacteria was unknown at the time, Snow recognizes the cholera poison as an organic substance and that "the disease is due to the crop or progeny". These insights may have aided discoveries in the field of germ theory, most notably by Louis Pasteur in 1859.[1]

1.2.3 Mechanisms and Conditions of Cholera Transmission

Snow's investigative prowess extends beyond identifying the pathology of cholera to tracing its mode of transmission. He observes that cholera spreads through close contact with bodily discharges from an infected person to a healthy individual, noting that medical professionals, who adhere to strict sanitization procedures, are less susceptible to the disease. Snow's ingenuity for causal inference is striking, as here he is describing the mechanisms of the treatment (i.e., 'bodily discharges') and how the treatment can be blocked through sanitization.

He sheds light on the relationship between occupational and living conditions and the spread of the disease by observing that poverty makes individuals more prone to cholera, particularly people living in cramped and poorly lit conditions, as it "prevents dirt from being seen". He notes that *'lunatic patients'* suffer greatly as "they are no more careful than children in the use of their hands. It is with the greatest difficulty that they can be kept even moderately clean".[2]

In his investigation of cholera deaths among those who bought stale meat from a vendor who died of cholera, Snow provides 'decisive proof' that air particles did not transmit cholera. He found that all those who further cooked that batch of meat from the vendor, treating it with heat, survived. Yet, most of those who consumed the meat with little processing died of cholera. This indicated that heat disinfected the poison and supported Snow's theory that contaminated water is the primary vehicle for Cholera transmission.

1.3 Cholera, a Waterborne Disease

Snow's investigation led him to identify the main culprit behind the spread of the disease: contaminated water. He gathers evidence from a cluster of cases that occurred during the 1849 epidemic on Thomas Street. In this area, the drinking water was

---

[1] Pasteur's contemporary Robert Koch, expounded on the germ theory a few years later. Hungarian-born Ignaz Semmelweis, a physician at Vienna General Hospital, further emphasized the importance of sanitization during medical procedures to prevent hospital deaths and disease spread in the following decade.

[2] Relatedly, he examines the case of miners, noting that they are more susceptible to cholera compared to other occupations as they work in close proximity and take meals with unwashed hands. While addressing an objection by Dr. Baly regarding the high incidence of cholera among miner's wives and children, Snow speculates that this may be attributed to the crowded living conditions in mining communities. He suggests that an inquiry would likely reveal that miners were affected first, followed by their families a day or two later, with women being more affected as they provide care for the sick. While Snow lacked empirical data to substantiate this claim, he wraps up with a flourish, "I leave this objection and Dr. Baly's to combat each other".

1.3 Cholera, a Waterborne Disease

supplied by Southwark and Vauxhall Waterworks Company. The first cases of cholera were reported on July 20th and 21st. Mr. Vinen, who attended to these cases stated that "evacuations were passed into the beds", and the water used for washing this linen was dumped back into the well that supplied drinking water for several members in the court (a group of houses around an open area). Subsequently, women and children living in seven of the fourteen houses in the court fell ill.[3]

Snow personally examined the water taken from the tanks located behind the houses affected by cholera in Albion Terrace. What he discovered was alarming. He found the water to be "offensive, and the deposit possessed the odor of privy soil," and "in it various substances which had passed through the alimentary canal, having escaped digestion," suggesting that fecal matter had contaminated the drinking water. Snow concludes that the 'cholera evacuations' getting into the water caused the disease to spread.

In making his case for waterborne spread at Albion Terrace, Snow challenges a fellow physician's report to the Board of Health that supported the Miasma theory. The report attributed cholera at Albion Terrace chiefly to three supposed causes: (1) foul odor carried by the wind from an open sewer in Battersea Fields, (2) unpleasant odors from kitchen sinks of houses, and (3) the accumulation of sewer water in one specific house ('the house No. 13'). Snow systematically rebuts each of these points, unraveling their flaws.

Regarding the first point, Snow notes that several streets and houses were exposed to the same wind and emanations, and "yet they were quite free from the malady", demonstrating that wind alone cannot explain the outbreak at Albion Terrace. Moving on to the second point, Snow observes that bad smells from the kitchen sinks were a common occurrence and of "almost universal prevalence". Therefore, they cannot explain the sudden and localized eruption in Albion Terrace. As for point three, Snow notes that the two houses (No. 8 and 9) that were flooded by a rainstorm and had the most offensive odors were actually less severely affected by cholera. This contradicts the claim that the accumulation of sewer water in house No. 13 was the specific cause of the outbreak.

In the light of these arguments, Snow firmly concludes that "it remains evident then, that the only special and peculiar cause connected with the great calamity .. was the state of the water". He contends that contaminated water, rather than the suggested causes led to this outbreak.

To reinforce the evidence for this theory of contaminated water as the cause of cholera, Snow presents several compelling examples. In a case in Rotherhithe, only one house out of seven houses remained unaffected by Cholera. The other six houses obtained their water from a ditch connected to the Thames, receiving "contents of the privies of all the seven houses". This resulted in twenty-five cases of Cholera and fourteen deaths, except for the single house that had access to its own water

---

[3] Interestingly, Snow observed that the men, who were likely away at work during the day, did not become sick. He suggests that the men did not drink the contaminated water, reinforcing the connection between water consumption and cholera transmission.

pump.[4] Snow recounts numerous such instances where houses that used one source of water suffered from Cholera while those that used another source escaped Cholera to underscore his causal claim.

1.4 The Interesting but Inconclusive Broad Street Pump Incident

Let's turn our attention to one of the most iconic aspects of Snow's study: the Broad Street water pump. As Snow (1855, p. 38) describes,

> The most terrible outbreak of Cholera which ever occurred in this kingdom is probably that which took place in Broad Street, Golden Square, and the adjoining streets, a few weeks ago. Within two hundred and fifty yards of the spot where Cambridge Street joins Broad Street, there were upwards of five hundred fatal attacks of Cholera in ten days.

This map of Broad Street created by Snow has become a landmark in the fields of data visualization, epidemiology, and causal inference (e.g., see Tufte 1997; Pearl and Mackenzie 2018). The two-dimensional map effectively portrays the relationship between the cause (the contaminated water pump) and the effect (the spatial distribution of cholera deaths) with great impact. By incorporating the spatial distribution of deaths, the map enhances our understanding of cause-effect relationship in a way that tables or graphs cannot achieve. In contemporary research, scholars continue to build upon Snow's ideas of causal inference leveraging spatial data, using advanced methods like spatial regression discontinuity design. We discuss the method of regression discontinuity design in Chap. 9.

During this investigation, Snow highlighted the concentration of deaths around the pump and the steep decline in areas farther away or inaccessible due to 'circuitous roads.' He noted that even when the deaths occurred at a distance from the pump, the victims were likely consuming the pump water, often due to work or schooling in close proximity. Snow clarifies that he was making an apples-to-apples comparison by noting that the outbreak affected people across different socio-economic classes from 'the poor Irish' to 'private houses.' However, the mortality rate was proportionate to the population of each class, emphasizing the strict relationship between the nature of water supply and cholera epidemic rather than due to other confounding causes.

To gather more detailed information, Snow conducted interviews with local residents, obtaining data on the timing of the cholera attacks and fatalities for over eighty deaths. Using this data, he constructed a timeline of the outbreak and determined that the peak of the epidemic had occurred before the removal of the pump handle. Based

---

[4] Similarly, Snow recounts an incident on a street in Salford, Manchester, where sewer water accidentally mixed up with well water, causing 26 cases of Cholera and twenty-five deaths in the thirty houses that used that well water. In contrast, sixty neighboring homes that used a different water source and did not experience any cases of cholera or deaths.

on the timing of cholera cases and his ingenious mapping of the spatial distribution of deaths in the area, Snow tentatively concludes that the pump on Broad Street may have been the source of the outbreak. While Snow cautioned against attributing the decline solely to the removal of the pump handle as the attacks were already diminishing, he believed that this intervention may have prevented a recurrence in the neighborhood (Coleman 2019).

Although Snow's physical inspection of the water from the Broad Street pump did not reveal any noticeable organic impurity that would have explained the cholera outbreak, he discovered that almost all the 90 deaths occurred near the pump. Even among the ten deaths closer to another pump, the majority still preferred water from the Broad Street pump, with three children attending school near the pump. He documented that 61 of the deceased who were closer to the pump indeed used the water source "either constantly or occasionally", and that the cause of death in only six cases could not be ascertained.[5]

Snow, as is his wont acknowledged the limitations of his Broad Street case study, recognizing the missing data on deaths of individuals who had moved away, become incapacitated, or died. However, he argued that these missing data did not diminish the topographical "correctness of the map" as they, i.e., both the observed and missing data, he assumes would be distributed proportionately within the affected district.

Finally, Snow emphasizes the importance of considering all available data, even if it contradicted the preferred hypothesis. He highlighted the case of a 59-year-old London resident living on West End Street, away from the Broad Street pump. Although her death initially seemed like an outlier, further investigation revealed that she preferred the taste of water from Broad Street and sent a cart to fetch it every morning. She died on 9 September, 1854, along with her ill-fated niece who had visited her. No other cases of cholera were reported during that time on West End Street. By tracing the cause of these deaths back to Broad Street pump, Snow demonstrated the significance of paying attention to seemingly isolated incidents (Tufte 1997). He credited Dr. Fraser, who had documented the West End deaths, emphasizing the importance of acknowledging and crediting the rightful sources of information. The story of the Broad Street pump (now Broadwick street) has become legendary and continues to be retold in various popular and academic publications. The John Snow Society even reenacts the events in London, to commemorate its historical significance (Pearl and Mackenzie 2018).

1.5 The Grand Experiment in London

In his 1855 research monograph, Snow expanded his focus to the broader context of densely populated London and the contamination of River Thames that flowed

---

[5] Furthermore, many food and drink establishments operated in the area and used the pump water, which could explain some of the other cases. For instance, a coffee shop owner in the vicinity reported that 9 of her customers were dead.

through it. He observed that the city's sewers discharged sewage into the Thames, leading to contamination downstream. Snow noted that in 1832, North and South London experienced differing mortality rates, with the higher death rate in the South attributed to its reliance on the contaminated Thames water. Two prominent water supply companies, the Southwark and Vauxhall Waterworks Company (SVC) and Lambeth Water Company (Lambeth), competed for customers in the same districts of London. SVC sourced its water from the Thames at Battersea Fields, downstream from where the London sewers entered the river. Lambeth obtained its supply opposite Hungerford Market, also downstream from the sewers.

However, during the middle of the 19th century, London underwent many changes in its water supply, which Snow saw as an opportunity for what he calls a 'Grand Experiment.' Between 1849 and August 1853, London remained free of cholera. Even so, in 1852, Lambeth changed its water source to the cleaner Thames Ditton upstream, north of London, removing it from the polluted waters near Hungerford Market. Snow observed a reduction in mortality due to the change by Lambeth, stating "It thus appears that the districts partially supplied with the improved water suffered much less than the others, although in 1849, when the Lambeth Company obtained their supply opposite Hungerford Market, these same districts suffered quite as much as those supplied entirely by the Southwark and Vauxhall Company". Snow's remark suggests that prior to the change to a cleaner source, areas served by Lambeth experienced cholera deaths similarly to deaths in areas served by SVC. However, this changed after Lambeth moved its supply to a cleaner source, now enjoying relatively lower deaths.

Snow further classified the regions into sub-districts to reveal the difference in mortality rates between the two water companies. Following the change in water source, Lambeth's rank in terms of mortality rates dropped significantly compared to 1849 (see Snow (1855), Table 5, p. 71). These facts provided "very strong evidence" of contaminated water from SVC being the cause of cholera. To provide "incontrovertible proof on one side or the other", Snow closes in on areas where the two companies' water supply is intermixed and both supply the "rich and poor; houses large and small".

Snow was delighted to find this intermixing situation created a natural experiment due to the accidental and even distribution of customers treated with clean (Lambeth) or dirty (SVC) water in the very same areas. He emphasized the large scale of the experiment, involving over 300,000 households, and highlighted that it yielded a balanced comparison,

> As there is no difference whatever, either in the houses or the people receiving the supply of water or in the physical conditions surrounding them, no experiment could be better than that which happened on a grandest scale by accident here. More than three thousand houses of both sexes, of every age and occupation, and of every rank and station, from gentlefolks down to the very poor, were divided into two groups without their choice, and, in most cases, without their knowledge; one group being supplied with water containing the sewage of London and, amongst it, whatever might have come from cholera patients, the other group having water free from such impurity (Snow, 1855, p. 75).

1.5 The Grand Experiment in London

Snow's careful arguments underscored the apples-to-apples comparisons afforded by the 'Grand Experiment.' He reasoned similarly to what Rosenbaum (2017, p. 101) describes as a natural experiment: "some key elements of a randomized experiment occur on their own, even though the investigator neither creates nor assigns the treatments". Rosenbaum (2017, p. 65) further describes the treatment assignment in a randomized experiment as if "a coin is flipped repeatedly, assigning one person to treatment, another to control. As in a fair lottery, everyone has the same chance: the coin flips favor no one. Rich or poor, wise or foolish, everyone suffers a fate determined by luck" (See more on this in Chap. 6 on Experiments).

1.5.1 Snow's Shoe-Leather Work for Identifying the Causal Links

Snow spared 'no exertion' to learn which houses received clean water (treated), and which suffered with water "containing the sewage of London", during the 1853 epidemic. He obtained permission from the authorities to access the addresses of cholera-afflicted individuals in districts where the water supply from the two companies was mixed. Specifically, in the Kennington and Lambeth sub-districts where both SVC and Lambeth supplied water, Snow found a significant disparity in cholera deaths. Out of 44 deaths, 38 occurred in houses supplied by SVC, only 4 in houses supplied by Lambeth, and the remaining 2 deaths in houses with private pump wells.

Snow extended his investigation to other sub-districts where both companies supplied water and found similar disproportionate numbers of deaths in houses supplied by SVC compared to Lambeth. To support his conclusions, Snow conducted tests on the water quality of the two companies. He found substantial differences in the 'chloride of silver' content, with SVC's water containing nearly 50 times more content than that of Lambeth.[6] The difference between the samples of these companies was visible to the naked eye. However, as a man of science, Snow relied on the test results to support his conclusions, while using ocular inferences as only corroborating evidence.

Personally, Snow enquired about every death in most of the sub-districts with mixed water supply, enlisting the help of "a medical man, Mr. John Joseph Whiting", to make enquires in the remaining areas. In the first four weeks of his investigation, Snow recorded 334 cholera deaths, of which a staggering 286 occurred in houses supplied by SVC and only 14 in houses supplied by Lambeth. The remaining deaths were attributed to other sources, including cases where water was directly obtained by "dipping a pail in the Thames".

During the 1853 epidemic, SVC supplied water to 40,046 houses, while Lambeth supplied water to 26,107 houses. Snow's investigation revealed a significant difference in the proportion of deaths between the two companies. For every 10,000 houses, there were 71 deaths in houses supplied by SVC to only 5 deaths in houses supplied by Lambeth, meaning there were fourteen times more fatalities when SVC

---

[6] This may be unrelated to cholera but indicates high sewage content in SVC.

Table 1.1 Deaths from Cholera in houses supplied water by different companies

	Number of houses	Deaths from cholera	Deaths per 10,000 houses
Southall and Vauxhall Company	40,046	1263	315
Lambeth Company	26,107	98	37
Rest of London	256,423	1,422	59

supplied water. In August 1853, over half of the 563 deaths in London were among SVCs customers, with most of the remaining deaths occurring among mariners or those who directly obtained drinking water from the Thames. Snow noted that as the epidemic progressed, the per capita deaths between the two companies began to converge due to other means of communication and high population density, which led to (what we now call) spillover effects from the treated to the control groups. However, even after seven weeks, there were still 8 to 9 times more deaths per 10,000 houses supplied by SVC compared to Lambeth as indicated in the difference-in-means table (Table 1.1) reproduced from Table 9 in Snow's (1855) original monograph.

1.6 Snow's Quasi-experimental Design

To assess the causal effect of the treatment, water quality on the outcome, and disease incidence, randomized controlled trials may not always be feasible. However, in RCTs, the treatment and control groups are randomized, which allows researchers to argue that the confounding factors are no longer an issue. If such biases are accounted for, one could use the difference in means between the outcome variable (cholera deaths) for the treated (Lambeth) and control groups as estimates of the causal impact of treatment (as we will see in Chap. 6). However, unobservable confounders can threaten causal inference in observational studies and even in quasi-experimental settings.

Snow was intuitively aware of these limitations. For instance, Snow observed that a third water company, Chelsea, obtained water from the Thames but used processes to clean it and supplied it to the 'most fashionable parts of London'. In contrast, SVC and Lambeth delivered it mostly without processing or cleaning the water. However, today's critics may argue the possibility of selection biases arising, even in this arguably apples-to-apples comparison.

Snow also recognized other threats to inference, such as changes in the river over time due to population, abolition of cesspools, and adoption of water closets (in his nod to time-varying effects, see Chap. 10 on Panel data). To address these concerns, Snow innovatively devised a quasi-experimental design by comparing the cholera deaths in 1849 and 1854 for SVC and Lambeth customers (see Table 1.2). Many consider Snow's design to be a precursor to the Difference-in-Differences (DID) method—a popular causal inference technique, particularly in policy studies (see more on DID in Chap. 11).

1.6 Snow's Quasi-experimental Design

Table 1.2 Difference in Cholera: comparing deaths in 1849 to 1854 by London sub-districts

Sub-districts (Number)	1849	1853	1854
Control (12)	2,261	2,458	197
Fully-treated (4)	162	37	−125
Partially treated (16)	3905	2547	−1358

Snow arranged the mortality table by which water companies served the districts (rows in Table 1.2) and by year (columns in Table 1.2). The treated group in this empirical design consisted of customers who received Lambeth's improved water, after the company changed its water source to a cleaner upstream location in 1852, with cholera deaths recorded in 1849, which was before the treatment (change in water source) and in 1854, which was after the treatment. Importantly, there was no cholera epidemic in London during the intervening years, which simplifies the empirical design and ensures a clean comparison between the two points.

In Snow's study, he compared the number of cholera deaths in districts served solely by SVC (control) to those served exclusively by Lambeth (treated), or by both Lambeth and SVC (partially treated). His meticulous comparison involved examining the differences in deaths before and after the implementation of the clean-water intervention in Lambeth treated districts and comparing them to equivalent differences in the control or partially treated districts. This approach is considered a prototype design of the DID (difference-in-differences) method for estimating causal effects.

Table 1.2 (adapted) from Snow's study illustrated a significant decrease in cholera deaths in fully treated sub-districts supplied by Lambeth between 1849 and 1854. The number of deaths decreased by 125, representing a sharp drop of 77%. In contrast, the control group (SVC) experienced an increase of 197 cholera deaths during the same period, which amounted to a notable increase of 9%. In the regions that were served by both Lambeth and SVC, considered as partially treated, there was a decline in cholera deaths from 3905 to 2547, signifying a significant reduction of 34% in cholera deaths. Snow interpreted these findings as evidence that adopting Lambeth's water sourcing policy from the upstream Thames could have potentially saved around 1000 lives if SVC had implemented it.

In our Difference-in-Differences chapter (Chap. 11), the comparative case of two banking districts during the Great Depression is very similar to Snow's analysis of the natural experiment in London. Similar to the intermingling of water supply in South London, the two banking districts within Mississippi adopted different policies immediately after the Depression. The treated banking district received generous liquidity aid, comparable to Lambeth's switch to a cleaner water source. The difference-in-differences estimate can be calculated by comparing the difference in bank collapses before and after the treatment in the treated district with the same difference in the control district.

1.6.1 Treatment Intensity and Comparative Cases

Snow's study of the treated sub-districts found that the higher the proportion of supply by Lambeth in the area, the greater the decrease in cholera. In other words, the reduction in cholera deaths was proportional to the intensity of the treatment effect. For example, within the partially treated sub-districts, the percentage reduction in cholera was close to but lower than the fully treated sub-districts. Curiously, Snow found that among the partially treated regions, for instance, Waterloo Road 1st had chiefly filthy and narrow streets but suffered little Cholera (69% decrease between 1849 to 1854); and Lambeth Church 1st despite hosting "a number of skinyards and other factories" witnessed an even sharper decline in cholera deaths (77% decrease). All these facts aligned with Snow's theory of waterborne transmission rather than the Miasma theory.

To further strengthen his comparisons, Snow identified controlled conditions such as prisons and workhouses (homeless shelters), where movements were restricted, and cleaner comparisons could be made. Workhouses like Newington and Lambeth (a district), supplied by Lambeth Company, recorded only three cholera deaths among their inmates, while St. George's workhouse, supplied by SVC, reported six cholera deaths among a smaller inmate population, which translated to six times higher mortality in St. George compared to the Newington and Lambeth. Snow highlighted the case of the workhouse in Poland Street, where despite being surrounded by houses experiencing severe cholera outbreaks, only thirty-five inmates out of five hundred died from Cholera. The workhouse had its pump well on the premises, providing cleaner water to the inmates.[7]

Similarly, Snow observed that some regions of North and East London where water was obtained from the upstream Thames, despite its poverty and density, were not affected as much by cholera as in South London. He noted the influence of seasonal factors, such as low Thames flow during the summer months, leading to increased concentration of sewage water and corresponding cholera cases. As the rains returned and the river flow increased, cholera cases began to decline.

Snow refuted the argument put forth by Dr. Farr that the elevation of a district from sea level determined cholera incidence. He provided counter-examples, such as high-lying Brixton experiencing higher cholera deaths compared to many low-lying districts. Snow points out that low-lying areas supplied with contaminated water suffered cholera greatly in 1849, while improved water supply in 1854 in the same regions provided them relative immunity compared to surrounding areas. In other words, Snow emphasized that changes in water quality, rather than elevation, played a significant role in determining the cholera outcomes.

In the case study of Newcastle-upon-Tyne, Snow described a policy intervention where the water company changed the water source (treatment) in response to public

---

[7] Similarly, none of the seventy men working at a Broad Street brewery suffered from Cholera. The workers were allowed a certain quantity of malt liquor which may have staved off Cholera attacks. Additionally, the brewery had a deep well on its premises and never obtained water from the Broad Street pump.

complaints about the unpleasant smell of their drinking water. The water company stopped drawing water from the River Tyne on 15 September. Within the next couple of days, the pipes ran out of water, coinciding precisely with the peak of deaths on 16 September, after which the Cholera deaths began to decline over the next week.

We conclude by revisiting the mysterious 1814 outbreak in Trichinopoly (now in Tamil Nadu), where the locals believed that one battalion suffered severe cholera attacks ('the wrath of heaven') due to the desecration of sacred tanks when the sepoys bathed in it. However, Snow examined archival materials and concluded that it was contaminated water and not outraged heavens that were the cause of the outbreak. The cholera-afflicted battalion of sepoys from the 9th Native Infantry had their water supplied from low-lying tanks likely contaminated with vibrio cholerae bacteria, while the fortunate 5th Native Infantry, received water from wells remained spared from the disease. Snow concluded the open-and-shut case "with a considerable degree of certainty, that each battalion was supplied with water from a source distinct from the other" (Snow 1855).

1.7 Archimedean Lever: Instrumental Variables

Doctor Snow's tireless investigation into the cholera outbreak in London is a remarkable example of the use of causal reasoning to uncover the true cause of a phenomenon. Beyond the case-by-case investigations, Snow found the metaphorical lever with the Grand Experiment in London and also literally where the pump handle at Broad Street was removed. The lever disengaged water contamination from the Miasma confounders, showing that the culprits were waterborne and without an alibi. In the London 'Grand Experiment,' the two water companies supplied clean and contaminated water in the same neighborhoods, giving Snow an external lever to refute the prevailing Miasma theory of cholera. Pearl and Mackenzie (2018) admire Snow's painstaking detective work with causal diagrams (see Chap. 5) to clarify the relationship between the water company, water quality and cholera.

Figure 1.2 illustrates the relationships between variables in Snow's Grand Experiment with causal graphs and clarifies the causal arrows between the water company, water quality, miasma, and cholera attacks. Importantly, the graph shows no causal arrow between Miasma in the air and the water supply by companies. Instead, there is a causal arrow between the water company (Lambeth) and water quality.

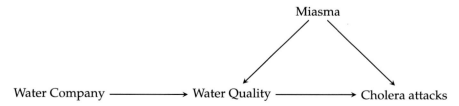

Fig. 1.2 Causal graph for cholera with instrumental variable, adapted from Pearl and Mackenzie (2018)

Additionally, Snow implies that the water company does not directly affect cholera, except through water quality. There is no causal arrow going from the Water company to Cholera. These three conditions are the essence of the modern method of instrumental variables, discussed in Chap. 8.

1.8 Potential Outcomes

Today's practitioners of causal inference in many fields, including epidemiology, extensively use the potential outcomes framework and causal graphs. Coleman (2019) brings in the potential outcomes framework while discussing Snow's work (p. 18): "The basic question for any treatment, say consuming clean water in the case of cholera, is whether the outcome (mortality) is different when the treatment is applied (clean water) versus when it is not (contaminated water). This is asking a hypothetical or counterfactual question—would an individual's chance of dying from cholera be lower when drinking clean water? This counterfactual is an important question but impossible to measure empirically because the individual drinks either clean water (treated) or contaminated (control). One cannot measure the same person both treated and not". In Chap. 4, we delve into the potential outcomes framework to help readers in thinking about causal questions.

1.9 The Chapters Ahead

This chapter highlighted the groundbreaking work of John Snow in epidemiology and how it has paved the way for many strands of modern causal inference. Today, we have affordable computing power and software capable of handling large datasets. In the upcoming chapters, we will use the R software and briefly discuss regression, a versatile statistical tool.

Two chapters will cover complementary frameworks for thinking about causal inference: potential outcomes and causal graphs. We then delve into specific designs and methods: experiments, matching, instrumental variables, regression discontinuity design, panel data, and difference-in-differences. In the final chapter, we will revisit public health applications, such as assessing the effectiveness of the Bacille Calmette-Guérin (BCG) vaccine, to address how policymakers can draw meaningful inferences from multiple studies. We will explore methods to integrate and generalize the findings from individual studies in Chap. 12. We will discuss the internal and external validity of studies.

References

Coleman, Thomas. 2019. Causality in the Time of Cholera: John Snow As a Prototype for Causal Inference. (March 2019).

Pearl, Judea, and Dana Mackenzie. 2018. *The Book of Why: The New Science of Cause and Effect*, 1st ed. Basic Books, New York. (May 2018).

Ramsay, Michael A.E. 2006. John Snow, MD: Anaesthetist to the Queen of England and Pioneer epidemiologist. *Proceedings* (Baylor University. Medical Center), 19 (1): 24–28. (January 2006).

Rosenbaum, Paul R. (2017). *Observation and Experiment: An Introduction to Causal Inference*. Cambridge, MA: Harvard University Press. (August 2017).

Snow, John. 1849. *On the Mode of Communication of Cholera*. John Churchill.

Snow, John. 1855. *On the Mode of Communication of Cholera*. John Churchill (2nd Ed), pp. 1–162. London.

Tufte, Edward R. 1977. *Visual Explanations: Images and Quantities*. Cheshire, Conn: Evidence and Narrative. Graphics Press. (January 1997).

RStudio and R

2.1 Introduction

R is an open-access software that has impressive data analysis capabilities. RStudio makes working with R easier. In this chapter, we provide an introduction to RStudio and working with R.

2.2 RStudio

RStudio has 4 panes (Fig. 2.1). The top left pane displays R script files when open. We recommend that you work in an R script and not in the console, which is the bottom left pane, although you can run commands there. Apart from R scripts, one can also work with R markdown files and other types of documents, all of which open in the top left pane. Output on running a command in R will display in the console, in the bottom left pane. The top right pane shows an Environment tab in which objects that are created or loaded are displayed. There is an Import Dataset icon which can be used to load data. The bottom right pane displays files in the Files tab, and Plots in the Plots tab. One can install packages via the Packages tab.

2.3 Use Projects and a Script

RStudio is convenient to use. We strongly urge the use of projects and scripts. Projects help us keep all relevant files in one place. Data, scripts, and output files are all in the project. We also suggest that scripts or other file types like R Markdown should be used. Certainly, the console should not be used directly.

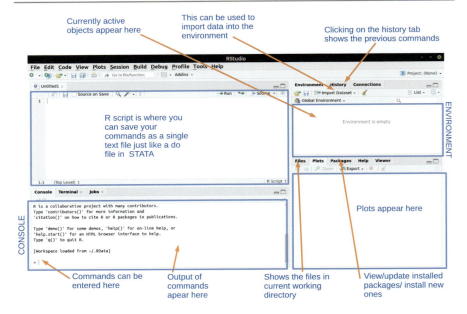

Fig. 2.1 RStudio

2.4 Typical R Code

In R, there are several ways of doing things.[1] And there are many things that we can do. It helps to remember that R code typically has this form:

| new object | ← | function | (| object or formula | , | object information | , | options |) |

In this section, we show some of the main ways that R is used. In the next section, we will work through a basic example where we go from creating a simple dataframe in R to working with data, running a regression, and plotting data.

2.4.1 Making a Vector

We can make a vector as follows.

```
X <- c(21, 31, 34)
```

This makes a vector called X, and the c function is concatenated. The three values 21, 31, and 34 are put in parentheses ( ).

---

[1] This section draws on Dayal (2020, Sect. 1.6).

2.4.2 Installing and Loading Packages

Working with R is all about working with packages. We need to install a package only once:

```
install.packages("tidyverse")
```

Here the function is install.packages. The 'tidyverse' package is the name of the package. Note that here the name of the package to be installed is in quotes.

We load the tidyverse package when we need to use it:

```
library(tidyverse)
```

The function used is the library function.

2.4.3 Data

We can get a data file called myfile into R, and name it myfile:

```
myfile <- read.csv("myfile.csv")
```

The data is read in with a function that reads CSV files, the name of the dataset is in quotes and a dataframe called myfile is created in R.

2.4.4 Graphs

We can draw a histogram of variable x with:

```
library(tidyverse) # to load the tidyverse package
ggplot(mydata, aes(x = x)) +
  geom_histogram()
```

The ggplot function is used, mydata is the dataframe, and we indicate which variable is to be plotted, and what geometric object with geom_histogram.

We can draw a scatterplot of y against x with:

```
ggplot(mydata, aes(x = x, y = y)) +
  geom_point()
```

Compare the code for the scatterplot with the code used for a histogram.

2.4.5 Regression

To regress y on x and z, we use:

```
reg.mod <- lm(y ~ x + z, data = mydata)
```

We store the results in an object after fitting a linear model with lm. We provide the formula and the data to be used.

To get regression output, we can use:

```
summary(reg.mod)
```

2.5 Bare Bones Example of Working with R

We will create some data, and first create some variables as vectors. We will then save the vectors as a dataframe. We then read the dataframe into R and work with it.

In what follows we use typewriter font for R commands, R output begins with ##.

We begin with a variable called Num for number. We create it as a vector in R.

```
Num <- c(1:6)
```

Num is created as an object in R and will be visible in the Environment panel (see Fig. 2.1).

We can print the vector:

```
Num
## [1] 1 2 3 4 5 6
```

To get the third value of num, we use:

```
Num[3]
## [1] 3
```

R is case-sensitive, and if we address Num as num, R protests that we have made an error:

```
num
```

```
## Error in eval(expr, envir, enclos): object 'num' not found
```

Errors can be frustrating. But we can learn from our errors. Everyone makes errors. Once we get a feel for R through repeated use, we make fewer errors and also can understand what went wrong. Persist!

2.5 Bare Bones Example of Working with R

We will now create another vector Y:

```
Y <- c(1000, 3000, 5000, 6000, 2000, 7000)
```

We print Y:

```
Y
## [1] 1000 3000 5000 6000 2000 7000
```

We can create another related vector Y2:

```
Y2 <- Y / 1000
Y2
## [1] 1 3 5 6 2 7
```

We will create a vector called Lev (for level):

```
Lev <- c("Low", "Low", "High", "High", "High", "High")
```

Another variable called X:

```
X <- c(22, 23, 21, 13, 15, 21)
```

We create a dataframe consisting of Num, Y, Y2, Lev, and X, using the data.frame function:

```
Data <- data.frame(Num, Y, Y2, Lev, X)
```

☞ **Your turn.** In order to learn more about data.frame, run ?data.frame. A help page will open up in the Help tab in RStudio (Fig. 2.1, bottom right pane). Read the page.

We print out Data, and can see the rows and columns; observations are in rows and variables are in columns:

```
Data
##    Num    Y Y2  Lev  X
## 1    1 1000  1  Low 22
## 2    2 3000  3  Low 23
## 3    3 5000  5 High 21
## 4    4 6000  6 High 13
## 5    5 2000  2 High 15
## 6    6 7000  7 High 21
```

We can view the second row of Data with:

```
Data[2, ]
##   Num    Y Y2 Lev  X
## 2   2 3000  3 Low 23
```

Notice that we use [2,] in the case of a dataframe. [2,] tells R that the second row is required, and because there is no number after 2, all columns are selected.

We will now load the `tidyverse` package, which is convenient for working with data and for graphing data.

We will first have to install tidyverse if it is not installed already, and then we load it every time we need to use it.

```
#install.packages("tidyverse")
library(tidyverse)
```

```
## ─ Attaching packages ─────────
## v ggplot2 3.4.0      v purrr   0.3.5
## v tibble  3.1.8      v dplyr   1.0.10
## v tidyr   1.2.1      v stringr 1.5.0
## v readr   2.1.3      v forcats 0.5.2
## ─ Conflicts ─ tidyverse_conflicts() ─
## x dplyr::filter() masks stats::filter()
## x dplyr::lag()    masks stats::lag()
```

Tidyverse is actually a collection of packages that work well together.

We now write our data to a csv file, using the `write_csv` function:

```
write_csv(Data, "Data2.csv")
```

We can read in the file, Data2.csv that we had created, after loading the `readr` package (contained in `tidyverse`):

```
Data2 <- read_csv("Data2.csv")
```

Because Data2.csv is in the project in which we are working, we do not need to provide a file path above. We confirm that we have the same data that we created:

```
Data2
## # A tibble: 6 x 5
##     Num     Y    Y2 Lev       X
##   <dbl> <dbl> <dbl> <chr> <dbl>
## 1     1  1000     1 Low      22
## 2     2  3000     3 Low      23
## 3     3  5000     5 High     21
## 4     4  6000     6 High     13
## 5     5  2000     2 High     15
## 6     6  7000     7 High     21
```

2.5 Bare Bones Example of Working with R

A `tibble` is a special type of a dataframe, and works with the `tidyverse`. We can extract the X and Lev variables from Data2 as follows:

```
Data2$X
## [1] 22 23 21 13 15 21
Data2$Lev
## [1] "Low"  "Low"  "High" "High" "High"
## [6] "High"
```

We can use a few data verbs to work with data; these data verbs are functions in the tidyverse package, and their names are suggestive of their function.

While using the tidyverse package, we can chain commands together with the pipe %>% symbol. See the following comments:

```
# is used for comments

# the pipe symbol is %>%
```

We can `filter` data:

```
Data2 %>%
  filter(Lev == "High")
## # A tibble: 4 x 5
##      Num     Y    Y2 Lev       X
##    <dbl> <dbl> <dbl> <chr> <dbl>
## 1     3  5000     5 High     21
## 2     4  6000     6 High     13
## 3     5  2000     2 High     15
## 4     6  7000     7 High     21
```

We took the tibble Data2, and then filtered it, so we are left only with those observations where Lev is 'High'. Note the use of a double equal to sign (==).

We can save the result of the filtering exercise above as DataHigh:

```
DataHigh <- Data2 %>%
  filter(Lev == "High")
DataHigh
## # A tibble: 4 x 5
##      Num     Y    Y2 Lev       X
##    <dbl> <dbl> <dbl> <chr> <dbl>
## 1     3  5000     5 High     21
## 2     4  6000     6 High     13
## 3     5  2000     2 High     15
## 4     6  7000     7 High     21
```

We can create a new variable with `mutate`:

```
Data2 <- Data2 %>%
  mutate(YbyY2 = Y/Y2)
Data2
## # A tibble: 6 x 6
##      Num     Y    Y2 Lev       X YbyY2
##    <dbl> <dbl> <dbl> <chr> <dbl> <dbl>
## 1     1  1000     1 Low      22  1000
## 2     2  3000     3 Low      23  1000
## 3     3  5000     5 High     21  1000
## 4     4  6000     6 High     13  1000
## 5     5  2000     2 High     15  1000
## 6     6  7000     7 High     21  1000
```

We saved the new variable to Data2 itself, Y/Y2 is 1000 for all observations, as expected.

We can arrange the data with `arrange`:

```
Data2 %>%
  arrange(Y)
## # A tibble: 6 x 6
##      Num     Y    Y2 Lev       X YbyY2
##    <dbl> <dbl> <dbl> <chr> <dbl> <dbl>
## 1     1  1000     1 Low      22  1000
## 2     5  2000     2 High     15  1000
## 3     2  3000     3 Low      23  1000
## 4     3  5000     5 High     21  1000
## 5     4  6000     6 High     13  1000
## 6     6  7000     7 High     21  1000
```

We can `select` the columns Y and X.

```
Data2 %>%
  select(Y, X)
## # A tibble: 6 x 2
##        Y     X
##    <dbl> <dbl>
## 1   1000    22
## 2   3000    23
## 3   5000    21
## 4   6000    13
## 5   2000    15
## 6   7000    21
```

We now summarize the data, grouping Y by Lev (using `group_by`).

2.5 Bare Bones Example of Working with R

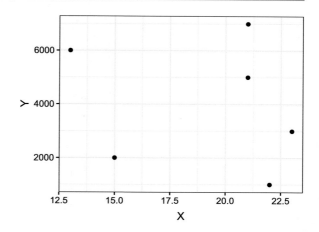

Fig. 2.2 Scatterplot of Y versus X

```
Data2 %>%
  group_by(Lev) %>%
  summarize(meanY = mean(Y))
## # A tibble: 2 x 2
##   Lev   meanY
##   <chr> <dbl>
## 1 High   5000
## 2 Low    2000
```

The mean of Y for the group where Lev is High is 5000, and the group where Lev is Low is 2000.

The R software is well known for its graphing capabilities, and the ggplot2 package is one of the most downloaded and popular packages.

We create a scatterplot of Y against X (Fig. 2.2):

```
ggplot(data = Data2, aes(x = X, y = Y)) +
  geom_point() +
  theme_bw()
```

We tell R that we want to use the `ggplot` function with the `tibble` Data2. We use `aes` (aesthetic) to communicate the variables in the data that are to be plotted. We also tell R that we want it to plot points (`geom_point`), which are one type of geom, or geometric object. We like to use the classic dark-on-light ggplot2 theme, `theme_bw`.

We can plot by Lev, using color (Fig. 2.3); we add a `col` option as an input in `aes`.

```
ggplot(data = Data2, aes(x = X, y = Y,
                         col = Lev)) +
  geom_point() +
  theme_bw()
```

Fig. 2.3 Scatterplot of Y versus X, color coded by Lev

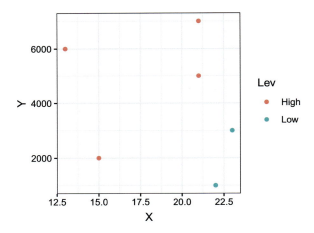

We can fit a linear model (lm):

```
lm(Y ~ X, data = Data2)
##
## Call:
## lm(formula = Y ~ X, data = Data2)
##
## Coefficients:
## (Intercept)            X
##      6033.4        -106.1
```

We can also plot the fitted line in the scatter plot (Fig. 2.4), using geom_smooth:

```
ggplot(data = Data2, aes(x = X, y = Y)) +
  geom_point() +
  geom_smooth(method = "lm", se = F) +
  theme_bw()
```

We often run several regressions. It is convenient to present regressions in a table. For this, we use the texreg package as follows. The package has very good documentation. We can present our very basic regression with texreg as follows (Table 2.1):

```
mod <- lm(Y ~ X, data = Data2)
library(texreg)
texreg(list(mod),
       caption = "Regression of Y on X",
       caption.above = TRUE,
       include.adjrs = FALSE)
```

2.5 Bare Bones Example of Working with R

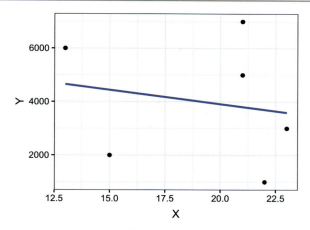

Fig. 2.4 Scatterplot of Y versus X, with line of fit

Table 2.1 Regression of Y on X

	Model 1
(Intercept)	6033.40
	(5514.16)
X	−106.09
	(282.31)
R^2	0.03
Num. obs.	6

***$p < 0.001$; **$p < 0.01$; *$p < 0.05$

Note that we are using texreg to produce output in a pdf document. Screenreg can be used, see below (it can also print in the console).

```
screenreg(list(mod),
         include.adjrs = FALSE)
## 
## ======================
##             Model 1   
## ----------------------
## (Intercept)  6033.40  
##             (5514.16) 
## X           -106.09   
##             (282.31)  
## ----------------------
## R^2           0.03    
## Num. obs.     6       
## ======================
## *** p < 0.001; ** p < 0.01; * p < 0.05
```

☞ **Your turn** Work through the bare bones example above, using an R script. Try changing the data while working through the example.

2.6 Resources

2.6.1 For Better Understanding

1. Datacamp's online course, Introduction to R, by Jonathan Cornelissen https://www.datacamp.com/courses/.
2. Datacamp's online course, Introduction to the Tidyverse, by David Robinson https://www.datacamp.com/courses/.

2.6.2 For Exploring Further

Grolemund and Wickham's (2017) book *R for Data Science*.

Packages Used in this Chapter

The citations for the packages used in this chapter are[2] :

```
## R Core Team (2021). _R: A Language and Environment for
## Statistical Computing_. R Foundation for Statistical
## Computing, Vienna, Austria. <URL: https://www.R-project.org/>.


## Wickham H, Averick M, Bryan J, Chang W, McGowan LD, François
## R, Grolemund G, Hayes A, Henry L, Hester J, Kuhn M, Pedersen
## TL, Miller E, Bache SM, Müller K, Ooms J, Robinson D, Seidel
## DP, Spinu V, Takahashi K, Vaughan D, Wilke C, Woo K, Yutani H
## (2019). "Welcome to the tidyverse." _Journal of Open Source
## Software_, *4*(43), 1686. doi: 10.21105/joss.01686 (URL:
## https://doi.org/10.21105/joss.01686).


## Xie Y (2022). _knitr: A General-Purpose Package for Dynamic
## Report Generation in R_. R package version 1.41, <URL:
## https://yihui.org/knitr/>.
```

---

[2] The tidyverse package itself contains several packages.

```
## Xie Y (2023). _formatR: Format R Code Automatically_. R
## package version 1.14, <URL:
## https://CRAN.R-project.org/package=formatR>.
```

References

Dayal, Vikram. 2020. *Quantitative economics with R: a data science approach*. Singapore: Springer.

Grolemund, Garrett, and Hadley Wickham. 2017. *R for data science: import, tidy, transform, visualize, and model data*. 1st edition. Sebastopol, CA: O'Reilly Media.

Regression and Simulation 3

3.1 Introduction

Entire books introduce the many aspects of regression. In this chapter, we emphasize the connection between regression and means and conditional means. We also describe P value functions. We introduce simulation as a tool for understanding causal and statistical inference. We use simulation extensively in this book.

3.2 Sampling Distribution and Simulation

In statistics, we use statistical procedures that have good properties. To understand statistical procedures, we need to understand sampling distributions. Kennedy (2008, pp. 403–404) persuaded us about the importance of the sampling distribution to understand what is going on in econometrics: "It cannot be stressed too strongly how important it is for students to understand the concept of a sampling distribution … Using $\beta*$ to produce an estimate of β can be conceptualized as the econometrician shutting her or his eyes and obtaining an estimate of β by reaching blindly into the sampling distribution of $\beta*$ to obtain a single number." This chapter discusses sampling distributions, means, and regressions using simulation.

Figure 3.1 shows a schematic diagram of a sampling distribution. We start with a population. We draw a sample, sample 1, and use a rule, or estimator, which gives us an estimate, estimate 1. We draw a large number (K) of samples and generate estimates, which we record. The distribution of the estimates is the sampling distribution of the estimator.

Simulation helps us understand the sampling distribution. Kennedy (2008, p. 22) writes that "a thorough understanding of simulation guarantees an understanding of the repeated sample and sampling distribution concepts, which are crucial to an

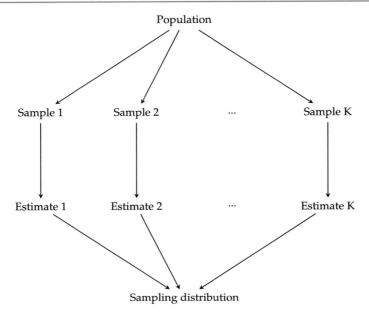

Fig. 3.1 Schematic of sampling distribution

understanding of econometrics." We can start at the top in the schematic of the sampling distribution (Fig. 3.1), in which we construct some data relating to a population, and because we construct the data, we know its features. Then we select samples and make estimates repeatedly. We end up with the sampling distribution that we can then examine, and see the properties of the estimator we have used. Because we generated the data, we know the true values and can see whether the estimator takes us close to the true values.

Barreto and Howland (2005, p. 216) express the value of simulation to "understand the properties of different statistics computed from sample data. ... we will test drive estimators, figuring out how different recipes perform under different circumstances. Our procedure is quite simple: In each case we will set up an artificial environment in which the values of important parameters and the nature of the chance process are specified; then the computer will run the chance process over and over; finally the computer will display the results."

3.3 Mean and Regression

3.3.1 Estimating the Mean is the Same as Regressing on a Constant

We first emphasize the connections between a mean and regression. Consider a box with numbered tickets in it. The ticket numbers are 1, 2, 3, 4, 5, 6, 7.

We can create this box in R:

3.3 Mean and Regression

```
Box <- 1:7
```

And find its mean:

```
mean(Box)
## [1] 4
```

Estimating the mean is the same as regressing on a constant term (we use the lm function):

```
lm(Box ~ 1)
## 
## Call:
## lm(formula = Box ~ 1)
## 
## Coefficients:
## (Intercept)
##           4
```

Note that the direct call to R for the mean of the Box, and regressing using a constant term with the lm function both give us an estimate = 4.

☞ **Your turn**   Change the tickets in Box so that they go from 2 to 8. Confirm that you can find the mean with mean and also by regression on a constant, using lm.

It is useful to see the connection between regression via least squares and the mean. If we take the tickets in the Box, shake the Box, and draw out just one ticket, the mean is the best guess about the value that will be drawn.

Following Gailmard (2014, p. 23), let the best guess of the value of the ticket be g. Since each draw could be y_i, the guess g will be off the mark by an error e_i:

$e_i = y_i - g$.

We now show that the mean $\bar{y}$ minimizes the mean squared error. If we take a sample of size n, the mean squared error, MSE, is:

$MSE(g) = \Sigma(y_i - g)^2/n$.

Now $(y_i - g)^2 = (y_i - \bar{y} + \bar{y} - g)^2$. This leads to

$$MSE = [\Sigma(y_i - \bar{y})^2 + \Sigma 2(y_i - \bar{y})(\bar{y} - g) + \Sigma(\bar{y} - g)^2]/n \quad (3.1)$$

The first term on the right hand side of equation (1) does not contain g. The second term is equal to zero since $\bar{y} - g$ can be brought out of the summation, and what is left after the summation is $\Sigma(y_i - \bar{y})/n$, which is zero. Choosing g to minimize the MSE is therefore choosing g to minimize the third term on the right hand side of equation (1). This implies that the best guess g is given by:

$g = \bar{y}$.

In other words, minimizing the MSE leads us to the mean.

3.3.2 Sampling Distribution of the Mean

We will now explore the sampling distribution of the mean via simulation. We load the tidyverse package:

```
library(tidyverse)
```

We create a population which is a large box of tickets, in which each of the tickets in the Box is repeated 10000 times:

```
Box <- 1:7
Box10000 <- rep(Box, 10000) # population
```

The first 10 observations are:

```
Box10000[1:10]
## [1] 1 2 3 4 5 6 7 1 2 3
```

We put our population into a dataframe:

```
Box10000dat <- data.frame(Box10000)
```

We plot the distribution of the population with the ggplot function (Fig. 3.2):

```
ggplot(Box10000dat, aes(x = Box10000)) +
  geom_bar(fill = "grey70", col = "black") +
  theme_bw()
```

The mean and standard deviation of our population are (we round to 2 digits:

```
round(mean(Box10000), 2)
## [1] 4
round(sd(Box10000), 2)
## [1] 2
```

We are going to take random samples using R. Each time we will get a different sample. By using the set.seed function, we can get the same random values each time we run the code:

Fig. 3.2 Distribution of population

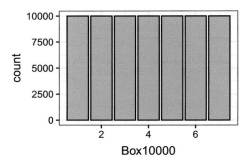

3.3 Mean and Regression

```
set.seed(123)
```

We now take a sample of size 25. We use the `sample` function:

```
# sample size N
N <- 25
samp1 <- sample(Box10000, N)
```

We list the sample (samp1) and calculate the average of the sample:

```
samp1
##  [1] 3 1 4 7 1 3 2 5 4 3 5 3 1 4 1 4 4 2
## [19] 2 5 7 1 6 6 6
mean(samp1)
## [1] 3.6
```

We are taking a sample of size 25. Because the sample is very small relative to the population, one draw of a ticket from the box is independent of the previous and succeeding draw. We can take another sample, and calculate the sample average:

```
samp2 <- sample(Box10000, N)
samp2
##  [1] 6 3 7 6 2 7 7 2 1 2 1 2 4 4 1 7 3 2
## [19] 5 7 3 4 1 1 4
mean(samp2)
## [1] 3.68
```

We reiterate that we can find the mean by regressing on a constant:

```
modsamp1 <- lm(samp1 ~ 1)
modsamp2 <- lm(samp2 ~ 1)
```

We use the `texreg` package to display the regressions:

```
library(texreg)

texreg(list(modsamp1, modsamp2),
       custom.model.names = c("Sample 1", "Sample 2"),
       caption = paste("Regression for dependent",    " variable tickets in Box"),
       caption.above = TRUE,
       stars = numeric(0),
       include.adjrs = FALSE,
       include.rsquared = FALSE,
       custom.note = "Standard errors in parentheses.")
```

Table 3.1 displays the means estimated via regression for our first two samples; we see that we get the same values as in a direct call to the mean function. We used the texreg package to create the table. It can create tables in a variety of formats, and is convenient for displaying regressions.

We can now repeatedly draw samples, and calculate the average. We use 'nreps' for the number of repetitions.

Table 3.1 Regression for dependent variable tickets in Box

	Sample 1	Sample 2
(Intercept)	3.60	3.68
	(0.39)	(0.45)
Num. obs	25	25

Standard errors in parentheses

```
nreps <- 1000
```

We create a vector samp_mean to store the calculated sample averages, with length equal to nreps.

```
samp_mean <- numeric(nreps)
str(samp_mean)
##  num [1:1000] 0 0 0 0 0 0 0 0 0 0 ...
```

Now we will use a for loop to repeatedly draw samples, calculate averages, and store values. Each of the positions in the samp_mean vector will be filled each time we cycle the loop (as i goes from 1 to the total number of repetitions):

```
for (i in 1: nreps) {
  samp <- sample(Box10000, N)
  samp_mean[i] <- mean(samp)
}
```

We create a data frame containing the sample averages so that we can plot the distribution of the sample averages:

```
mean_dat <- data.frame(samp_mean)
```

We now use ggplot to plot the distribution of the sample averages (Fig. 3.3). Notice that we draw a vertical red line (with geom_vline) to show the true mean in the population, which equals 4:

```
library(tidyverse)
ggplot(mean_dat, aes(x = samp_mean)) +
  geom_histogram(bins = 10, fill = "grey70", col = "black") +
  geom_vline(xintercept = 4, col = "red") +
  theme_bw()
```

We calculate the mean of the sample means; the mean of the sample means is very close to 4, the true value:

```
mean(samp_mean)
## [1] 3.99796
```

3.3 Mean and Regression

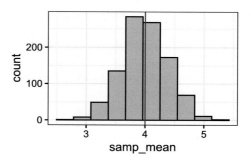

Fig. 3.3 Sampling distribution of the sample means. Samples were taken from the population (Fig. 3.2) 1000 times, and each time the mean was estimated

We calculate the standard deviation of the sample means, and compare the value to the estimate of the standard error from the standard deviation of the tickets in the Box:

```
sd(samp_mean)
## [1] 0.3910601
sd(Box10000)/(N^0.5)
## [1] 0.4000029
```

☞ **Your turn.** Work through the code of this subsection, create a new Box that has tickets from 2 to 8, then a new Box10000 and work your way to the plot of the sampling distribution of the means.

Through simulation, we have illustrated the following ideas, expressed formally:

We denote a random sample from a population by $Y_1, Y_2, ..., Y_n$. An estimator of the population mean μ is the sample average $\bar{Y} = \Sigma Y_i / n$.

The estimator $\bar{Y}$ is a rule that gives us an estimate $\bar{y}$, the average of a sample. We examine the distribution of an estimator, its sampling distribution, to establish the properties of an estimator. We can show that the expectation of $\bar{Y}$ is equal to the population average, μ:

$E(\bar{Y}) = E(\Sigma Y_i/n) = (1/n)(\Sigma E(Y_i)) = (1/n)\Sigma\mu = \mu.$

Thus the sample average $\bar{Y}$ is an unbiased estimator.

The central limit theorem tells us that if Y has an unknown distribution, $Y \sim (\mu, \sigma^2)$, then $\bar{Y}$ is approximately normally distributed, $\bar{Y} \sim N(\mu, \sigma^2/n)$.

3.4 Bivariate Regression

3.4.1 Bivariate Regression and Conditional Means

We use simulation to get a feel for regression, using a simple bivariate example. We create a variable X, that takes values 1, 2, 3, 4, and 5, repeated 20 times, using `rep`:

```
X <- rep(1:5, 20)
X[1:10]
## [1] 1 2 3 4 5 1 2 3 4 5
```

We create an error Uy, normally distributed with mean 0 and standard deviation one, with `rnorm`:

```
Uy <- rnorm(100)
```

We create Y as a function of X and Uy:

```
Y <- 1.5 + 3 * X + 10 * Uy
```

We create a dataframe:

```
reg_dat <- data.frame(Y, X)
```

We will plot a scatterplot of Y against X (Fig. 3.4):

```
ggplot(reg_dat, aes(x = X, y = Y) ) +
  geom_point(col = "grey50") +
  theme_bw()
```

We (1) take the dataframe, `reg_dat`, create a `factor` (categorical variable) Xfac, with `mutate`, (2) group by Xfac, and then for each group calculate the mean of Y:

```
reg_dat <- reg_dat %>%
  mutate(Xfac = factor(X)) %>%
  group_by(Xfac) %>%
  mutate(mean_Y = mean(Y))
```

We can plot the regression line, and points showing the mean of Y for each value of X, and the observations (Fig. 3.5). The conditional means of Y are close to the regression line. Note that we use `geom_point` twice below, and `geom_smooth` once. We specify the x-axis limits with `xlim`:

3.4 Bivariate Regression

Fig. 3.4 Y versus X

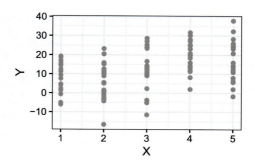

Fig. 3.5 Y versus X, with conditional means of Y for different values of X, and line of fit (OLS)

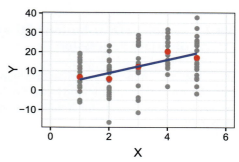

```
ggplot(reg_dat) +
  geom_point(aes(x = X, y = Y), col = "grey50") +
  geom_point(aes(x = X, y = mean_Y), col = "red", size = 2) +
  geom_smooth(aes(x = X, y = Y), method = "lm",
              se = F) +
  xlim(c(0,6)) +
  theme_bw()
```

We regress Y on X:

```
mod1 <- lm(Y ~ X, data = reg_dat)
```

We display the results (Table 3.2):

```
texreg(list(mod1),
       caption ="Regression of Y on X, true value of coefficient is 3.",
       caption.above = TRUE,
       stars = numeric(0),
       include.adjrs = FALSE,
       custom.note = "Standard errors in parentheses.")
```

Table 3.2 Regression of Y on X, true value of coefficient is 3

	Model 1
(Intercept)	2.00
	(2.31)
X	3.49
	(0.70)
R^2	0.20
Num. obs	100

Standard errors in parentheses

3.4.2 Sampling Distribution of the Regression Coefficient in a Bivariate Regression

We will now examine the sampling distribution of the coefficient of X in the regression of Y on X. We use a for loop as we did in Sect. 3.2. We will use 1000 repetitions. We need to create vectors for X and for storing the coefficient estimates before the loop begins:

```
lmreps <- 1000
X <- rep(1:5, 20)
coeff_estim <- numeric(lmreps)
set.seed(123)
for(i in 1:lmreps) {
Uy <- rnorm(100)
Y <- 1.5 + 3 * X + 10 * Uy
mod2 <- lm(Y ~ X)
coeff_estim[i] <- mod2$coeff[2]
}
```

We create a data frame containing the coefficient estimates and then plot the sampling distribution (Fig. 3.6):

```
coeff_dat <- data.frame(coeff_estim)
ggplot(coeff_dat, aes(x = coeff_estim)) +
  geom_histogram(bins = 10, col = "black", fill = "grey70") +
  geom_vline(xintercept = 3, col = "red") +
  theme_bw()
```

The mean and standard deviation of the regression coefficients are:

```
mean(coeff_estim)
## [1] 2.982361
sd(coeff_estim)
## [1] 0.704011
```

3.4 Bivariate Regression

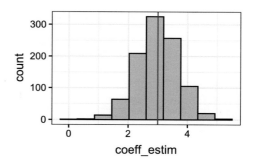

Fig. 3.6 Sampling distribution of coefficient of X. Data for Y and X were generated (see text) 1000 times and each time Y was regressed on X

We can see that the mean of the regression coefficient is close to the true value, which is 3.

☞ **Your turn**   Use the code in Sects. 4.1 and 4.2, but change the relationship of Y to Y = 2 - 2.5 * X + 10 * Uy. What do you observe?

3.4.3 Estimating a Difference is the Same as Regressing on an Indicator Variable

We show that if we have measures of Y for two different groups, and the mean of Y for those two groups is different, a regression of Y on the group indicator gives us an estimate of the difference in means.

We generate some data for two groups, 1 and 2. The mean of the first group is 7, and of the second is 10:

```
samp_size <- 50
Y1 <- rnorm(samp_size, mean = 7, sd = 1)
Y2 <- rnorm(samp_size, mean = 10, sd = 1)
Y <- c(Y1, Y2)
groupnum <- c(rep(1, samp_size), rep(2, samp_size))
groupfac <- factor(groupnum)
modgroup <- lm(Y ~ groupfac)
groupdat <- data.frame(Y, groupfac, groupnum)
```

Table 3.3 shows the estimated difference in means, which is close to the true value.

Table 3.3 Regression of Y on group indicator, true difference in means of groups is 3

	Model 1
(Intercept)	7.05
	(0.15)
groupfac2	2.82
	(0.22)
R^2	0.64
Num. obs	100

Standard errors in parentheses

Fig. 3.7 Scatterplot of Y against group. The line connects the mean of the group = 0 with the mean of the group = 1. The points have been plotted with some random noise or jitter

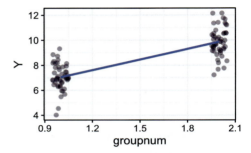

```
texreg(list(modgroup),
       caption = "Regression of Y on group indicator, true difference in means of groups is 3.",
       caption.above = TRUE,
       include.adjrs = FALSE,
       stars = numeric(0),
       include.ci = FALSE,
       custom.note = "Standard errors in parentheses.")
```

We can of course also estimate the difference with the mean function:

```
mean(Y2) - mean(Y1)
## [1] 2.823377
```

We display the data and the regression (Fig. 3.7 and Table 3.3):

```
ggplot(groupdat, aes(x = groupnum, y = Y)) +
  geom_jitter(width = 0.05, alpha = 0.3, height = 0.05) +
  geom_smooth(method = "lm", se = F) +
  theme_bw()
```

In this chapter, we stressed the connection between regression and conditional means. Gelman et al. (2020, p. 85) suggest that we can always interpret regressions as comparisons, but only under certain circumstances, as effects: "Regression coefficients can sometimes be interpreted as effects, but they can always be interpreted as average comparisons." When can we interpret a regression coefficient as a causal effect? The potential outcomes framework (Chap. 4) and causal graphs (Chap. 5) help us with this question.

3.5 The P Value Function: A Tool for Inference

Researchers often present regression results in tables with stars, which highlight statistical significance. With or without stars, people often zoom in on 'significance'. In his highly regarded text, the econometrician Wooldridge (2019, p. 742) writes: "we have produced three kinds of evidence concerning population parameters: point estimates, confidence intervals, and hypothesis tests. These tools for learning about population parameters are equally important. There is an understandable tendency for students to focus on confidence intervals and hypothesis tests because these are things to which we can attach confidence or significance levels. But in any study, we must also interpret the magnitudes of point estimates." In his highly regarded text, the statistician Wasserman (2004, p. 150) writes: "Warning! There is a tendency to use hypothesis testing methods even when they are not appropriate. Often, estimation and confidence intervals are better tools. Use hypothesis testing only when you want to test a well-defined hypothesis."

There is a large literature on the different tools for statistical inference, and how they may be misleading and misinterpreted (see Rothman et al. (2008) for a clear and enlightening discussion). The economist David Romer (2020) has praised confidence intervals. He writes that our interest is often not in whether a point estimate is zero or not. He takes the example of the rate of return to education, or the percentage increase in earnings from an extra year of schooling. There is sufficient evidence that it is positive, so a new study should discuss whether the evidence in that study is compatible with estimates like the median value of 9.4% found in studies that used instrumental variables, or with other estimates in the literature.

In this book, we present regression tables with standard errors in parentheses below the estimated coefficients. We typically have multiple models to compare and regression tables provide a compact format.

In this section, we present one graphical device that conveys all the information you get from point estimates, confidence intervals, and hypothesis tests, the P value function or confidence interval function. Infanger and Schmidt-Trucksass (2019, p. 1) call the P value function an underused method to present research results. They write, "P value functions ... display confidence limits and P values for any confidence level for a parameter. P value functions accessibly display a wealth of information."

The P value function is a plot of P values for not just the hypothesis that the regression coefficient is zero, but for a range of values of the coefficient around the estimated coefficient value. It also can be seen as a visualization of confidence intervals.

The P value function helps us understand the connection between point estimates, confidence intervals, and P values. In what follows, the P value function plot is built up from basic calculations using R code.

We first create some synthetic data. We assume that the data generation process is:

$Y = \alpha + \beta x + \epsilon$

We assume numerical values: $\alpha = 3$ and $\beta = 3$, and for ϵ, we draw random numbers from a normal distribution. Our interest is in inferring β.

We load packages:

```
library(knitr)
library(tidyverse)
```

Note that for replicability, we use the set.seed function, and provide 10 as an input:

```
# synthetic data
set.seed(10)
N <- 50
x1 <- rnorm(N)
y1 <- 3 + 3*x1 + 9*rnorm(N)
```

We collect the data in a dataframe:

```
datasim <- data.frame(x1, y1)
head(datasim)
##              x1          y1
## 1   0.01874617  -0.5494994
## 2  -0.18425254  -0.5637667
## 3  -1.37133055  11.1975939
## 4  -0.59916772  20.4424008
## 5   0.29454513   8.4360088
## 6   0.38979430  11.2464644
```

We regress y1 on x1 using the lm function. We further use the summary function to see the regression output:

```
# regression of y1 on x1
mod1 <-  lm(y1 ~ x1)
sum1 <- summary(mod1)
sum1
##
## Call:
## lm(formula = y1 ~ x1)
##
## Residuals:
##     Min      1Q   Median      3Q     Max
## -15.334  -5.688    1.092   5.550  20.013
##
## Coefficients:
##              Estimate Std. Error t value
## (Intercept)     3.768      1.350   2.791
## x1              3.453      1.463   2.360
##              Pr(>|t|)
## (Intercept)   0.00752 **
```

3.5 The P Value Function: A Tool for Inference

```
## x1            0.02236 *
## ---
## Signif. codes:
##   0 '***' 0.001 '**' 0.01 '*' 0.05
##   '.' 0.1 ' ' 1
##
## Residual standard error: 8.871 on 48 degrees of freedom
## Multiple R-squared:  0.104,	Adjusted R-squared:  0.08534
## F-statistic: 5.572 on 1 and 48 DF,  p-value: 0.02236
```

We can get the 95% confidence interval with `confint`:

```
confint(mod1)
##                 2.5 %    97.5 %
## (Intercept) 1.0533764 6.483282
## x1          0.5117422 6.393932
```

We produce a typical regression table (with stars!) for the model (Table 3.4). Often we will zoom in on the star next to the estimate 3.45 (note that $\beta = 3$):

```
library(texreg)
texreg(list(mod1),
       caption = "Regression of y1 on x1.",
       caption.above = TRUE,
       include.adjrs = FALSE)
```

Wooldridge reminds us that we should also discuss the magnitude from a contextual and subject matter perspective. In some disciplines, for example, epidemiology (Rothman et al. 2008) (and as advocated by the economist David Romer (2020)), we may present the coefficient values and the 95% confidence interval. We now build up a P value function using R. We can pull out the regression coefficient for x1 and the standard error as follows. You can confirm by comparing with the regression summary above:

Table 3.4 Regression of y1 on x1

	Model 1
(Intercept)	3.77**
	(1.35)
x1	3.45*
	(1.46)
R^2	0.10
Num. obs	50

***$p < 0.001$; **$p < 0.01$; *$p < 0.05$

pull out estimate of coefficient
sum1$coefficients[2,1]
[1] 3.452837
pull out standard error
sum1$coefficients[2,2]
[1] 1.462769
```

We rename the pulled out values:

```
# rename the pulled out values
# beta below is an estimate
beta <- sum1$coefficients[2,1]; beta
## [1] 3.452837
se <- sum1$coefficients[2,2]; se
## [1] 1.462769
```

On the x-axis, we will be plotting different possible values of beta around the point estimate of beta:

```
# to get the range of values on x axis
(beta + 3*se); (beta - 3*se)
## [1] 7.841145
## [1] -0.9354708
ulim <- ifelse(beta + 3*se > beta - 3*se,
               beta + 3*se,
               beta - 3*se); ulim
## [1] 7.841145
llim <- ifelse(beta + 3*se < beta - 3*se,
               beta + 3*se,
               beta - 3*se); llim
## [1] -0.9354708
```

We illustrate a P value calculation below for the hypothesis that beta = 0:

```
# illustrating p value calculation for
# hypothesis that x is zero
xiszero <- 0 ; xiszero
## [1] 0
t <- (beta - xiszero) / se; t
## [1] 2.36048
2*pt(-abs(t),df= N - 2)
## [1] 0.02236218
```

We can check with the regression summary above. Satisfied that we have the correct code, we generalize and plot P values for different possible values of beta (Fig. 3.8):
```

3.5 The P Value Function: A Tool for Inference

Fig. 3.8 P value function

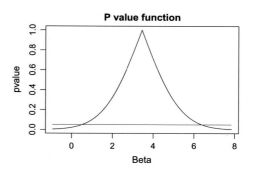

```
# now use curve to plot p value function
curve(expr = 2*pt(-abs((beta - x) / se),
                df=N-2),
      from = llim, to = ulim,
      main = "P value function",
      ylab = "pvalue",
      xlab = "Beta")
# add red line for 0.05 p value
curve(expr = 0.05 + 0*x, from = llim,
      to = ulim,
      add = TRUE, col = "red")
```

The black line shows how the P value varies across possible beta values. The red line shows the P value = 0.05 and the intersection with the black line gives us the 95 percent confidence interval.

We can also use ggplot for a more stylish figure, with annotations. The code may look complex, but one can think of it as adding layers and details to the plot:

```
pvalfun <- function(x){
  2*pt(-abs((beta - x) / se),df=48)
}


ggplot(data.frame(x = c(llim, ulim)),
       aes(x = x)) +
  stat_function(fun = pvalfun) +
  geom_hline(yintercept = 0.05,
             col = "red", linetype = "dashed") +
  geom_vline(xintercept = 0,
             col = "blue", linetype = "dashed") +
  ylab("p value") +
  xlab("Beta") +
  xlim(c(-3, 10)) +
  ylim(c(-0.5, 1.5)) +
```

```
scale_y_continuous(
  breaks = seq(0, 1, by = 0.1),
  name = "P value",
  # Add a second axis and specify its features
  sec.axis = sec_axis( trans=~.*-100 + 100,
                      name="Confidence Level",
                   breaks = seq(0, 100, by = 10))
) +
annotate("text", x = 5.2, y = 0.95,
         label = "Point Estimate \n= 3.45") +
annotate("text", x = 1.7, y = 0.01,
         label = "P value  = 0.02") +
annotate("text", x = 3.3, y = 0.16,
         label = "Confidence \nInterval \n[0.51, 6.39]") +
theme_bw()
```

☞ **Your turn.** Try decoding the code above, searching online. For example, search for 'ggplot annotate'.

In Fig. 3.9, the P value function is the black solid line. The peak of the function is the point estimate, 3.45. The lower and upper limits of the 95% confidence interval are given by the intersection of the 95% confidence level line (see the Y-axis on the

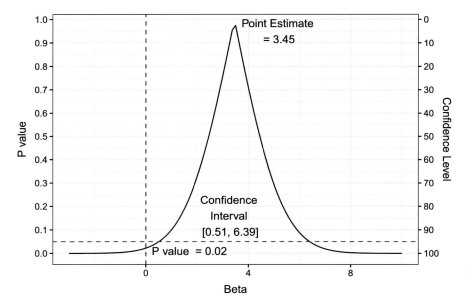

Fig. 3.9 P value function

3.6 Systematic and Random Error

Table 3.5 Regression of y1 on x1, with a different sample

	Model 1
(Intercept)	3.08*
	(1.30)
x1	2.12
	(1.48)
R^2	0.04
Num. obs	50

***$p < 0.001$; **$p < 0.01$; *$p < 0.05$

right) and the P value function. The P value for the null hypothesis is 0.02, and is given by the intersection of the P value function and the Beta = 0 line. Note that the P value for the hypothesis that Beta is 7 is similar to the P value for the null hypothesis. So Beta = 7 and beta = 0 are equally incompatible with the data. This is an example of how the P value function provides more information than the null hypothesis P value.

The beauty of simulation is that since we create the data, we know the correct answer, a luxury we do not have while analyzing data. We will now generate the data once again by changing the set.seed value to 11.

☞ **Your turn** Replicate the code above and change the set.seed value to 11. What do you observe?

Table 3.5 shows the new estimate. Note that the star against x1 has disappeared although the data generating process is the same; we have only generated a new sample.

Our new point estimate is 2.12, the 95% confidence interval is now [−0.86, 5.10], but the P value is 0.15 (Fig. 3.10). The P value has jumped from 0.02 to 0.15. Note that we used the same code for generating the data and only generated a new sample of y1 and x1. Motulsky (2017) used a simulation to demonstrate that P values jump around a lot.

3.6 Systematic and Random Error

In our investigations, we are faced with the possibilities of both systematic and random error (Rothman et al. 2008). Following Westreich (2019), we illustrate with a bulls-eye diagram. In Fig. 3.11, the large red dot shows the target, the small black dots our attempts to hit the target. We usually miss the target a bit, though on average we may hit the target.

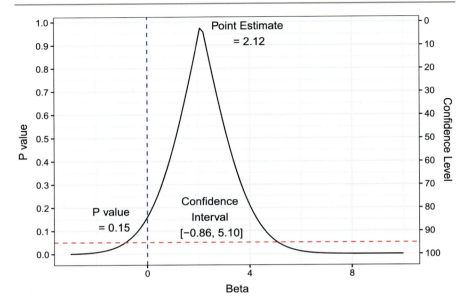

Fig. 3.10 P value function with new sample

Fig. 3.11 Random error

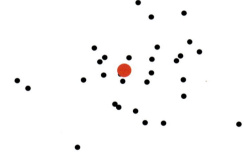

Systematic error would lead us to miss the target on average, even if random error is low, as in Fig. 3.12. Random error will get smaller as the sample size decreases. But systematic error will not.

In causal inference, while recognizing random error, we study the assumptions required for us to overcome systematic error, or achieve causal identification. We study causal identification in the next two chapters, using two complementary approaches—potential outcomes and causal graphs.

3.7 Resources

Fig. 3.12 Lower random error, but with systematic error. Compare with Fig. 3.11

3.7.1 For Better Understanding

1. Gailmard's (2014) book *Statistical Modeling and Inference for Social Science*.
2. Goldberger's (1998) book *Introductory Econometrics*.
3. Rothman et al.'s (2008) chapter *Precision and study size*.

3.7.2 For Going Further

Gelman, Hill and Vehtari's (2020) book *Regression and Other Stories*.

Packages Used in this Chapter

The citations for the packages used in this chapter are[1]:

```
## R Core Team (2021). _R: A Language and Environment for
## Statistical Computing_. R Foundation for Statistical
## Computing, Vienna, Austria. <URL: https://www.R-project.org/>.


## Makowski D, Lüdecke D, Patil I, Thériault R, Ben-Shachar M,
## Wiernik B (2023). "Automated Results Reporting as a Practical
## Tool to Improve Reproducibility and Methodological Best
## Practices Adoption." _CRAN_. <URL:
## https://easystats.github.io/report/>.
```

---

[1] The tidyverse package itself contains several packages.

```
## Wickham H, Averick M, Bryan J, Chang W, McGowan LD, François
## R, Grolemund G, Hayes A, Henry L, Hester J, Kuhn M, Pedersen
## TL, Miller E, Bache SM, Müller K, Ooms J, Robinson D, Seidel
## DP, Spinu V, Takahashi K, Vaughan D, Wilke C, Woo K, Yutani H
## (2019). "Welcome to the tidyverse." _Journal of Open Source
## Software_, *4*(43), 1686. doi: 10.21105/joss.01686 (URL:
## https://doi.org/10.21105/joss.01686).


## Xie Y (2022). _knitr: A General-Purpose Package for Dynamic
## Report Generation in R_. R package version 1.41, <URL:
## https://yihui.org/knitr/>.


## Xie Y (2023). _formatR: Format R Code Automatically_. R
## package version 1.14, <URL:
## https://CRAN.R-project.org/package=formatR>.
```

References

Barreto, Humberto, and Frank Howland. 2005. *Introductory econometrics: using Monte Carlo simulation with Microsoft excel*. Har/Cdr edition: Cambridge University Press.

Gailmard, Sean. 2014. *Statistical modeling and inference for social science*. New York, NY: Cambridge University Press.

Gelman, Andrew, Jennifer Hill, and Aki Vehtari. 2020. *Regression and other stories*. 1st edition. Cambridge University Press.

Goldberger, Arthur S. 1998. *Introductory econometrics: Cambridge*. MA: Harvard University Press.

Infanger, Denis, and Arno Schmidt-Trucksäss. 2019. P value functions: an underused method to present research results and to promote quantitative reasoning. *Statistics in Medicine*, 38(21): 4189–4197. https://onlinelibrary.wiley.com/doi/pdf/10.1002/sim.8293.

Kennedy, Peter. 2008. *A guide to econometrics*. 6th edition. Blackwell.

Motulsky, Harvey. 2017. *Intuitive biostatistics: a nonmathematical guide to statistical thinking*, 4th ed. New York: Oxford University Press.

Romer, David. 2020. In praise of confidence intervals. *AEA Papers and Proceedings* 110: 55–60.

Rothman, Kenneth J., Sander Greenland, and Timothy L. Lash. 2008. Precision and study size. In *Rothman, Kenneth J, Sander Greenland, and Timothy L Lash*, ed. Modern Epidemiology. New York: Wolters Kluwer.

Wasserman, Larry. 2004. *All of statistics: a concise course in statistical inference*. New York, Berlin, Heidelberg: Springer.

Westreich, Daniel. 2019. *Epidemiology by design*. New York, NY: Oxford University Press.

Wooldridge, Jeffrey M. 2019. *Introductory econometrics: a modern approach*, 7th ed. Boston, MA: Cengage Learning.

Potential Outcomes

4.1 Introduction

The potential outcomes approach or the Neyman-Rubin causal model (Rubin 2008) provides a conceptual basis for causal inference. Causal inference builds on statistical inference, and the Neyman-Rubin causal model guides us in thinking about causal estimands and in estimating causal effects. In this chapter we provide an intuitive introduction to the Neyman-Rubin causal model.

We may have data on an outcome Y, a treatment W, and other variables X. A statistical analysis, for example, a regression of Y on W and X may show an empirical relation. We may reason informally and intuitively about whether this relation is causal or not. Or, we may aim to anchor our reasoning with a formal causal framework, the Neyman-Rubin model. We use the symbol $Y_i(W)$ to denote the potential outcome for unit i when experiencing a treatment W.

4.2 Basic Ideas

What is a causal effect? In the Neyman-Rubin causal model, a causal effect is defined as follows: for each unit, the comparison of the potential outcome under treatment and the potential outcome under control.

We consider an example: Does aspirin cause a reduction in the severity of headaches? A person, Ram, has a headache and may take an aspirin, in the hope of reducing the pain. Here, Ram is the unit of analysis, headache after an hour is the outcome, and aspirin is the treatment, which may be either 0 if aspirin is taken, or 1 if not. Ram has two potential outcomes corresponding to whether he takes the aspirin now or not. For Ram, aspirin potentially leads to a reduction in his severity score for headaches from 5 (if he does not take aspirin) to 1 (if he takes it). The potential outcomes model uses formal notation corresponding to the outcome, unit, and the treatment. The outcome here is headache, unit is Ram, and the treatment is aspirin (Asp). In symbols, $Y_i(W)$, where Y is the outcome, i is the unit, and W is the treatment. We can translate Ram's potential outcomes as follows, substituting Ram for i and Asp for W: $Y_{RAM}(Asp = 0) = 5$; $Y_{RAM}(Asp = 1) = 1$. The causal effect for Ram is $Y_{RAM}(Asp = 1) - Y_{RAM}(Asp = 0) = -4$.

For Sam, aspirin potentially leads to a reduction in his severity score for headaches from 1 (if he does not take aspirin) to 0 (if he takes it). Translated into potential outcomes notation: $Y_{Sam}(Asp = 0) = 1$; $Y_{Sam}(Asp = 1) = 0$. The causal effect for Sam is –1.

We have made a key assumption above: Ram's and Sam's potential outcome is defined in terms of their *own* treatment assignment. Ram's potential outcome is not defined in terms of whether Sam takes an aspirin or not, and vice versa. This assumption is known as the Stable Unit Treatment Value Assumption (SUTVA).[1] We have to think carefully about the context of our study and the related treatment and potential outcomes.

A key idea in the Neyman-Rubin causal model is the "Fundamental problem of causal inference"; only one of the two potential outcomes for Ram or Sam can be observed. Ram either takes the aspirin or does not. If he takes the aspirin, then we will observe $Y_{Ram}(Asp = 1)$. Then $Y_{Ram}(Asp = 0)$ will not be observed, it is counterfactual.

We can try to use the observed outcomes for Ram and Sam; we consider two scenarios as follows.

- Ram takes the aspirin because of his proneness to headaches, and Sam does not because headaches do not affect him much. We observe that the aspirin taker (Ram) has a value of Y = 1, and Sam has a value of Y (headache) = 1. The effect of aspirin on Ram's headache is –4, but if we only compare Ram's and Sam's values of Y, we think it has no effect.
$Y_{Ram}(Asp = 1) - Y_{Sam}(Asp = 0) = 1 - 1 = 0$.
- Ram is generally careless about his health, and does not take the aspirin, while Sam is the opposite and takes the aspirin. So we observe Y for Ram = 5, and Y for Sam = 0. Now aspirin looks really strong, we think aspirin has an effect of –5! $Y_{Sam}(Asp = 1) - Y_{Ram}(Asp = 0) = 0 - 5 = -5$.

In the two scenarios above, we get very different answers; we need to be careful if we simply use observed values of the outcome for those treated and not treated.

---

[1] See Gelman et al. (2020) for an excellent discussion.

4.3 Basic Identity of Causal Inference

Because of the fundamental problem of causal inference, we will observe $Y_i(1)|W_i = 1$ and not observe $Y_i(1)|W_i = 0$ for the ith unit. We therefore consider the average treatment effect, ATE = $E[Y(1) - Y(0)]$. Note that the average treatment effect is defined in terms of potential outcomes and we call it the causal effect in what follows.

We now consider what Varian (2016) calls the basic identity of causal inference:

$$\text{Observed effect} = \text{causal effect} + \text{selection effect}. \tag{4.1}$$

Note that observed Y is a mixture of potential outcomes:
$Y_i = Y_i(0) + [Y_i(1) - Y_i(0)]W_i$.
We now see how we get the basic identity, using potential outcomes notation:

$$\text{Observed effect} = E[Y_i|W_i = 1] - E[Y_i|W_i = 0]. \tag{4.2}$$

The first term on the right-hand side of equation (2) above, $E[Y_i|W_i = 1]$, equals $E[Y_i(1)|W_i = 1]$, since we assume that if a unit is treated, the observed outcome will equal the potential outcome with treatment. The second term on the right-hand side of equation (2) above, $E[Y_i|W_i = 0] = E[Y_i(0)|W_i = 0]$:

$$\text{Observed effect} = E[Y_i(1)|W_i = 1] - E[Y_i(0)|W_i = 0]. \tag{4.3}$$

Subtract $E[Y_i(0)|W_i = 1]$ from, and add to, the RHS of equation (4.3) above.
$E[Y_i(1)|W_i = 1] - E[Y_i(0)|W_i = 1] + E[Y_i(0)|W_i = 1] - E[Y_i(0)|W_i = 0] =$ causal effect (for treated) + selection effect (how treated and control differ without treatment).

An example of this: Observed health outcomes among those hospitalized = causal effect of hospitalization + how hospitalized and non-hospitalized differ in absence of hospitalization.

4.4 Rubin Doctor Example

Rubin (2008) provided an intriguing hypothetical example. Units: patients; treatment: surgery; outcome: years lived (Table 4.1). The true average effect is –2.

Note that both potential outcomes cannot be observed; and constant effects are not assumed. We now consider the random assignment of treatment.

Two possible random assignments, Assignments A and B, would imply different treatment/control groups and therefore different estimates:

- Assignment A is displayed in Table 4.2. We get an estimated average treatment effect of –4.5.
- Assignment B is displayed in Table 4.3. We get an estimated average treatment effect of –6.75.

Table 4.1 Perfect doctor example

Y1	Y0	Unit_Effect
14	13	1
0	6	−6
1	4	−3
2	5	−3
3	6	−3
1	6	−5
10	8	2
9	8	1

Table 4.2 Perfect doctor example, treatment assignment A

Y1	Y0	Unit_Effect	AssignmentA	ObservedYA
14	13	1	0	13
0	6	−6	0	6
1	4	−3	1	1
2	5	−3	0	5
3	6	−3	1	3
1	6	−5	1	1
10	8	2	0	8
9	8	1	1	9

Table 4.3 Perfect doctor example, treatment assignment B

Y1	Y0	Unit_Effect	AssignmentB	ObservedYB
14	13	1	0	13
0	6	−6	1	0
1	4	−3	0	4
2	5	−3	1	2
3	6	−3	1	3
1	6	−5	1	1
10	8	2	0	8
9	8	1	0	8

☞ **Your turn.** Consider a treatment assignment: the first four rows are treated, the rest are not. Create a table like Tables 4.2 and 4.3. Now what is the average treatment effect?

We now consider a large number of random assignments, and collect the results and plot the histogram (Fig. 4.1). The mean of the estimated mean effects is −2.0365. We see that random assignment leads to unbiased estimation of the causal effect.

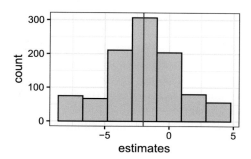

Fig. 4.1 Perfect doctor, estimates of treatment effect from many random assignments of treatment

4.5 Assumptions for Causal Inference Using Potential Outcomes

Being aware and careful about assumptions is one of the characteristics of contemporary causal inference. Imbens and Wooldridge (2009, p. 11) write that the potential outcomes approach helps us state assumptions in a manner that makes the assumptions easier to assess: "the potential outcomes approach allows us to formulate probabilistic assumptions in terms of potentially observable variables, rather than in terms of unobserved components."

Consider a randomized experiment. If we have $i = 1, ..., N$ units, and we randomly decide whether the ith unit gets treated ($W = 1$) or not ($W = 0$) by flipping a fair coin, then the probability of the ith unit getting treatment is 0.5. Clearly, the treatment received is independent of the potential outcomes: $(Y(0), Y(1)) \perp W$, where $\perp$ signifies independence.

Now consider the situation where among the N units J are women and N - J are men, and X = 1 for women and X = 0 for men. We use a randomized assignment to treatment for the J units such that among the $i = 1, ..., J$ women, each woman has a probability = 0.45 of getting treated. For the men, each now has a probability of getting treated = 0.7. We can call this randomization based on a covariate. Symbolically, we can say $(Y(0), Y(1)) \perp W | X$.

Finally, consider an observational study in which we observe data on Y, X and W for each unit. An analyst examines the effect of W on Y by adjusting for X as the analyst would when analyzing data when randomization is based on a covariate. Implicitly, the analyst is assuming $(Y(0), Y(1)) \perp W | X$. Or, the analyst may assert the assumption based on a view or theory of how Y, W, and X are generated.

The assumption $(Y(0), Y(1)) \perp W | X$ is a key assumption, which helps us interpret an estimate as causal. Different study designs or statistical methods help us get causal effects from observational data, and involve some variant of this assumption. The plausibility of assumptions depends on the context, evidence that can be brought to bear, is partly a matter of judgment, and is often debated.

4.6 Manski Bounds: Recidivism

Manski has used potential outcomes to shed light on causal effect estimation. He is a critic of strong and not credible assumptions used for the identification of causal effects. Manski has developed a way of estimating causal effects that aims to find bounds on the causal effect, and uses a variety of assumptions going from minimal to stronger.

We first provide some intuition of how one gets minimal assumption bounds following Aronow and Miller (2019). Consider potential outcomes Y(1) and Y(0). The outcomes are binary. We have potential outcomes for six units (Table 4.4).

Consider a treatment assignment indicator W, and a specific assignment of treatment (Table 4.5). For the first unit, it is assigned to control (W = 0), so we only observe Y(0), not Y(1). The fourth observation is assigned to treatment (W = 1), so we only observe Y(1), not Y(0).

The causal effect for a unit is Y(1) - Y(0). For the units assigned to control, the causal effect is ? - Y(0), and for the units assigned to treatment, the causal effect is Y(1) - ?. Since Y is binary it is either 0 or 1. We can get an upper bound of the treatment effect by using 1 for the missing Y(1) values and 0 for the missing Y(0) values as in Table 4.6.

☞ **Your turn** We can get a lower bound of the treatment effect by using 0 for the missing Y(1) values and 1 for the missing Y(0) values. Fill in values as we did with Table 4.6.

Table 4.4 Hypothetical potential outcomes

Y1	Y0
0	1
1	1
0	0
1	0
0	1
0	1

Table 4.5 Treatment assignment and observed outcomes, given potential outcomes in Table 4.4

W	Observed Y1	Observed Y0
0	?	1
0	?	1
0	?	0
1	1	?
1	0	?
1	0	?

Table 4.6 Imputed potential outcomes for upper bound

W	ObservedY1	ObservedY0	ImputedY1	ImputedY0
0	?	1	1	1
0	?	1	1	1
0	?	0	1	0
1	1	?	1	0
1	0	?	0	0
1	0	?	0	0

We get bounds of [−4/6, 2/6] from the data alone. The difference in the lower bound and upper bound is 1. This shows the logic of estimating Manski bounds with minimal assumptions.

Manski and Nagin (1998) looked at the effect of treatment (1 = residential treatment, 0 = nonresidential treatment) on the outcome recidivism (or repeat offense) among juveniles in the state of Utah in the United States. If the offender repeated the offense, then the outcome y = 1, if not then the outcome y = 0.

The average treatment effect (called classical treatment effect by Manski and Nagin 1998) is given by $P[y(1) = 1] - P[y(0) = 1]$, the difference in recidivism if all the offenders were sentenced to residential treatment versus if all were sentenced to nonresidential treatment. Since probabilities vary between 0 and 1, we can have extremes of average treatment effect varying between −1 (0 - 1) and 1 (1 - 0). Thus, without data the range of values has a width of two. With data, we can narrow this down to a width of 1, as demonstrated in the numerical example above. Using their data, Manski and Nagin (1998) find that the no-assumptions bounds for the average treatment effect (ATE) are $-0.56 \leq ATE \leq 0.44$.

4.7 R Code (Corresponding to Section 4.4)

Perfect Doctor hypothetical example by Rubin Units: patients; treatment: surgery; outcome: years lived (Table 4.1).

We produced the table using the knitr package:

```
library(knitr)
Y0 <- c(13,6,4,5,6,6,8,8)
Y1 <- c(14,0,1,2,3,1,10,9)
Unit_Effect <- Y1- Y0
perdoc1 <- data.frame(Y1,Y0,Unit_Effect)
kable(perdoc1, caption = "Perfect doctor example",
      booktabs = TRUE)
```

We estimate the treatment effect:

```
mean(Y1) - mean(Y0)
```

We generated Assignments A and B:

```
W    <- c(rep(1,4),rep(0,4))
AssignmentA <- sample(W, replace = F); AssignmentA
AssignmentB <- sample(W, replace = F); AssignmentB
```

We produced the table for Assignment A:

```
ObservedYA <- Y0 * (1-AssignmentA) + AssignmentA*Y1
ObservedYA
perdocA <- data.frame(Y1, Y0, Unit_Effect, AssignmentA,
                ObservedYA)
kable(perdocA,
      caption = "Perfect doctor example, assignment A",
      booktabs = TRUE)
  modA <- lm(ObservedYA~AssignmentA)
  modA
```

We produced the table for Assignment B:

```
ObservedYB <- Y0 * (1-AssignmentB) + AssignmentB*Y1
ObservedYB
perdocB <- data.frame(Y1,Y0,Unit_Effect, AssignmentB, ObservedYB)
kable(perdocB,
     caption = "Perfect doctor example, assignment B",
     booktabs = TRUE)
  modB <- lm(ObservedYB ~ AssignmentB)
  modB
```

We simulated a large number of random assignments, using a for loop:

```
draws <- 1000
mean.effect.1000 <- numeric(draws)
for (i in 1:draws) {
  Ass  <- sample(W, replace = FALSE)
  Out <- Y0 * (1-Ass) + Ass*Y1
  mod.r <- lm(Out~Ass)
  mean.effect.1000[i]   <- mod.r$coeff[2]
}
mean(mean.effect.1000)
```

4.8 Resources

We plotted the sampling distribution:

```
library(tidyverse)
data.frame(estimates = mean.effect.1000) %>%
  ggplot(aes(x = estimates)) +
  geom_histogram(bins = 7, fill = "grey",
                 col = "black") +
  geom_vline(xintercept = -2, col = "red") +
  theme_bw()
```

4.8 Resources

4.8.1 For Better Understanding

Chapter 18 in Gelman, Hill and Vehtari's (2020) book *Regression and Other Stories*.

4.8.2 For Going Further

Aronow and Miller's (2019) book *Foundations of Agnostic Statistics*.

Packages used in this chapter

The citations for the packages used in this chapter are[2]

```
## Makowski D, Lüdecke D, Patil I, Thériault R, Ben-Shachar M,
## Wiernik B (2023). "Automated Results Reporting as a Practical
## Tool to Improve Reproducibility and Methodological Best
## Practices Adoption." _CRAN_. <URL:
## https://easystats.github.io/report/>.


## R Core Team (2021). _R: A Language and Environment for
## Statistical Computing_. R Foundation for Statistical
## Computing, Vienna, Austria. <URL: https://www.R-project.org/>.


## Wickham H, Averick M, Bryan J, Chang W, McGowan LD, François
## R, Grolemund G, Hayes A, Henry L, Hester J, Kuhn M, Pedersen
## TL, Miller E, Bache SM, Müller K, Ooms J, Robinson D, Seidel
## DP, Spinu V, Takahashi K, Vaughan D, Wilke C, Woo K, Yutani H
## (2019). "Welcome to the tidyverse." _Journal of Open Source
```

---

[2] The tidyverse package itself contains several packages.

```
## Software_, *4*(43), 1686. doi: 10.21105/joss.01686 (URL:
## https://doi.org/10.21105/joss.01686).


## Wickham H, Averick M, Bryan J, Chang W, McGowan LD, François
## R, Grolemund G, Hayes A, Henry L, Hester J, Kuhn M, Pedersen
## TL, Miller E, Bache SM, Müller K, Ooms J, Robinson D, Seidel
## DP, Spinu V, Takahashi K, Vaughan D, Wilke C, Woo K, Yutani H
## (2019). "Welcome to the tidyverse." _Journal of Open Source
## Software_, *4*(43), 1686. doi: 10.21105/joss.01686 (URL:
## https://doi.org/10.21105/joss.01686).


## Xie Y (2022). _knitr: A General-Purpose Package for Dynamic
## Report Generation in R_. R package version 1.41, <URL:
## https://yihui.org/knitr/>.
```

References

Aronow, Peter, and M., and Benjamin T. Miller. 2019. *Foundations of agnostic statistics*. Cambridge: Cambridge University Press.

Gelman, Andrew, Jennifer Hill, and Aki Vehtari. 2020. *Regression and other stories*. Publisher: Cambridge University Press 9781139161879.

Imbens, Guido W., and Jeffrey M. Wooldridge. 2009. Recent developments in the econometrics of program evaluation. *Journal of Economic Literature* 47 (1): 5–86.

Manski, Charles F., and Daniel S. Nagin. 1998. Bounding disagreements about treatment effects: A case study of sentencing and recidivism. *Sociological Methodology* 28 (1): 99–137. https://onlinelibrary.wiley.com/doi/pdf/10.1111/0081-1750.00043.

Rubin, Donald. 2008. Statistical inference for causal effects, with emphasis on applications in epidemiology and medical statistics. In *Handbook of statistics*, ed. C.R. Rao, J.P. Miller, and D.C. Rao. Amsterdam: Elsevier.

Rubin, Donald B. 2004. Teaching statistical inference for causal effects in experiments and observational studies. *Journal of Educational and Behavioral Statistics* 29 (3): 343–367. Publisher: American Educational Research Association.

Varian, Hal R. 2016. Causal inference in economics and marketing. *Proceedings of the National Academy of Sciences* 113 (27): 7310–7315. Publisher: Proceedings of the National Academy of Sciences.

Causal Graphs 5

5.1 Introduction

Causal graphs help us understand issues in causal inference. Although anchored in mathematics, they provide visual cues that aid intuition and understanding (Elwert 2013).

We may have data on an outcome Y, a treatment A, and other variables X. A statistical analysis, for example, a regression of Y on A and X may show an empirical relation. We may reason informally and intuitively about whether this relation is causal or not. Or, we may use a structural causal model (Pearl et al. 2016). We use an arrow to clearly represent the effect of the treatment on the outcome: $A \rightarrow Y$. Other variables are also represented in the causal graph, if relevant.

The structural causal model has been influential, like the potential outcomes framework. Although researchers may prefer one over the other, several researchers combine causal graphs and potential outcomes (Morgan and Winship 2015, Hernan and Robins 2023). In this chapter, we use simulation and the ggdag package to get a feel for causal graphs.

5.2 Concepts and Examples

The causal graphs we consider are part of Pearl's structural causal model (Pearl et al. 2016). A feature and strength of the structural causal model is that we do not need to assume specific functional forms. However, both for ease of exposition and for simulation, we will assume simple functional forms.

5.2.1 Causal Graphs for Two Variables

The causal graphs we consider are part of Pearl's structural causal model (Pearl, Glymour, and Jewell 2016).

We consider the case of a structural causal model with two variables: (1) a cause W and (2) an outcome S.

The structural causal model in this case consists of:

- set of variables U (exogenous): U_w, U_s.
- set of variables V (endogenous): W, S.
- set of functions F that assigns each variable in V a value based on the other variables in the model: f_w, f_s.

The functions in this structural model are as follows: $f_w : W = U_w$ $f_S : S = \alpha + \beta W + U_s$ We use U here to denote unknown factors or 'errors'.

The causal graph corresponding to the structural equations is shown in Fig. 5.1. In this graph, the arrow shows that there is a direct causal effect of W on S.

We conducted a simulation for the structural causal model $W \to S$. Note that the true causal effect β is 2 by construction, and we estimate β when we regress S on W (Table 5.1 and Fig. 5.2). The regression coefficient of W is the estimate of β.

We also regress W on S (Table 5.2 and Fig. 5.3). However, the regression coefficient of S is not an estimate of an effect (or causal effect) because S does not cause

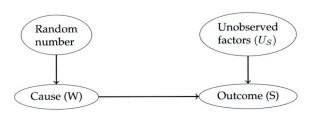

Fig. 5.1 Causal graph for W and S. W causes S, W is generated randomly

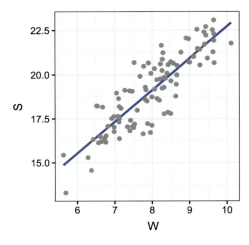

Fig. 5.2 Scatter plot of S versus W, with line of fit from regression of S on W

5.2 Concepts and Examples

Table 5.1 Regression of Outcome (S) on Cause (W), true causal effect = 2

	Model 1
(Intercept)	4.74
	(0.85)
W	1.80
	(0.11)
R^2	0.75
Num. obs	100

Standard errors in parentheses

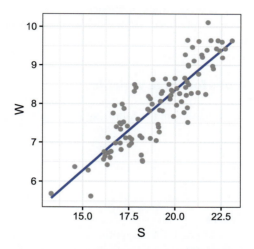

Fig. 5.3 Scatter plot of W versus S, with line of fit from regression of W on S

Table 5.2 Regression of Cause (W) on Outcome (S). Does not have a causal interpretation

	Model 1
(Intercept)	0.07
	(0.47)
S	0.41
	(0.02)
R^2	0.75
Num. obs	100

Standard errors in parentheses

Fig. 5.4 Common cause: W is a common cause of S and I

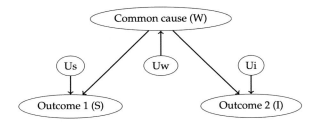

W. Note that the data by themselves do not tell us whether what we have estimated is causal or not.

Causal inference builds on statistical inference. In Table 5.1, the statistical inference translates into causal inference. In Table 5.2 statistical inference cannot be interpreted as causal.

5.2.2 Causal Graphs for Three Variables

We now examine three variables, in the following hypothetical cases:

- Common cause.
- Intermediate variable.
- Collider.

5.2.2.1 Common Cause

Figure 5.4 shows the causal graph for a hypothetical example of common cause.

The structural equations are:

$$W := U_w$$
$$S := \alpha_S + \gamma_S W + U_S$$
$$I := \alpha_I + \gamma_I W + U_I$$

Note that I has no effect on S; the structural equation for S does not contain I. We generated data for W, S, and I.

Outcome 1 (S) and outcome 2 (I) are not causally related; the true effect of I on S is zero. In Table 5.3, Model 2 gives us an estimate that is closer to the true effect. The intuition is that there is a path $S \leftarrow W \rightarrow I$; since this points into I, we call it a backdoor path and need to block it. When we block it, our effect estimate reflects the true effect.

We need to control for common cause. Most textbooks have emphasized omitted variable bias. Analysts often put in more 'control' variables, erring on the side of more to avoid the perceived threat of omitted variable bias. But in the next two cases we see that we should not control for intermediate or collider variables.

5.2 Concepts and Examples

Table 5.3 Common cause case, Dependent variable is S, true effect of I on S is 0

	Model 1	Model 2
(Intercept)	21.42	14.33
	(4.15)	(2.93)
I	0.91	0.12
	(0.09)	(0.10)
W		2.79
		(0.27)
R^2	0.50	0.77
Num. obs	100	100

Standard errors in parentheses

5.2.2.2 Intermediate Variable

Figure 5.5 shows the causal graph. J causes H, and C lies between J and H on the path $J \to C \to H$.

The structural equations are:

$$J := U_j.$$
$$C := \alpha_C + \gamma_C J + U_c.$$
$$H := \alpha_H + \gamma_H C + U_h.$$

We generated data. When we regress H on J, we get an estimate close to the true effect (Table 5.4). However, when we regress H on J and C, C blocks the effect of J on H (Table 5.4). We should not control for the intermediate variable.

5.2.2.3 Collider

In Fig. 5.6, Cause 1 (S) is independent of Cause 2 (H). The structural equations corresponding to Fig. 5.6 are:

$$H := Uh.$$
$$S := Us.$$
$$B = \alpha + \gamma_H H + \gamma_S S + Ub.$$

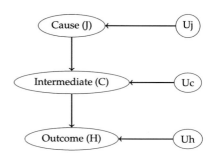

Fig. 5.5 Intermediate variable hypothetical example. C lies between J and H on the path $J \to C \to H$

Table 5.4 Intermediate variable is C, Dependent variable is H, true effect of J on H is 6

	Model 1	Model 2
(Intercept)	9.08	5.17
	(3.59)	(1.73)
J	6.37	−0.47
	(0.24)	(0.39)
C		3.21
		(0.18)
R^2	0.88	0.97
Num. obs	100	100

Standard errors in parentheses

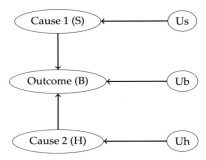

Fig. 5.6 Collider example. Arrows from S and H into B collide

Table 5.5 Dependent variable is S. True effect of H on S is zero

	Model 1	Model 2
(Intercept)	1.05	−0.71
	(0.61)	(0.45)
H	0.10	−0.49
	(0.10)	(0.09)
B		0.54
		(0.05)
R^2	0.01	0.54
Num. obs	100	100

Standard errors in parentheses

We generated data. In Table 5.5, we see that Model 1 gives us a truer picture, while model 2 gives us a misleading picture. Table 5.5 illustrates that we should not control for a collider.

We have considered several simple cases with two and three variables. These cases are the building blocks for larger causal graphs.

5.2 Concepts and Examples

5.2.3 Causal Graphs with ggdag Package

The ggdag package in R can be used to explore causal graphs or directed acyclic graphs (dags); in a later section, we discuss the R code. We create our dag. We plot the dag with the exposure or treatment and outcome variable highlighted (Fig. 5.7).

We now shift our attention to consider different paths in a causal graph with the help of the ggdag package. In terms of paths, there is a path from x to y, and we are interested in the effect of x on y. According to a theorem (Pearl et al. 2016), backdoor paths should be blocked. The first backdoor path, $y \leftarrow w \rightarrow x$ can be blocked by adjusting for w. The second backdoor path, $y \rightarrow m \leftarrow z \rightarrow x$ is blocked because m is a collider; colliders block paths when left alone, and open paths when adjusted for.

We can find out which variables to adjust for, and see how the adjustment set works in terms of blocking paths (Fig. 5.8), using a function in the dagitty package.

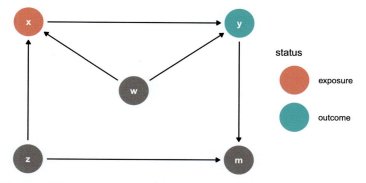

Fig. 5.7 Causal graph created with ggdag, the exposure or treatment variable and the outcome are color coded

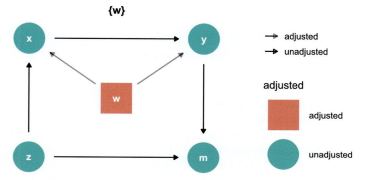

Fig. 5.8 Adjustment set for the same causal graph as in Fig. 5.7. When w is adjusted the grayed out backdoor path with nodes x, w and y is blocked. The other backdoor path with nodes x, z, m and y is blocked without adjustment because m is a collider

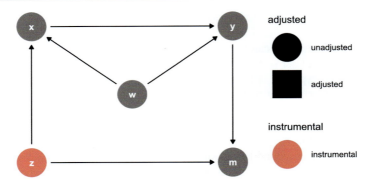

Fig. 5.9 Instrumental variables in the same causal graph as that shown in Fig. 5.7: z can be an instrumental variable for x because z causes x and affects y only through x

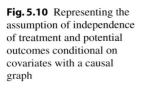

Fig. 5.10 Representing the assumption of independence of treatment and potential outcomes conditional on covariates with a causal graph

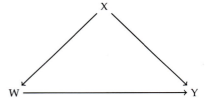

```
## { w }
```
,

There is only one adjustment set, w (Fig. 5.8). So we should adjust for w.

We can also check whether an instrumental variable can be used. Here (Fig. 5.9), z is a candidate instrumental variable because z causes x and only affects y via x (since m is a collider along $z \to m \leftarrow y$).

5.2.4 Assumptions for Causal Inference Using Causal Graphs

In the earlier chapter on potential outcomes, we saw that the assumption that potential outcomes are independent of treatment conditional on covariates, $(Y(0), Y(1)) \perp W|X$ is a key assumption in causal inference. Whether this is true or not depends on the context. Translating this assumption into its causal graph form helps the applied researcher understand the assumption.

For $(Y(0)Y(1)) \perp W|X$, we have in mind the causal graph in Fig. 5.10, and we adjust for X to close the backdoor path $Y \leftarrow X \to W$. The assumption is indicated by missing arrows. A critic may argue that we have left out a variable J, and it should be part of the causal graph. There is another backdoor path, $Y \leftarrow J \to W$, and since this has not been adjusted for the assumption $(Y(0), Y(1)) \perp W|X$ does

5.2 Concepts and Examples

not hold, because $(Y(0), Y(1)) \perp W|X, J$, the potential outcomes are independent of treatment conditional on X and J.

5.2.5 Electoral Systems

Keele et al. (2020) provide a real example based on research in electoral systems to illustrate that not every regression coefficient can be interpreted as a causal effect. The authors assume that a researcher is interested in estimating the effect of district magnitude on the effective number of parties.

The variables are:

- parts: effective number of legislative parties. This is the outcome variable.
- dist: district magnitude. This is the treatment variable.
- U: unmeasured common cause.
- soci: social cleavages.
- seat: upper tier seat allocation.
- rule: electoral rules.
- pres: effective number of presidential parties.

Based on their reading of the literature, the authors present a causal graph (or DAG) that is a possible causal structure. We input the dag for their example and use ggdag (Fig. 5.11).

We list the adjustment sets that can be used to estimate the causal effect of dist on parts.

```
## { seat, soci }
```

Adjusting for seat and soci blocks the two backdoor paths into dist. If we use a regression: parts = b0 + b1 dist + b2 seat + b3 soci + b4 rule + b5 pres, b1 can be interpreted as an estimate of the causal effect of dist on parts because the backdoor paths between parts and dist are blocked. However, we need to be cautious with the other coefficients. For example, b3 cannot be interpreted as a causal effect—the backdoor path $parts \leftarrow U \rightarrow soci$ is not blocked. We need to carefully consider the relevant backdoor paths and whether they are blocked.

The authors essentially caution against interpreting all regression coefficients of control variables causally. To interpret a regression coefficient one must see whether, given a causal graph that one believes to be true, the regression in question is adequate for identifying the effect of the variable on the outcome.

5.2.6 Collider Bias in Public Health

Collider bias rears its head repeatedly in public health. We briefly look at two cases.

5.2.6.1 COVID-19

Gareth et al. (2020) wrote a paper titled "Collider bias undermines our understanding of COVID-19 disease risk and severity." One of the examples discussed in the paper is the relation between ACE inhibitors and COVID-19. A concern was that people using ACE inhibitors could be more susceptible to COVID-19 infection. Some studies aimed to use data from apps where people self-reported data.

In Fig. 5.12, App is a collider, since infection and use of ACE inhibitors may lead people to self-report. Even if use of ACE inhibitors and infection are not related, use of self-reported data will show an association between ACE use and infection.

☞ **Your turn.** Go through the paper by Griffith et al. (2020). What other examples do they provide of collider bias?

5.2.6.2 The Obesity Paradox

Consider the causal graph in Fig. 5.13. Obesity (Ob) causes both cardiovascular disease (CVD) and mortality directly. U is unobserved direct causes of both CVD and mortality. Given this causal graph, if we use data on those with CVD, since CVD

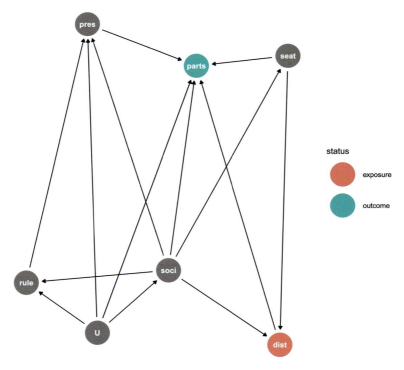

Fig. 5.11 Causal graph of electoral systems (Keele et al. 2020), researchers want to estimate the effect of district magnitude (dist) on effective number of parties (parts)

5.3 R code

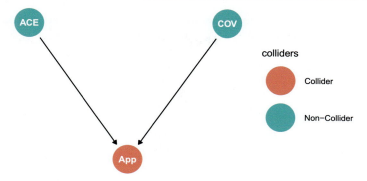

Fig. 5.12 COVID-19 infection (COV) is a cause of self-reporting in the App. Use of ACE inhibitors is likely to be associated with self-reporting in the App. App is a collider. Because the data generation is conditional on self-reporting in the app, ACE and COV could appear to be associated, even if they actually are not

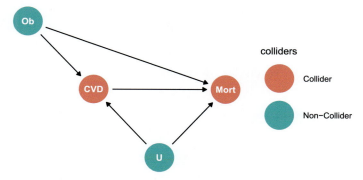

Fig. 5.13 Obesity (Ob) and Mortality (Mort). Cardiovascular disease is a collider because Ob and unobserved variable U both directly cause CVD. This could explain the paradox where obesity appears to reduce mortality

is a collider, the results are going to be biased. This is one possible explanation for the obesity paradox, in which obesity appears to be protective (Banack and Kaufman 2014).

5.3 R code

5.3.1 Causal Graphs for two Variables (Corresponding to Section 5.2.1)

We conduct a simulation for the structural causal model $W \to S$. We translate the structural equations into R code to generate artificial data.

First, for U_w, which is an error, we use the rnorm function to get random draws from a normal distribution. We provide the sample size and the mean and standard deviation:

```
ss <- 30
Uw <- rnorm(ss, mean = 8, sd = 1)
W <- Uw
```

Then, U_s and S (we give α a value of 3, and β a value of 2):

```
Us <- rnorm(ss)
S <- 3 + 2*W + Us
```

Two variables relationship: we make a scatter plot:

```
library(tidyverse)
data2 <- data.frame(W, S)
ggplot(data2, aes(x = W, y = S)) +
  geom_smooth(method = "lm", se = F) +
  geom_point()
```

We regress S on W. We display with texreg:

```
library(texreg)
mod1 <- lm(S ~ W)
texreg(list(mod1), caption = "Regression of S on W.")
```

Now we plot W versus S:

```
ggplot(data2, aes(x = S, y = W)) +
  geom_smooth(method = "lm", se = F) +
  geom_point()
```

We regress W on S:

```
mod1 <- lm(W ~ S)
texreg(list(mod1), , caption = "Regression of W on S.")
```

5.3.2 Causal Graphs for Three Variables (Corresponding to section 5.2.2)

5.3.2.1 Common Cause
We generate data for W, S, and I.

```
Uw <- runif(100, min = 10, max = 20)
W <- Uw
Us <- rnorm(100, 10, 5)
```

5.3 R code

```
S <- 7 + 3 * W + Us
Ui <- rnorm(100, 10, 5)
I <- 3 + 2 * W + Ui
```

We run regressions.

```
m_com1 <- lm(S ~ I)
m_com2 <- lm(S ~ I + W)
texreg(list(m_com1, m_com2), caption = "Common cause, true effect)
( is 0", caption.above = T)
```

5.3.2.2 Intermediate
We generate data:

```
J <- runif(100, min = 10, max = 20)
C <- 3 + 2*J + 2*rnorm(100)
H <- 5 + 3*C + 3*rnorm(100)
```

We run regressions:

```
lm_inter1 <- lm(H ~ J)
lm_inter2 <- lm(H ~ J + C)
texreg(list(lm_inter1, lm_inter2),
  caption = "Intermediate variable, true effect is 6.",
  caption.above = T)
```

5.3.2.3 Collider
We generate data:

```
Uh <- rnorm(100, 6, 1)
H <- Uh
Us <- rnorm(100, 2, 1)
S <- Us
Ub <- rnorm(100)
B <- 2 + H + S + Ub
```

We run regresssions:

```
mod_coll1 <- lm(S ~ H)
mod_coll2 <- lm(S ~ H + B)
texreg(list(mod_coll1, mod_coll2),
  caption = "True effect of H on S is zero.",
  caption.above = T)
```

5.3.3 ggadag use (Corresponding to section 5.2.3)

We load the dagitty and ggdag packages; both have good documentation:

```
library(dagitty)
library(ggdag)
```

We create our dag with the dagify function. We specify what variables we want in the dag and how they are related. In what follows, x and w are direct causes of y, for example:

```
simple_dag <- dagify(
  y ~ x + w,
  x ~ w + z,
  m ~ z + y,
  exposure = "x",
  outcome = "y"
)
```

We plot the dag, with the exposure or treatment and outcome variable highlighted, using the ggdag_status function:

```
# plot dag, with exposure and treatment variable
ggdag_status(simple_dag, stylized = FALSE) +
  theme_dag()
```

We can find out which variables to adjust for; and we see how the adjustment set works in terms of blocking paths:

```
# which variables to adjust for:
adjustmentSets(simple_dag)
# graph of how adjustment set blocks paths:
ggdag_adjustment_set(simple_dag, shadow = FALSE) +
  theme_dag()
```

> **Your turn**   Replicate the code above for using ggdag. Create a dag of your own by hand with several variables, with paper and pen. Then use ggdag to plot it, and find adjustment sets, etc., Look up the ggdag documentation, which is quite accessible.

5.3.4 Electoral Systems (Corresponding to section 5.2.5)

We input the dag for the example in Keele et al. (2020):

```
parties_dag <- dagify(
  parts ~ seat + dist + soci + pres + U,
  pres ~ U + rule + soci,
  rule ~ U + soci,
  soci ~ U,
  dist ~ soci + seat,
  seat ~ soci,
  exposure = "dist",
  outcome = "parts"
)
```

We can highlight which is the exposure and which is the outcome variable thus:

```
ggdag_status(parties_dag) +
  theme_dag()
```

We can list the adjusment sets that can be used to estimate the causal effect:

```
adjustmentSets(parties_dag)
```

5.4 Resources

5.4.1 For Better Understanding

Elwert's (2013) paper titled *Graphical Causal Models*.

5.4.2 For Going Further

The Primer by Pearl, Glymour, and Jewell (2016).

Packages Used in this Chapter

The citations for the packages used in this chapter are[1] :

```
## Barrett M (2021). _ggdag: Analyze and Create Elegant Directed
## Acyclic Graphs_. R package version 0.2.4, <URL:
## \url{https://CRAN.R-project.org/package=ggdag}.}


## Leifeld P (2013). "texreg: Conversion of Statistical Model
## Output in R to LaTeX and HTML Tables." _Journal of Statistical
## Software_, *55*(8), 1-24. <URL:
## \url{http://dx.doi.org/10.18637/jss.v055.i08>.}
```

---

[1] The tidyverse package itself contains several packages.

```
## Textor J, van der Zander B, Gilthorpe MS, Li?kiewicz M,
## Ellison GT (2016). "Robust causal inference using directed
## acyclic graphs: the R package 'dagitty'." _International
## Journal of Epidemiology_, *45*(6), 1887-1894. doi:
## 10.1093/ije/dyw341 (URL: \url{https://doi.org/10.1093/ije/dyw341}.}


## R Core Team (2021). _R: A Language and Environment for
## Statistical Computing_. R Foundation for Statistical
## Computing, Vienna, Austria. <URL: \url{https://www.R-project.org/>.}

print(citation("tidyverse"), style = "text")
## Wickham H, Averick M, Bryan J, Chang W, McGowan LD, François
## R, Grolemund G, Hayes A, Henry L, Hester J, Kuhn M, Pedersen
## TL, Miller E, Bache SM, Müller K, Ooms J, Robinson D, Seidel
## DP, Spinu V, Takahashi K, Vaughan D, Wilke C, Woo K, Yutani H
## (2019). "Welcome to the tidyverse." _Journal of Open Source
## Software_, *4*(43), 1686. doi: 10.21105/joss.01686 (URL:
## \url{https://doi.org/10.21105/joss.01686}).}

print(citation("knitr")[[1]], style = "text")
## Xie Y (2022). _knitr: A General-Purpose Package for Dynamic
## Report Generation in R_. R package version 1.41, <URL:
## \url{https://yihui.org/knitr/>.}

print(citation("formatR"), style = "text")
## Xie Y (2023). _formatR: Format R Code Automatically_. R
## package version 1.14, <URL:
## \url{https://CRAN.R-project.org/package=formatR>.}
```

References

Banack, Hailey R., and Jay S. Kaufman. 2014. The obesity paradox: Understanding the effect of obesity on mortality among individuals with cardiovascular disease. *Preventive Medicine* 62: 96–102.

Elwert, Felix. 2013. Graphical causal models. In *Handbook of causal analysis for social research*, ed. Stephen L Morgan, 245–274. New York: Springer.

Griffith, Gareth J., Tim T. Morris, Matthew J. Tudball, Annie Herbert, Giulia Mancano, Lindsey Pike, Gemma C. Sharp, Jonathan Sterne, Tom M. Palmer, George Davey Smith, Kate Tilling, Luisa Zuccolo, Neil M. Davies, and Gibran Hemani. 2020. Collider bias undermines our understanding of COVID-19 disease risk and severity. *Nature Communications*, 11(1):5749. Number: 1 Publisher: Nature Publishing Group.

Hernan, Miguel A., and James M. Robins. 2023. *Causal inference: What if*. Boca Raton: CRC Press.

Pearl, Judea, Madelyn Glymour, and Nicholas P Jewell. 2016. *Causal inference in statistics: A primer | Wiley*. Wiley.

Keele, Luke, Randolph T. Stevenson, and Felix Elwert. 2020. The causal interpretation of estimated associations in regression models. *Political Science Research and Methods*, 8(1):1–13. Publisher: Cambridge University Press.

Morgan, Stephen L., and Christopher Winship. 2015. *Counterfactuals and causal inference*. Cambridge University Press. Google-Books-ID: Q6YaBQAAQBAJ.

Experiments

6.1 Introduction

Have you wondered how researchers evaluate the effectiveness of vaccines or answer public policy questions, such as whether quotas for women in political leadership positions make a difference in policy outcomes, or whether smaller classes lead to better student learning outcomes? The answer often would be the experimental method. Researchers use this method to investigate cause-and-effect relationships by randomly assigning units, such as individuals, schools, and villages, to different treatments.

Random assignment involves using a randomizer, such as a coin toss, to determine which units receive a treatment or intervention in an experiment. For instance, when conducting an experimental study to test the effectiveness of an oral antiviral pill, researchers may use a coin toss to determine whether an individual receives the treatment pill or a placebo pill (i.e., a dummy pill with no therapeutic value). In a single-blind study, participants are not aware if they are assigned to the treatment group, receiving the antiviral pill, or the control group, receiving the placebo pill. This helps mitigate issues such as placebo effects. However, in some cases, single- or double-blinding is not feasible, such as when randomizing the reservation of villages for women's leadership. Nonetheless, the experimental method remains a powerful tool for gaining knowledge about cause and effect.

Random assignment of treatment is a central feature of many disciplines that aim to understand cause and effect. Economists, for instance, have investigated racial discrimination by sending identical resumes with randomly assigned white- or black-sounding names in response to job advertisements (Bertrand and Mullainathan 2004). Botanists use random assignment to measure the effectiveness of a new compound on plant growth. By comparing the outcomes of the treated and control groups after treatment, researchers can learn about the magnitude of causal effects. Researchers and policymakers are also interested in the size of causal effects, such as the fertilizer

© The Author(s), under exclusive license to Springer Nature Singapore Pte Ltd. 2023
V. Dayal and A. Murugesan, *Demystifying Causal Inference*,
https://doi.org/10.1007/978-981-99-3905-3_6

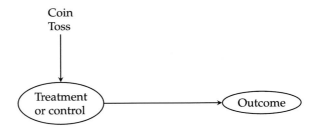

Fig. 6.1 General Experiment where the treatment is randomly assigned by a coin toss

compounds' ability to produce small or large blooms in treated plants, the impact of distributing deworming drugs on lengths of school children's absenteeism, and the extent to which reserving local leadership positions for women improves welfare outcomes.

The randomized assignment of treatment can be achieved by flipping a coin to decide who gets the treatment and who does not (see Fig. 6.1). Randomness in the assignment of treatment is a crucial element of the experimental design as it severs the link between unit characteristics and the likelihood of treatment. All units have an equal chance of treatment, independent of their characteristics such as race, gender, and wealth, enabling an apples-to-apples comparison of the treated and control groups.

Maintaining this even balance is critical because then the treated and control groups are similar before treatment. This similarity before treatment allows researchers to estimate the effect of the treatment. Following treatment, the researchers can then compare the average difference in outcomes, such as the size of the sapling blooms, between the treated and control groups to measure the impact of the treatment.

6.2 Examples and Concepts

6.2.1 Anchoring Affects Judgments

Let's start with a simple laboratory experiment before exploring larger policy questions using large-scale experiments. Consider a randomizer similar to flipping a coin, such as spinning a wheel of fortune,[1] numbered 0–100. Nobel laureate Daniel Kahneman and his collaborator Amos Tversky used a similar wheel to demonstrate how people's judgments or estimates can be influenced by starting points, commonly known as 'anchors'.

Let's explore how anchors can influence our estimates. Begin by writing down the last two digits of your phone number, and have a friend do the same with their phone number. Next, both of you should quietly make your best guesses of the number of

---

[1] A long-running American television game show, where participants spin the titular *Wheel of Fortune*, a roulette-style wheel with several slices labeled with dollar amounts to determine the dollar prize. The participants can win the prize if they answer word puzzles correctly.

6.2 Examples and Concepts

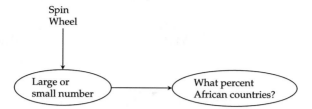

Fig. 6.2 Anchoring experiment by Tversky and Kahneman (1974). A large or small number is randomly assigned to the participant, who is then asked about the percentage of countries that are African

African countries in the United Nations without discussing it with each other. Write down your guesses. Don't read on until both of you have recorded the numbers. Have you completed the task?

The numbers you wrote down can reveal the influence of anchors on your estimates. Specifically, your guesses are likely anchored closer to the starting points, which were the last two digits of your phone numbers. A behavioral economics instructor at Harvard Business School often conducts this experiment in her executive education course, which is attended by management experts from various industries (Lewis 2016). She collects the papers with the two numbers—the phone number and the guess of each student—to demonstrate that people whose phone numbers have the last two digits closer to 100 tend to have higher estimates of the number of African countries in the United Nations. Assuming that your phone number's last two digits were randomly assigned to you, the experiment highlights the phone number's anchoring effect on your estimate of African nations.

The anchoring effect was first demonstrated by Tversky and Kahneman (1974) in a lab experiment in which participants were divided into two groups. Before participants in each group were asked to estimate the percentage of African countries in the United Nations, a number between 0 and 100 was determined by spinning a wheel in the subject's presence.[2] The wheel randomly stopped at 10 or 65, and the subjects then had to indicate whether the percentage of African countries in the UN was higher or lower than the value of the number at which the wheel stopped. Finally, the participants estimated the percentage by moving up or down from the starting point, which was either 10 or 65, depending on their group (Fig. 6.2). According to Tversky and Kahneman (1974), the median estimates of the percentage of African countries in the UN were 25 for groups that started with 10 and 45 for groups that started with 65. The researchers found that incentives for accurate guessing did not reduce the anchoring effect in their experiment.

We wanted to test whether the Kahneman and Tversky experiment would yield similar results in two of our classes. Figure 6.3 displays the results for the Indian Economic Service (IES) and The Energy and Resources Institute (TERI) classes.

---

[2] The wheel was rigged to randomly stop only at either 10 or 65 in their experiment to allow comparison between a low and a high starting point, rather than continuous starting points ranging from 0 to 100. Whether it stopped at 10 or 65 was random.

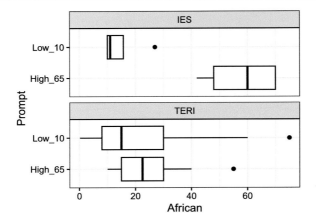

Fig. 6.3 Anchoring Experiment: Comparison of the distribution of estimates of African countries in the UN by class and by treatment

In both cases the results were similar to Tversky and Kahneman (1974). In the IES class, there was a clear difference in the estimate given the starting point, while in the TERI class, the difference was not so marked. It's important to note that these classroom experiments were only conducted for illustrative purposes and that there were differences in the number of students in each class. The IES class was small with only eight students. Researchers conducting a careful experimental study must ensure that they have a sufficient number of participants in both the treated and control groups to make valid statistical inferences.

The Tversky and Kahneman (1974) experiment demonstrated how random anchoring points can systematically bias people's predictions. They used a roulette wheel to assign different starting points to different groups, making it a transparent method of randomizing treatments.[3] While other experiments use simpler methods like coin tosses, die rolls, or computer-based random number generators, the key idea remains the same: randomization can break any link between unit characteristics and the chance of treatment. By using randomization, we create a balanced comparison of the treated and control groups, allowing us to estimate the effect of the treatment on the outcome in an apples-to-apples comparison.

6.2.2 Women as Policymakers

In the 1990s, the Indian government began conducting a far-reaching policy experiment by randomly reserving one-third of its village council head positions for women. This randomization creates an ideal setting for answering many policy questions. Chattopadhyay and Duflo (2004) utilized this randomization to show that the

---

[3] Even if the wheel was rigged!

6.2 Examples and Concepts

gender of the village head affects the types of public goods provided in the village. For instance, they found that women leaders invest more in drinking water projects than men on roads.

You may still wonder why the randomized policy experiment provides an ideal setting for causal inference. Can't we just compare average outcomes in regions or villages headed by men versus women to determine the effect of gender on policy decisions? The answer lies in the possibility that differences in outcomes between regions with different proportions of women in leadership positions could be caused by factors other than just the gender of the leaders. For instance, the political preferences of the group that elected them could be different. Without randomization, the fact that women came to power in one region and not the other means that comparing the two regions may not be an apples-to-apples comparison.

To examine the impact of women's representation on policies, let's imagine that you have the ability to conduct an experimental study on the elections in a country where few women hold leadership positions. Seeking advice from a statistician, you learn that you can use a policy of reserving seats in villages for women, based on coin toss results, to gain insight into this impact. For each village council head position, if the coin lands on heads, the seat is reserved for a woman, and if it lands on tails, it remains unreserved, likely be filled by a man. In reality, the Indian policy of randomly assigning one-third of the seats to women since the 1990s created a natural experiment. The experiment delinked the role of village characteristics from the chance of having a woman as their head due to seat reservation. By randomly determining if women would hold power through a coin toss, the experiment evened out the characteristics of reserved and unreserved villages. Whether the village invests in drinking water or roads after treatment arises from the leaders' choices and is not systematically related to the characteristics of the village.

In the Indian natural experiment, the random assignment of reservations in a large sample of village council seats balances covariates across randomly treated and control units, enabling an apples-to-apples comparison.[4] The assignment would even out pre-treatment differences in factors such as preference for women leaders or drinking water projects. Chattopadhyay and Duflo (2004) (hereafter CD) present a table that displays no statistical difference in covariates such as female or male literacy rate, dirt or metal road, and tube well availability between the treated and control units before the natural experiment began. Randomization balances both observed and unobserved covariates in expectation, allowing CD to make inferences about the effect of women leaders, all else being equal.

To study the influence of women political leaders, CD collected primary data from Gram Panchayats (GP) in Birbhum (West Bengal, India) and Udaipur (Rajasthan, India). GPs are typically made up of multiple villages. CD interviewed the GP Pradhan (elected head) first and then conducted surveys in three villages in each GP, with two villages randomly selected and the third village being the one where the GP Pradhan resided. The participants in the survey were asked to identify the types of

---

[4] Unlike the anchoring experiment in IES classroom which had very few students.

infrastructure (public goods) constructed or repaired during the GP Pradhan's tenure. CD asked the same questions to the GP Pradhan and in the village surveys wherever possible. CD noted that the village-level information is likely to be more reliable as the Pradhan may provide biased responses, but the information given by the Pradhan refers to the entire GP and is free from sampling error.[5] The authors analyze the data separately and compare the results given the trade-off.

The empirical strategy of the authors is transparent: the natural experiment by randomly assigning the treatment to villages allowed them to compare the means of outcomes in reserved (treated) and unreserved (control) GPs. The difference in means is the effect of reservations.[6],[7]

In the districts CD studied, they found that all reserved GPs had a female Pradhan, while barely any of the unreserved GPs had elected a female Pradhan. As the treatment assignment was compliant with the reservation policy, CD argue that they are estimating a causal effect of the policy. They found that when the Pradhan was a woman, the percentage of women participating in the Gram Samsad (townhall meetings) was significantly higher (9.8% vs. 6.9%). Additionally, women in villages with a female Pradhan were twice as likely to have voiced their grievances about village issues in the last 6 months compared to women in villages with a male Pradhan. The CD study showed that having a female Pradhan increased the participation of other women in village political affairs.

CD analyzed the formal requests made by villagers to the Panchayat in the 6 months before the survey. They found that women in the reserved villages complained more about drinking water than men. Furthermore, GPs reserved for women made substantially more investments in drinking water (see Fig. 6.4), and gender of the women leader significantly affected the type of public good investments made in the GP. These results suggest that the reservation policy has a meaningful impact on local policy decisions.

---

[5] Sampling error is the difference between a sample's characteristics and the characteristics of the population from which the sample was drawn. It can be reduced by increasing the sample size and using appropriate sampling techniques.

[6] Following the authors, we denote Y_{ij} as the value of the outcome of interest for good i (e.g., investment in drinking water between 1998 and 2000) and R_j is an indicator (typically called dummy) variable. The variable R_j is equal to 1 if the GP is reserved for a woman and 0 if it is not. Therefore, the difference or the effect of the reservation is

$$E[Y_{ij}|R_j = 1] - E[Y_{ij}|R_j = 0],$$

which the authors use to make inferences about the effect of women leaders, all else equal.

[7] The simple difference in means estimate does not account for possible correlation within GPs. To address this concern, the authors estimate reduced form village-level regressions with errors clustered at the GP level. Clustering standard errors is important for two reasons, as argued by Abadie et al. (2020): (1) sampling design, because you have sampled data from a population using clustered sampling, and want to make inferences about the general population; and (2) experimental design, where the assignment mechanism for the causal treatment of interest is clustered at a particular level.

6.2 Examples and Concepts

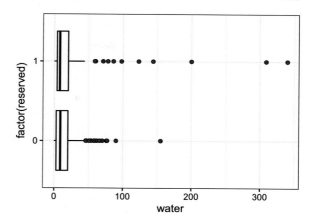

Fig. 6.4 Distribution of drinking water facilities in reserved and not reserved villages in Birbhum

☞ **Discussion.** Identify the other types of public goods where the authors found a difference (or no difference) between the reserved and unreserved villages.

Data from Birbhum district in West Bengal, a subset of the data CD collected, was analyzed and presented in Imai (2018). We present Fig. 6.4 using this data to compare treatment and control groups.

CD noted that women who serve as Pradhans may differ from male Pradhans in several ways, such as their level of political experience, likelihood of re-election, and socioeconomic status. This raises questions about whether the study's policy conclusions are weakened. However, the authors rely on the strength of randomization to address these concerns. By randomly assigning seats to women, the policy disentangled the gender effect from other effects. The authors control for the characteristics of the Pradhan in their regression specification.[8] Moreover, when comparing investments in GPs reserved for women to those in GPs with new male Pradhans, the authors found that none of the results on public goods provisions were affected, suggesting that the effect of reservation for women on policy cannot solely be attributed to the fact that these women are new Pradhans.

To address concerns about whether women Pradhan's decisions may be influenced by their (lower) likelihood of re-election, CD compared outcomes in GPs reserved for women to those under male Pradhans who are less likely to serve a consecutive term because the seat would be reserved for a woman in the next election. The comparison groups were similar in terms of re-electability incentives for the serving Pradhans, regardless of gender. CD found that the main results were not affected

---

[8] Furthermore, CD control for the characteristics of the Pradhans and their interactions with women's reported preferences for public goods. The coefficient of the interaction between the reservation and the intensity of women's preference remained unchanged and significant.

by these comparisons. Additionally, CD compared differences in GPs reserved for Scheduled Castes (SC) and Scheduled Tribes (ST) and found that the gender result remains unchanged.[9]

CD utilized a natural policy experiment in India to overcome selection biases that may arise when comparing villages led by women to those led by men. By randomizing who led the village, the authors were able to mitigate any selection biases in the treated and control villages. With a sufficient sample size of randomized villages, they were able to balance observed covariates, and possibly unobserved covariates as well, across the reserved and unreserved villages. Since the CD study included only the sample where the villages entirely complied with the treatment, a simple difference in means of outcomes under reserved and unreserved can provide useful insights.

Overall, the CD study demonstrated that the randomized policy experiment of reserving seats for women in India provided an ideal setting for causal inference. Through randomization, the authors were able to create an apples-to-apples comparison of treated and control villages, thereby overcoming selection biases. The empirical approach isolated the gender effect from other effects and estimated the causal effect of the policy. The results revealed that women Pradhans had a significant impact on policy outcomes, such as the availability of drinking water.

What's more, the results on the influence of women leaders on policy outcomes remained consistent when the authors restricted the comparison groups, such as newly elected Pradhans only or SC/ST seats. All of these findings were made possible by the "flip of a coin" in a natural experiment, highlighting the power of randomization to make causal inferences.

6.2.3 Small Class Size and Student Learning Outcomes

Many countries, regardless of their level of economic development, face the policy question of how much to invest in public education for children. While an extensive literature examined the relationship between school resources and student achievement, the findings on the impact of class size on student learning were inconclusive until the Governor of Tennessee funded Project STAR (Student-Teacher Achievement Ratio) in the 1980s. Project STAR was a large-scale policy experiment that randomly assigned primary school children to small or regular class sizes. The Tennessee legislature authorized a four-year study, following a smaller study in Indiana that found improved student learning in smaller classes.

In Tennessee, about 6,500 pupils in 330 classrooms were assigned to either a small, regular, or regular class with an aide assisting the teacher. A team of academics and members of the Tennessee Department of Education found that smaller classes

---

[9] The SC and ST are official designations used in India for historically marginalized communities who have faced social, economic, and political exclusion due to their caste or tribal status. The Indian government has proportionately reserved seats in village council elections for these groups.

6.2 Examples and Concepts

led to significant early learning improvements. The effect of small class size on achievements was larger for minority children than for other children in the early years.

Why did earlier studies on class size and student achievement produce inconclusive and conflicting results? To answer the question, we must consider the issue with simple comparisons based on non-experimental data. Typically, schools with small class sizes were located in wealthier regions or districts and had greater resources than those with larger class sizes. Children from affluent neighborhoods enjoyed advantages that contributed to their academic performance, such as better nutrition, better-educated parents, and higher quality teachers. These other factors, both observable and unobservable, such as access to private tutoring, could also affect academic performance, leading to a bias in the estimate of the effect of class size. Consequently, a simple comparison of average test scores from small and large classes would not isolate the class size effects from other factors, resulting in a distorted estimate of the causal effect of class size.

What if we could control or account for these other factors? Accounting for *all* the factors that affect schooling outcomes can reduce or even eliminate the bias in estimating the effect of class size on student performance. A multiple regression framework that includes class size and all relevant factors can address the issue of conflated effects. However, is it possible to observe, measure, and control for *all* the relevant factors? The simple answer is no. Even if we account for the observable factors, there may still be unobservable ones. As Krueger (1999) argues, there are likely to be *omitted* factors in the "education production function", which is complex and uncertain (p. 498). Krueger (1999) used the classical experiment structure in the STAR project. Students in Project STAR were randomly assigned to different class sizes, essentially by coin tosses.

Discussion. Identify some of the unobservable or difficult to measure factors that would affect both class size and test scores. Would randomization of treatment address the bias arising from these unobservable factors?

Project STAR was a randomized controlled policy experiment that was conducted on an unprecedented scale. It cost the Tennessee government approximately $ 12 million over four years and covered students from various backgrounds attending schools in inner-city, rural, urban, and suburban areas. The study began in the 1985–1986 school year, where kindergarten students and their teachers were randomly assigned to one of three groups: small classes (13–17 students per teacher), regular-size classes (22–25 students), and regular-aide classes (22–25 students) where an aide assisted the full-time teacher. Over the four years, the sample included 11,600 students from 80 schools, split among 330 classrooms.

While the STAR experiment was designed to be nearly ideal, as with any policy experiment of this scale, there were implementation issues that affected the ideal randomization. For example, some parents expressed discontent when their children were initially not assigned to the smaller classes, as they believed that the districts had unevenly (and unfairly) allocated school resources. To relieve such parental concerns, re-randomization was conducted after the kindergarten year. However, this re-randomization posed challenges for causal inference of the effect of class size through simple comparisons across treated and control groups, as changing the peer groups could potentially affect student achievement.

Another issue with conducting a simple comparison of mean differences among the three different classes (small, regular, regular-aide) in the STAR experiment is that around 10% of students switched between small and regular classes between grades "primarily because of behavioral problems or parental complaints" (Krueger p. 499). This non-random transitioning could compromise experimental comparisons. Additionally, families relocating during the school year could lead to variations in the student composition and class size. Furthermore, longitudinal studies of schooling are subject to sample attrition over the years. Krueger (1999) addresses these limitations in implementing the ideal experimental design and attempts to calculate the benefits and costs of having a small class size.

Project STAR sought to minimize selection effects by inviting all Tennessee schools with K-3 classes (Kindergarten to class 3) to participate, ensuring that various types of schools were represented. To qualify for the study, each school had to have enough students for at least one of each three class types: small, regular, and regular with an aide. This design allowed the researchers to control for school-level differences when comparing student achievement by class size, essentially studying the difference of means across treatments within each school. In total, 79 schools from diverse locations, including inner-city, rural, urban, and suburban areas, met the requirements of Project STAR, providing a large and representative sample to study.

Students and teachers were randomly assigned to their respective class type within each school, which alleviated concerns that better or worse teachers were matched with a particular type of class. Notably, no child received fewer resources due to the experiment, as the average regular class size was maintained from previous years. However, students in the treated groups, i.e., small classes and regular classes with an aide, were allocated more resources. To protect the privacy and confidentiality of human subjects, individual student results were never reported by investigators, and only the average outcomes at the treatment level were reported.

Krueger (1999) applies econometric methods to strengthen the analysis of the STAR experiment. To assess the quality of randomization, he manually verifies whether the students were enrolled in their randomly assigned class type. The compliance was almost perfect, with only 0.3% of students (i.e., 3 in 1000) *not* enrolled in

Fig. 6.5 Covariates are balanced across treated and control groups in project STAR

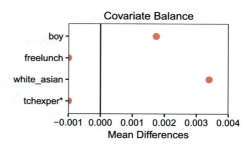

their assigned class type.[10] However, despite the randomization, differences could exist in the baseline characteristics of students across class types. Unfortunately, baseline test results were not available to confirm that it was an apples-to-apples comparison.

Krueger addressed concerns of systematic differences at the beginning of the experiment across groups by testing for differences in means on other measurable covariates. He controlled for school-level effects and found that the random assignment produced relatively similar treated and control groups, such as students on free lunch, race, and age. Figure 6.5 illustrates that observable variables, such as gender and race, are balanced (mean differences very close to zero) across the treatment and control groups. To check whether teacher assignment was random, Krueger regressed each of the three teacher characteristics (experience, race, or education) on class type dummies, but found no significant correlation suggesting that teachers were randomly assigned to different class types. Krueger's thorough approach provides policymakers with confidence in the validity of the study's findings.

To assess student learning of the treated and control groups, Krueger (1999) used standardized tests administered in March or April of each year. These tests evaluated reading, word recognition, and math skills for grades K-3, while the Tennessee Basic Skills First test evaluated reading and math achievement in grades 1–3.[11]

Krueger (1999) estimates the effect of small class size on the scores by controlling for observed student and teacher characteristics, such as gender and race, as well as school effects in some specifications. The regression model of the differences estimator has two treatment groups: small class and regular-aide class, implemented

---

[10] Only one student assigned to a regular or regular-aide class was enrolled in a small class, which means compliance was near perfect.

[11] Since the test results do not have natural units, Krueger scaled them into percentile ranks ranging from 0 (lowest score) to 100 (highest score) to compare scores across different class sizes. To determine each student's percentile score in the small class for each subject test, Krueger placed them in the comparative distribution of percentile scores of the regular-class students (including regular-aide). He found that the average test scores of all class types tended to be lower for students who entered the experiment in higher grades, likely because higher achieving students were more likely to attend kindergarten (which was optional in Tennessee at the time of the study). To address this issue, Krueger controlled for the grade in which the student entered Project STAR.

as two dummy variables indicating whether the student was in a small class or regular-aide class (see equation below):

$$Y_i = \beta_1 SmallClass_i + \beta_2 RegAid_i + \epsilon_i.$$

Krueger's findings support earlier estimates, which found that students in small classes tend to perform better than those in regular and regular-aide classes in Project STAR. The simple regression results without controlling for covariates show an average performance gap of about five percentile points in kindergarten, 8.6 points in first grade, and 5–6 points in second and third grades. The modest effect of including covariates on the class-size coefficients suggests that the class size was randomly assigned according to the experimental ideal.[12]

Krueger's (1999) analysis of Project STAR indicates that students in regular classes with an aide perform slightly better (one or two percentile points, on average) than those in regular classes without an aide. However, this difference is statistically significant in only one grade level, suggesting that the teacher aide has a small effect on student scores. On the other hand, the difference between small and regular classes (with or without an aide) is consistently statistically significant. Krueger estimates that the impact on students assigned to small kindergarten classes is about 64%, which is as large as the white-black test score gap. In third grade, the impact is 82%. The effects are substantial, with smaller classes having a more significant effect in the early years, but a smaller cumulative effect for boys than girls. Less privileged students, particularly those on free lunch or black students, benefit most from attending smaller classes. Krueger's results inform the implementation of progressive policies.

Krueger's findings from his rigorous analysis were in the same ballpark as the estimates from simpler studies using the Project STAR data, highlighting the strength of the randomized experiment design. As Krueger (1999, p. 528) emphasizes, "one well-designed experiment should trump a phalanx of poorly controlled, imprecise observational studies based on uncertain statistical specifications." Despite adjustments made for school effects, attrition, re-randomization after kindergarten, and other deviations from an ideal experiment, Krueger's findings did not contradict findings from simpler studies using the same experimental data. Project STAR's success in answering a long-standing policy question conclusively demonstrates the potential of randomized experiments in informing policymaking.

6.2.4 Simulate to Understand

We will try to understand key ideas related to the working of randomized experiments via simulation.

We consider an observed Treatment $Treat\_obs$ that affects an outcome y_out.

---

[12] The standard errors may be correlated at the class level (e.g., a few exceptional students may have a common influence, good or bad, on the whole class), so Krueger accounts for this correlation in estimating the standard errors.

6.2 Examples and Concepts

Fig. 6.6 Observed treatment and outcome

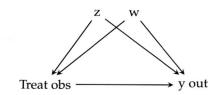

Fig. 6.7 Sampling distribution of estimated effects with observational data. The true effect is given by the red line, and equals 2. In subfigure (**a**), we do not control for z, and in subfigure (**b**) we control for z. Controlling for z reduces but does not eliminate bias because we cannot control for the unobserved variable w

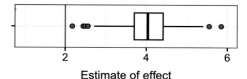

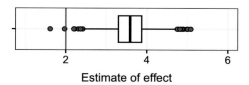

Figure 6.6 shows the causal graph for how the observed treatment affects the outcome. The variable z, which is observed and w, which is not observed, also affect both the observed treatment and the outcome.

We generated data that is consistent with Fig. 6.6:

```
# w = sample(c(0,1),ssize, replace = TRUE)
# z = rnorm(n = ssize, mean = 5),
# Tstar = 3*w + z + rnorm(n = ssize)
# Treat_obs = ifelse(Tstar > 6.5,1,0)
# y_out = 2 * Treat_obs + 2 * w + z + rnorm(n = ssize)
```

We run regressions of the outcome variable on the treatment variable and of the outcome variable on the treatment variable and z, the observed covariate:

```
# regressions
# m1_obs <- lm(y_out ~ Treat_obs, data = sim_obs_data)
# m2_obs <- lm(y_out ~ Treat_obs + z, data = sim_obs_data)
```

In Fig. 6.7, we see that with observational data with 900 observations, we have bias. The sampling distribution of the estimated coefficient is away from the true value of 2 (red line) whether we control for z or not. Controlling for z reduces the bias, but since we do not observe w, a confounding variable is still not controlled for.

Fig. 6.8 Randomly assigned treatment and outcome

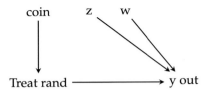

With observational data, there may be a confounding variable that we have not adjusted for (though that does not necessarily imply that we should put as many variables as possible in a regression). For example, children studying in smaller classes may live in relatively wealthy neighborhoods and are raised by parents with relatively higher levels of education.

Figure 6.8 shows the causal graph for how the randomly assigned treatment affects the outcome. Because of random assignment, the variables z and w no longer affect the treatment, since it is randomly assigned. The variable z, which is observed and w, which is not observed, also affect both the observed treatment and the outcome.

We generated data for the variables consistent with Fig. 6.8. The main change now is that the treatment is randomly assigned, and we denote it as *treat_rand*; it no longer is influenced by w and z:

```
# w = sample(c(0,1),ssize, replace = TRUE)
# z = rnorm(n = ssize, mean = 5)
# Treat_rand = sample(c(0,1),ssize, replace = TRUE)
# y_out = 2 * Treat_rand + 2 * w + z + rnorm(n = ssize)
```

We ran regressions of the outcome variable on the treatment variable and of the outcome variable on the treatment variable and z, the observed covariate:

```
# regressions
# m1_exp <- lm(y_out ~ Treat_rand, data = sim_exp_data)
# m2_exp <- lm(y_out ~ Treat_rand + z, data = sim_exp_data)
```

Figure 6.9 shows that the difference estimator with observational data is biased in contrast to the difference estimator with experimental data. In both cases the sample size is 900. In the case of randomized assignment of treatment, it is possible that we do not have bias even without using a covariate in a regression.

Figure 6.10 shows that when using experimental data, controlling for variables may not be needed so much to improve the point estimate as to improve precision. In subfigure A, we see that the difference estimator with experimental data without controlling for z is less precise than the regression estimate with experimental data that controls for z.

6.2 Examples and Concepts

Fig. 6.9 Sampling distribution of estimated effects with observational and experimental data. The red line gives the true effect, and equals 2. In subfigure (**a**), we see that the difference estimator with observational data is biased, but in subfigure (**b**) we see that the difference estimator with experimental data is unbiased

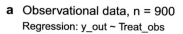
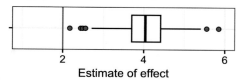

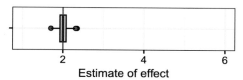

Fig. 6.10 Sampling distribution of estimated effects with experimental data. The red line gives the true effect, and equals 2. In subfigure (**a**), we see that the difference estimator with experimental data without controlling for z is less precise than the regression estimate with experimental data that controls for z

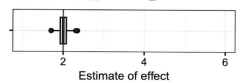

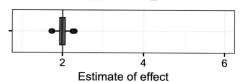

Figure 6.11 shows that if the sample size is small, some estimates with experimental data could be at some distance from the true effect. With larger sample sizes the precision is high.

Fig. 6.11 Sampling distribution of estimated effects with experimental data with small (30) and larger (900) sample sizes. The individual estimates with small sample size with experimental data may be off the mark though they are unbiased

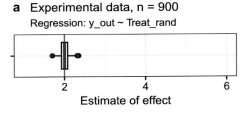

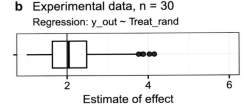

6.3 R Code

We load the packages we need to analyze the data:

```
library(knitr)
library(tidyverse)
library(texreg)
library(formatR)
library(estimatr)
library(POE5Rdata)
library(cobalt)
library(gridExtra)
library(ggpubr)
```

6.3.1 Anchoring Affects Judgments

We start with data from a version of the Kahneman and Tversky experiment one of the authors conducted. Participating students in the experiment were asked to fill out a paper questionnaire.

The number X was randomly assigned within a class, with a high X (65) being assigned to the treatment group, and a low X (10) being assigned to a control group. X was recorded as the variable `Prompt`.

Participants were told:

- We chose (by computer) a random number between 0 and 100.
- The number selected and assigned to you is $X = $ .....

6.3 R Code

Participants were then asked the following questions:

- Do you think the percentage of countries, among all those in the United Nations, that are in Africa is higher or lower than X?............
- Give your best estimate of the percentage of countries, among all those in the United Nations, that are in Africa. ....

The data in the file `anchor` contains the following variables:

- `Prompt`. High if $X = 65$, low if $X = 10$.
- `African`. Best guess of the percentage of countries in Africa among all the countries in the United Nations.
- `Class`. Which of the two classes the participating students belonged to—IES or TERI.

In R, we read in the data, and can check the kinds of variables we have from the displayed message.

We get a glimpse of the data:

```
glimpse(anchor)
## Rows: 41
## Columns: 4
## $ ...1       <dbl> 1, 2, 3, 4, 5, 6, 7, 8~
## $ Prompt     <chr> "Low_10", "High_65", "~
## $ African    <dbl> 25.0, 14.0, 15.0, 15.0~
## $ Class      <chr> "TERI", "TERI", "TERI"~
```

We generate means of the variable African by Class and Prompt. In the case of the IES class, there is a big difference in means, but there are only 4 observations each in the treatment and control groups. In the case of the TERI class, the treatment group (Prompt of 65) has a slightly higher mean (Table 6.1):

```
anchor %>%
  group_by(Class, Prompt) %>%
  summarize(count = n(),
            mean_AF = mean(African)) %>%
  kable(format = "latex", digits = 2,
        caption ="Mean guess for African
        countries percentage by class and prompt",
        booktabs = TRUE)
```

Table 6.1 Mean guess for African countries' percentage by class and prompt

Class	Prompt	Count	Mean_AF
IES	High_65	4	58.00
IES	Low_10	4	14.75
TERI	High_65	16	24.50
TERI	Low_10	17	21.89

Table 6.2 Dependent variable is African, class TERI

	Model 1
(Intercept)	24.50
	(4.28)
PromptLow_10	−2.61
	(5.97)
R^2	0.01
Num. obs.	33

Standard errors in parentheses

The following code gives us the figure we saw in Sect. 6.1:

```
ggplot(anchor, aes(y=African,
                   x = Prompt)) +
  geom_boxplot() +
  facet_wrap(~ Class, ncol = 1) +
  coord_flip() +
  theme_bw()
```

We now do a more formal analysis for the TERI class, so we filter the data for it:

```
anchor2 <- anchor %>%
  filter(Class == "TERI")
```

We regress the variable African on Prompt (Table 6.2):

```
mod2 <- lm(African ~ Prompt, data = anchor2)
library(texreg)
texreg(list(mod2),
  caption = "Dependent variable is African, class TERI",
       caption.above = TRUE,
       stars = numeric(0),
       include.ci = FALSE,
       include.adjrs = FALSE,
       custom.note = "Standard errors in parentheses.")
```

6.3 R Code

☞ **Your turn**   Print out the Kahneman anchoring questions and make a few copies. Ask a small group of people you know to fill out the questions. For a twist, you can ask them to note the last two digits of their phone number before their guess. Record the data, and then analyze it.

6.3.2   Women as Policymakers

We use a subset of the CD (2004) data corresponding to the data for the Birbhum district in West Bengal presented in Imai (2018). The data can be accessed as follows (remove the hash symbol):

```
#library("devtools")
#install_github("kosukeimai/qss-package", build_vignettes = TRUE)
#data(women, package = "qss")
```

We already have the data on our computer, so we read it:

```
women <- read.csv("women.csv")
```

A glimpse of the data:

```
glimpse(women)
## Rows: 322
## Columns: 6
## $ GP         <int> 1, 1, 2, 2, 3, 3, 4~
## $ village    <int> 2, 1, 2, 1, 2, 1, 2~
## $ reserved   <int> 1, 1, 1, 1, 0, 0, 0~
## $ female     <int> 1, 1, 1, 1, 0, 0, 0~
## $ irrigation <int> 0, 5, 2, 4, 0, 0, 4~
## $ water      <int> 10, 0, 2, 31, 0, 0,~
```

```
women %>%
  group_by(reserved) %>%
  summarize(count_res = n(),
            mean_female = mean(female),
            mean_water = mean(water)) %>%
  kable(caption = "Mean for female and water by reserved",
        booktabs = TRUE)
```

Table 6.3 Mean for female and water by reserved

Reserved	Count_res	Mean_female	Mean_water
0	214	0.0747664	14.73832
1	108	1.0000000	23.99074

Table 6.4 Effect of women on water

	Model 1
(Intercept)	14.74
	(1.53)
Factor(reserved)1	9.25
	(5.07)
R^2	0.02
Num. obs.	322
N Clusters	161

Standard errors in parentheses

Means are compared in Table 6.3. The code for Fig. 6.3 used in the introduction is

```
ggplot(women, aes(x = water,
                 y = factor(reserved))) +
  geom_boxplot() +
  theme_bw()
```

We estimate the effect of reservation with the following regression:

```
women$reserved <- factor(women$reserved)
#library(estimatr)
mod_water_r <- lm_robust(water ~ factor(reserved),
                        clusters = GP, data = women)
```

We make a table for the regression (Table 6.4):

```
library(texreg)
texreg(list(mod_water_r),
       caption = "Effect of women on water",
       caption.above = TRUE,
       stars = numeric(0),
       include.ci = FALSE,
       include.adjrs = FALSE,
       include.rmse = FALSE,
       custom.note = "Standard errors in parentheses.")
```

6.3 R Code

6.3.3 Small Class Size and Student Learning Outcomes

The data can be accessed as follows (Table 6.5):

```
#devtools::install_github("ccolonescu/POE5Rdata")
data(star)
write_csv(star, "star.csv")
#str(star)
```

We use only a subset of the data:

```
star <- star %>%
  filter(aide == 0) %>%
  dplyr::select(totalscore, small, tchexper,
                boy, freelunch, white_asian, schid) %>%
  mutate(small_fac = ifelse(small == 1, "small", "regular"),
         sch_fac = factor(schid))
star <- as_tibble(star)
```

We examine the mean of total score by treatment (small class) (Table 6.5):

```
star %>%
  group_by(small_fac)  %>%
  summarize(mscore = mean(totalscore),
            sdscore = sd(totalscore)) %>%
  kable(caption = "Mean of totalscore by small fac",
        booktabs = TRUE)
```

We produce a graphical comparison of total score by the treatment group:

```
ggplot(star, aes(x = small_fac, y = totalscore)) +
  geom_boxplot() +
  coord_flip() +
  theme_bw()
```

Table 6.5 Mean of total score by small fac

small_fac	score	sdscore
Regular	918.0429	73.13799
Small	931.9419	76.35863

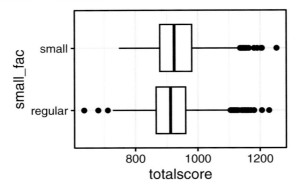

We compare means of covariates:

```
star %>%
  group_by(small_fac)   %>%
  summarize(mboy = mean(boy),
            mlunch = mean(freelunch),
            mw_a = mean(white_asian),
            mexper = mean(tchexper))
## # A tibble: 2 x 5
##   small_fac  mboy mlunch  mw_a mexper
##   <chr>     <dbl>  <dbl> <dbl>  <dbl>
## 1 regular   0.513  0.474 0.681   9.07
## 2 small     0.515  0.472 0.685   9.00
```

Figure 6.5 we used in Sect. 6.1:

```
library(cobalt)
bal.plot(small ~ boy + freelunch +
           white_asian + tchexper,
         data = star, var.name = "boy")
```

Regression for covariate balance (Table 6.6):

```
mod_star_check <- lm(small ~ boy +
    white_asian + tchexper + freelunch,
    data = star)
library(texreg)
texreg(mod_star_check,
       caption = "Checking balance",
       caption.above = TRUE,
       stars = numeric(0),
       include.ci = FALSE,
       include.adjrs = FALSE,
       custom.note = "Standard errors in parentheses.")
```

6.3 R Code

Table 6.6 Checking balance

	Model 1
(Intercept)	0.47
	(0.03)
Boy	0.00
	(0.02)
white_asian	0.00
	(0.02)
tchexper	−0.00
	(0.00)
Freelunch	−0.00
	(0.02)
R^2	0.00
Num. obs.	3743

Standard errors in parentheses

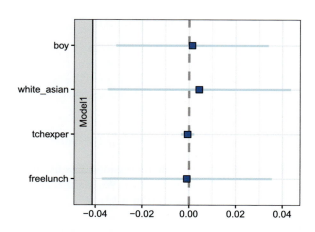

Fig. 6.12 Confidence intervals for covariate balance

Confidence intervals for covariate balance (Fig. 6.12):

```
plotreg(list(mod_star_check), omit.coef=
        c("Intercept"),
     custom.note = "")
```

We run regressions:

```
mod_star_1 <- lm(totalscore ~ small_fac, data = star)
mod_star_2 <- lm(totalscore ~ small_fac + boy +
                   freelunch + white_asian, data = star)
mod_star_3 <- lm(totalscore ~ small_fac + boy +
                   freelunch + white_asian +
              tchexper + sch_fac, data = star)
```

Table 6.7 Effect of small class on total scores

	Model 1	Model 2	Model 3
small_facsmall	13.90	13.81	16.06
	(2.45)	(2.34)	(2.13)
Boy		−15.64	−13.46
		(2.34)	(2.09)
Freelunch		−34.19	−36.34
		(2.60)	(2.50)
white_asian		12.58	25.26
		(2.79)	(4.41)
tchexper			0.82
			(0.22)
R^2	0.01	0.09	0.30
Num. obs.	3743	3743	3743

Standard errors in parentheses

The table of regressions (Table 6.7):

```
texreg(list(mod_star_1, mod_star_2, mod_star_3),
       omit.coef = "Intercept|sch_fac",
       caption = "Effect of small class on total scores",
       caption.above = TRUE, stars = numeric(0),
       include.ci = FALSE,
       include.adjrs = FALSE,
       custom.note = "Standard errors in parentheses.")
```

Especially with multiple regressions, it is useful to plot the confidence intervals for the estimated effects together. We see that changing the specification does not change the estimates much (Fig. 6.13):

```
plotreg(list(mod_star_1, mod_star_2, mod_star_3),
    signif.light = "black",
    custom.coef.map =
    list("small_facsmall" = "Small class"),
    custom.note = "")
```

Fig. 6.13 Confidence intervals for effect of small size, three models

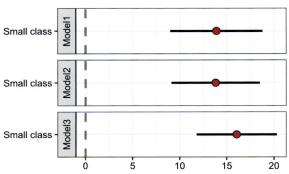

6.3.4 Simulate to Understand

The following is the code and corresponding output for the observational data. We can modify the code and use it again for the rest of the scenarios:

```
set.seed(111)
# make function
sim_regression_obs = function(ssize) {

  # consistent with causal graph

  sim_obs_data = tibble(
    w = sample(c(0,1),ssize, replace = TRUE),
    z = rnorm(n = ssize, mean = 5),
    Tstar = 3*w + z + rnorm(n = ssize),

    Treat_obs = ifelse(Tstar > 6.5,1,0),

    y_out = 2 * Treat_obs + 2 * w + z + rnorm(n = ssize),
  )

  # models

  m1_obs <- lm(y_out ~ Treat_obs, data = sim_obs_data)

  m2_obs <- lm(y_out ~ Treat_obs + z, data = sim_obs_data)

  # results

  tibble(
    b1_m1_obs = coef(m1_obs)[2],
    b1_m2_obs = coef(m2_obs)[2]
  )
}

# run function
sim_regression_obs(30)
## # A tibble: 1 x 2
##   b1_m1_obs b1_m2_obs
##       <dbl>     <dbl>
## 1      3.24      3.17

# now iterate
sim_results_obs =
  rerun(1000, sim_regression_obs(30)) %>%
  bind_rows()
```

```
# check
sim_results_obs
## # A tibble: 1,000 x 2
##    b1_m1_obs b1_m2_obs
##        <dbl>     <dbl>
##  1      4.66      3.77
##  2      3.37      3.33
##  3      3.45      3.36
##  4      4.12      3.64
##  5      4.17      3.98
##  6      3.79      3.61
##  7      5.31      4.66
##  8      4.08      3.63
##  9      3.68      3.47
## 10      3.81      3.59
## # ... with 990 more rows

GG1 <- ggplot(sim_results_obs, aes(x = b1_m1_obs)) +
  geom_boxplot() +
  geom_vline(xintercept = 2,
             col = "red") +
  labs(
    subtitle = "y_out ~ Treat_obs",
    title = "(a) Observational, n = 30"
  ) +
  xlim(1,6) +
  theme_bw()
GG1
```

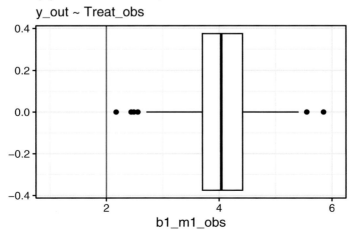

☞ **Your turn** Replicate the code above. Now change the data generation so that it incorporates random assignment of treatment (see the simulation section earlier in the chapter).

6.4 Resources

6.4.1 For Better Understanding

1. Rosenbaum's (2017) book *Observation and Experiment*.
2. Chapters 18 and 19 in Gelman et al.'s (2020) book *Regression and Other Stories*.

6.4.2 For Going Further

The book by Imbens and Rubin (2015), *Causal Inference for Statistics, Social and Biomedical Sciences: An Introduction*.

Packages Used in This Chapter

The citations for the packages used in this chapter are[13]

```
## Auguie B (2017). _gridExtra: Miscellaneous Functions for ##
"Grid" Graphics_. R package version 2.3, <URL: ##
https://CRAN.R-project.org/package=gridExtra>.

## Blair G, Cooper J, Coppock A, Humphreys M, Sonnet L (2022). ##
_estimatr: Fast Estimators for Design-Based Inference_. R ## package
version 1.0.0, <URL: ##
https://CRAN.R-project.org/package=estimatr>.

## Colonescu C (2017). _POE5Rdata: R Data Sets for Principles of
## Econometrics Fifth Edition_. R package version 0.1.0.

## Greifer N (2022). _cobalt: Covariate Balance Tables and ##
Plots_. R package version 4.3.2, <URL: ##
https://CRAN.R-project.org/package=cobalt>.

## Kassambara A (2020). _ggpubr: 'ggplot2' Based Publication ##
Ready Plots_. R package version 0.4.0, <URL: ##
https://CRAN.R-project.org/package=ggpubr>.

## Leifeld P (2013). "texreg: Conversion of Statistical Model ##
Output in R to LaTeX and HTML Tables." _Journal of Statistical ##
Software_, *55*(8), 1-24. <URL: ##
http://dx.doi.org/10.18637/jss.v055.i08>.
```

---

[13] The tidyverse package itself contains several packages.

```
## Makowski D, Lüdecke D, Patil I, Thériault R, Ben-Shachar M, ##
Wiernik B (2023). "Automated Results Reporting as a Practical ##
Tool to Improve Reproducibility and Methodological Best ## Practices
Adoption." _CRAN_. <URL: ## https://easystats.github.io/report/>.

## R Core Team (2021). _R: A Language and Environment for ##
Statistical Computing_. R Foundation for Statistical ## Computing,
Vienna, Austria. <URL: https://www.R-project.org/>.

## Wickham H, Averick M, Bryan J, Chang W, McGowan LD, François ##
R, Grolemund G, Hayes A, Henry L, Hester J, Kuhn M, Pedersen ## TL,
Miller E, Bache SM, Müller K, Ooms J, Robinson D, Seidel ## DP,
Spinu V, Takahashi K, Vaughan D, Wilke C, Woo K, Yutani H ## (2019).
"Welcome to the tidyverse." _Journal of Open Source ## Software_,
*4*(43), 1686. doi: 10.21105/joss.01686 (URL: ##
https://doi.org/10.21105/joss.01686).

## Xie Y (2022). _knitr: A General-Purpose Package for Dynamic ##
Report Generation in R_. R package version 1.41, <URL: ##
https://yihui.org/knitr/>.

## Xie Y (2023). _formatR: Format R Code Automatically_. R ##
package version 1.14, <URL: ##
https://CRAN.R-project.org/package=formatR>.
```

References

Abadie, Alberto, Susan Athey, Guido W. Imbens, and Jeffrey M. Wooldridge. 2020. Sampling-based versus design-based uncertainty in regression analysis. *Econometrica* 88 (1): 265–296.

Bertrand, Marianne, and Sendhil Mullainathan. 2004. Are Emily and Greg more employable than Lakisha and Jamal? A field experiment on labor market discrimination. *American Economic Review* 94 (4): 991–1013.

Chattopadhyay, Raghabendra, and Esther Duflo. 2004. Women as policy makers: evidence from a randomized policy experiment in India. *Econometrica* 72 (5): 1409–1443.

Gelman, Andrew, Jennifer Hill, and Aki Vehtari. 2020. Regression and Other Stories. ISBN: 9781139161879. Publisher: Cambridge University Press. (July 2020).

Imai, Kosuke. 2018. *Quantitative social science: an introduction*. Illustrated edition. Princeton: Princeton University Press. (February 2018)

Imbens, Guido W., and Donald B. Rubin. 2015. *Causal inference for statistics, social, and biomedical sciences: an introduction*. Cambridge: Cambridge University Press.

Krueger, Alan B. 1999. Experimental estimates of education production functions. *The Quarterly Journal of Economics* 114 (2): 497–532.

Lewis, Michael. 2016. *The undoing project: a friendship that changed the world*. Penguin UK.

Rosenbaum, Paul R. 2017. *Observation and experiment: an introduction to causal inference*. Cambridge, MA: Harvard University Press. (August 2017)

Tversky, Amos, and Daniel Kahneman. 1974. Judgment under uncertainty: heuristics and biases. *Science* 185 (4157): 1124–1131.

Matching   7

7.1 Introduction

Matching is a method to uncover 'hidden experiments' in observational data, as conceived by King and Nielsen (2019). It involves processing observational data to create a comparison group where treated and control units are similar on observed characteristics. Advocates of matching argue that creating observably similar groups allows for an apples-to-apples comparison, which can be used to estimate the causal effect of a treatment, be it an intervention, a policy, or a program. Matching is an appealing method to estimate causal effects as it offers the promise of using readily available observational data, without the need for randomized experiments, which can be expensive and time-consuming. In this chapter, we will explore how matching methods can deliver on this promise of finding causal effects from non-experimental data.

Randomized trials can be expensive, infeasible, or raise ethical concerns. Therefore, the idea of estimating causal effects without randomization is an alluring prospect, almost like magic. One method to estimate causal effects is matching, which involves carefully selecting control units that resemble the treated units in relevant characteristics to create matched pairs of similar units. However, the credibility of the estimated causal effect with matching depends on the validity of key assumptions, such as unconfoundedness.[1] This implies that the treatment assignment must

---

[1] Other assumptions, such as the Stable Unit Treatment Value Assumption (SUTVA), play a role in getting an accurate causal estimate. The SUTVA states that the potential outcome of a unit, such as an individual, is defined in terms of only their own treatment assignment (Gelman 2020). In other words, the treatment assigned to one unit should not affect the potential outcomes of other units. Violations of the SUTVA can occur in various situations, such as spillover effects of a vaccine that have positive externalities for others beyond the benefits for the individual receiving the treatment.

be independent of the potential outcomes once the treated and control groups have been matched on their observed characteristics (Abadie and Imbens 2016). To illustrate the differences between estimates from experimental and observational data, we discuss Robert J. Lalonde's seminal paper.

☞ **Discussion.** Provide a case where the unconfoundedness assumption is arguably valid to estimate the causal effect with matching on observed characteristics. What are the observed characteristics that make the assumption valid in your case? Also discuss a case where the unconfoundedness assumption is invalid.

7.2 Concepts and Examples

7.2.1 Lalonde's Study

Lalonde (1986) conducted a comparative analysis of the impact of a labor training program on post-training income levels using both experimental and observational data. He analyzed data from the National Supported Work Demonstration (NSW), a federally sponsored program in the United States that *randomly* assigned qualified applicants to job training programs. The treatment group received the temporary employment training program, while the control group "were left to fend for themselves (p. 605)." The baseline characteristics of the treatment and control groups were similar, indicating that the groups were *balanced* due to the random assignment of treatment to a sufficient sample from the population. For instance, the pre-training earnings of the two groups were essentially identical. The unobserved characteristics were probably similar, as they are identical in expectations for an RCT. The similarity in the pre-treatment covariates provided further confidence that the experimental design should give us an unbiased estimator of the causal effect, as we are comparing apples to apples.

Lalonde (1986) found that post-treatment earnings were about 28% higher (equivalent to almost 900 dollars) for the treatment group compared to the control group. The robustness of the estimates was demonstrated by their lack of change when using different econometric procedures, such as varying the models or including control variables. Such stubborn persistence of estimates, also known as robustness, is expected when the treatment is randomly assigned under ideal experimental conditions.

☞ **Discussion.** Examine Table 7.4 in Lalonde's (1986) paper and determine if the estimates change when using another causal inference method, such as the difference-in-differences (which is discussed in Chap. 11). What does this reveal about the robustness of the estimates from the experimental data?

7.2 Concepts and Examples

Lalonde (1986) having established the benchmark results from the experimental data proceeded to evaluate observational data from the general training program that did not use randomized treatment of participants. His evaluation instead involved "some of the econometric procedures found in studies of the employment and training programs (p. 609)." This econometric evaluation involved selecting a comparison group and making model choices, such as choosing covariates in the regression specifications to estimate the effect of the training program on incomes. Previous researchers had estimated the benefits of training programs with regression analysis, which controlled for observable characteristics of the trainees and attempted to adjust for unobservable characteristics with econometric methods (e.g., fixed effects with panel data; see Chap. 10).

Lalonde found that unlike the estimates from the experimental data, the results from the non-experimental data were sensitive to the composition of the comparison group and the econometric procedures used. He found that the order of sensitivity was large with observational data, ranging from replicating the experimental results to finding more than double the effect. Lalonde (1986, p. 617) warned that non-experimental evaluations might contain "large and unknown biases resulting from specification errors."[2]

Lalonde's 1986 study rang alarm bells about the pitfalls of evaluating policies and programs using observational data. However, in a positive turn, Dehejia and Wahba (1999) revisited the data in Lalonde's study and, through the 'magic' of matching, replicated the robustness of the experimental data results with observational data. They illustrated that one could identify causal effects if the data is processed such that treated and control units are matched based on specified criteria.[3]

In the upcoming sections, we will uncover the 'magic' behind matching and discuss several methods of processing and pruning data to create an apples-to-apples comparison and estimate causal effects of a treatment. But first, we start with a simple numerical example to intuit the basic idea of creating matched pairs.

7.2.2 Simple Numerical Example

Let's use a simple numerical example to illustrate matching. We create some artificial data, as shown in Table 7.1. The outcome variable, Y, is dependent on two variables,

---

[2] In Lalonde's study, the use of longitudinal data instead of cross-sectional data reduced the potential for specification errors, resulting in improved estimates. We discuss how these improvements occur in our related Chap. 10 on Panel data).

[3] Diamond and Sekhon (2013) have raised concerns that the Dehejia and Wahba matching method may not always result in balanced groups. They replicated the related Dehejia and Wahba (2002) study and found that, while the matching satisfied conventional notions of balance, performing statistical tests across the treated and control covariates showed significant differences. Similarly, Smith and Todd (2005) noted that the results from the propensity score matching methods in Dehejia and Wahba (1999) study are sensitive to both the set of variables included in the scores and the particular analysis sample used in the estimation.

X, the covariate and, W, the treatment variable: $Y = 2 + 0.5W + X + error$. The first five observations in Table 7.1 have low values of X, and are all in the control group.

We can consider only those observations in the treatment and control group where X is equal, i.e., we do 'exact' matching. That leaves us with two observations (see Table 7.2). The difference in the outcome between these two observations is 1.

When the data is sparse, we may not be able to rely on strict standards of exact matching. In such cases, we can use coarsened exact matching which relaxes the exactness requirements and settles for closeness instead. For instance, we can consider matches within ranges – X = 1 to 2, X = 3 to 4, and so on (Table 7.3). Alternatively, we can match observations if the distance between the control and treatment group observation in X is less than 0.3, which yields the observations in Table 7.3.

In Table 7.4, what distinguishes the different estimates is not a difference in specification (they are same), but a difference in the preprocessing of the data. As shown in Table 7.4, Model 1 (with unmatched data) gives us a misleading picture of the estimate (where the true effect is 0.5). Model 2, which uses only exactly matched observations, with only two observations, yields a poor estimate. Model 3 uses 'coarsened exact' or close matching data and now the estimate is close to the true effect.

Figure 7.1 illustrates the key points of the numerical example. The black line joins the means of the control and treated observations with all the observations (those in

Table 7.1 Observed data: Y is the outcome, W is the treatment, and X is a covariate

Obs_num	X	W	Y
1	1.0	0	2.83
2	1.1	0	3.03
3	1.4	0	3.87
4	2.1	0	4.12
5	2.3	0	4.34
6	4.5	1	7.51
7	4.7	0	6.84
8	5.5	0	7.12
9	5.7	1	7.99
10	6.0	0	7.87
11	6.0	1	8.87
12	7.3	1	9.91
13	7.4	0	9.52
14	8.6	0	10.63
15	8.8	1	11.13
16	9.2	1	12.24
17	9.4	0	11.55
18	10.2	1	12.11
19	10.3	0	12.51

7.2 Concepts and Examples

Table 7.2 Data after exact matching

Obs_num	X	W	Y
10	6	0	7.87
11	6	1	8.87

Table 7.3 Data after close or coarsened matching

Obs_num	X	W	Y
6	4.5	1	7.51
7	4.7	0	6.84
8	5.5	0	7.12
9	5.7	1	7.99
10	6.0	0	7.87
11	6.0	1	8.87
12	7.3	1	9.91
13	7.4	0	9.52
14	8.6	0	10.63
15	8.8	1	11.13
16	9.2	1	12.24
17	9.4	0	11.55
18	10.2	1	12.11
19	10.3	0	12.51

Table 7.4 Regression of Y on W, where the true effect is 0.5

	Model 1	Model 2	Model 3
(Intercept)	7.02	7.87	9.43
	(0.86)		(0.79)
W	2.95	1.00	0.53
	(1.42)		(1.11)
R^2	0.20	1.00	0.02
Num. obs.	19	2	14

Standard errors in parentheses

Table 7.1, and Model 1 in Table 7.4). The red line joins the means of the control and treated observations after discarding the blue points (as in Table 7.3, and Model 3 in Table 7.4).

7.2.3 Generating Apples to Apples

As demonstrated in the simulation example, matching involves pairing control and treatment units with similar pre-treatment covariates, creating balanced comparison

Fig. 7.1 Illustrating matching. The black line is joining the means of the control and treated group observations, with all observations. The red line joins the means of the control and treated observations after discarding the blue points, i.e., after matching

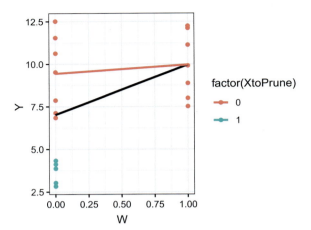

groups. To better understand this idea, consider an observational dataset of school students in a city who are enrolled in different class sizes. A student in a smaller class size may have different characteristics than a student in a regular-sized classroom, such as a higher household income or a parent with higher education.

However, by finding pairs of students who are similar in the characteristics we are interested in, such as age, gender, and parental income, but who differ only in the class size (our independent variable of interest), we can create similar matched pairs. Each pair contains a student who was treated (in a smaller class) and another who was not (in a regular-sized class). We discard the unmatched pairs, leaving us with a dataset containing only 'identical pairs' of students. This process of pruning observational data to create apples-to-apples comparisons is known as matching.

There are several methods to find the matches, including exact matching, coarsened exact matching, propensity score matching, and genetic matching. In our examples of school students and simulation, we briefly discussed the exact or coarsened exact matching methods proposed by Iacus et al. (2012). Once we have created balanced groups of treated and control units, we can compare the means between the two groups, as we do in randomized experiments, to estimate the causal effects.

The estimated causal effects with data on matched pairs rely on the fundamental assumption that treatment assignment is unconfounded, conditional on the observed covariates. In other words, once we have matched pairs on observable attributes, any difference in their outcomes we assume are solely due to the treatment itself, and not some other factor. Sekhon (2011, p. 4) formalizes this as follows: "one can assume that conditional on X, treatment assignment is unconfounded ($\{Y_0, Y_1 \perp T\}|X$) and there is overlap: $0 < Pr(T = 1|X) < 1$." Here, Y_0 and Y_1 represent potential outcomes, T is the treatment, and X represents covariates.

The assumption that treatment assignment is unconfounded, conditional on covariates, allows us to rule out potential confounding factors that could bias our results and close backdoors in the causal graph by matching on these covariates. Cunningham (2021) refers to this assumption as a 'leap of faith' (p. 240) that some researchers are reluctant to make. However, advocates of matching argue that this assumption is valid in various settings. Although this assumption cannot be empirically tested, sensitivity tests are available to help researchers examine the robustness of their findings to possible deviations from the strict assumption of unconfoundedness or conditional independence.

While Lalonde (1986) starkly demonstrated the biases inherent in structural estimates derived from observational data compared to estimates from RCTs, Dehejia and Wahba (1999) rekindled hope for mitigating these biases using a matching method on the same observational dataset. In the next sections, we will discuss popular matching methods that can potentially uncover 'hidden experiments' in observational data.

7.2.4 Exact Matching

The *exacting* procedure of exact matching involves pairing each treated unit with a control unit that has identical pre-treatment covariates. For example, we might compare a 24-year-old female with a college-education, majoring in philosophy, employed, and living in Pest County, Budapest,[4] who received a scholarship (the treatment), to a 24-year-old, female with the exact same characteristics and living in Pest except that she did not receive the scholarship. This approach allows us to create precisely matched treated and control groups. However, finding exact matches becomes challenging when dealing with multiple covariates in smaller datasets.

If an analyst wants to match and balance a few covariates between the treated and control groups, she is likely to find adequate samples of matched pairs in a dataset. However, when faced with richer covariates that require exact matching between individuals in the treatment and control groups (as illustrated in the numerical example in Sect. 7.2), the curse of dimensionality becomes an issue. In such cases, the analyst may end up with too few matched pairs to conduct statistical tests. For instance, it would be unlikely to find an exact match for a 24-year-old scholarship recipient with an income of 22,475 euros per month who has identical attributes to someone who did not receive the scholarship but earns exactly the same amount, 22,475 euros per month. The curse of dimensionality is severe for continuous covariates, such as income. Even with only 30 categorial covariates and three different categories for each variable (e.g., low, medium, and high), finding matches becomes difficult. In this setup, there simply aren't enough people on earth to guarantee an exact match for each individual.

> **Your turn** Elaborate on this thought experiment. Take the case of 5 categorical variables and 10 categorical variables with three levels and argue why finding exactly matched pairs becomes challenging.

---

[4] The spectacular capital of Hungary was formerly two cities, Buda and Pest, divided by the Danube river.

To address the issue of too few matched pairs, we must compromise on how identical the matched pairs appear with the size of the statistical sample we can generate. Instead of aiming for an exact match based on age and income, we can create brackets for these variables and match individuals if they belong to the same bracket. By coarsening the covariates, as we describe next, we can mitigate the impact of the curse of dimensionality.

7.2.5 Coarsened Exact Matching

Iacus et al. (2012) propose coarsening continuous covariate data as the solution to the curse of dimensionality. Coarsening involves grouping similar values into brackets, such as age groups or income brackets, rather than using the raw continuous values. For instance, age data may be coarsened into age brackets like 0–5, 5–12, 12–18, 18–30, 30–45 years, while income may be grouped into 0–10 k, 10–20 k, 20–30 k brackets. By using meaningful brackets, we increase the likelihood of finding a match for a treated person with a control person. For example, it is easier to find a match for a treated person who is 18–30 years old and earning 20–30 k with an untreated person who is also 18–30 and earning 20–30 k, compared to finding a match for a treated 24-year-old earning 22,475 in the control group.

However, it's important to note that the increased chance of matching treated units to control units through coarsening comes at a cost. The increased probability of finding matches is traded off with a loss in the balance of covariates. The larger the brackets used for coarsening, the less balanced the covariates will be. This means that the treated and control groups may differ in ways that are not captured by the coarser brackets. Conversely, using smaller brackets or bins leads to more balanced covariates, but it results in fewer matches being made.

To better understand how this method works, let's look at an empirical example of decentralized forest management in the Indian Himalayas.

7.2.6 Decentralized Forest Management

Conserving forests and wild areas have heightened importance today, due to the threat of global warming. Developing countries offer the potential for cost-effective conservation, while simultaneously increasing the benefits of biological diversity. However, national governments in these countries may not prioritize such conservation due to the associated costs, even if it is justifiable on a global scale. Transfers from developed to developing countries are fraught with incentive compatibility and political economy problems, and it is not surprising that such transfers have not occurred frequently. To tackle the issue of cost-effective conservation at local levels in developing countries, Somanathan et al. (2009) compared the costs of state-managed forests to the decentralized management of forests by village councils in India.

7.2 Concepts and Examples

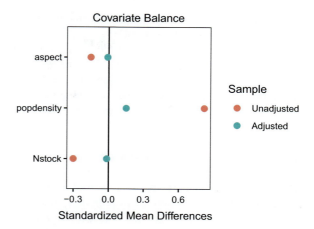

Fig. 7.2 Balance between treatment and control groups in the forest conservation example

Decentralization has been a popular political trend in many parts of the world, offering better targeting and access to public services (Ostrom 1990; Amel et al. 2017). It can also increase cost-sharing (Centofanti and Murugesan 2022) and improve the effectiveness of managing resources (Somanathan et al. 2009). To explore these benefits, Somanathan et al. (2009) compared the cost-effectiveness of council-managed forests versus state-managed forests in Uttarakhand, a Himalayan state in India, where large areas of forests have been nationalized and state-managed since the 1930s. Their study examined the long-term consequences of switching some of these forests to council management as part of the decentralization process.

Somanathan et al. (2009) first compare the costs of state management to the costs of council management. They use data from the government to calculate the cost per hectare of managing state forests, and primary survey data to estimate the cost of council-managed forests. They find that the cost of managing forests by local village councils was seven times lower than that of managing state forests. With this established, the authors move on to compare the effectiveness of state-managed forests versus council-managed forests.

In these parts of the Indian Himalayas, state forest lands were demarcated in the early twentieth century, and historical evidence indicated that they had more tree cover than those allocated for management by village councils. However, using satellite image data from 1998 on forest crown coverage, Somanathan et al. (2009) show that after adjusting for relevant covariates, there is no difference in the crown cover between state-managed and village council-managed forests. The authors employ both regression and matching methods to make inferences, making an apples-to-apples comparison. To illustrate their arguments, we will use coarsened exact matching to balance treatment and control groups.

Figure 7.2 depicts that coarsened exact matching greatly improved balance in the covariates of the two management groups. Once the data was pre-processed, the results indicated that there was virtually no difference in crown cover between state and village council-managed forests, even though village council-managed forests incurred far lower management costs. In conclusion, Somanathan et al. (2009)

suggest that decentralized forest management can offer a cost-effective solution to conservation in developing countries.

In the following section, we discuss the pros and cons of a popular matching method, propensity score matching. The method has been around since the early 1980s when it was introduced by Rosenbaum and Rubin (1984), but it gained renewed attention for its potential for causal inference after Dehejia and Wahba (1999) used it to analyze Lalonde's (1986) observational data.

7.2.7 Propensity Score Matching

Propensity score matching is a widely used method for matching pairs, especially in policy research. The reason for its popularity may lie in the ease of implementation with observational data. The method involves creating a propensity score (π) that compresses multiple dimensions of covariates of a unit into a single dimension. This score represents the probability of treatment for each unit, such as an individual. If we find pairs of people with the same propensity score, where one is in the treatment group and the other in the control group, the method assumes that they are a profoundly similar pair. In theory, the score suggests that they were equally likely to be treated; however, in reality, only one of them was treated. We can use this similarity to estimate the treatment effect. The fundamental idea behind using propensity scores is that it can help balance the treated and control groups by creating similar pairs of individuals. For more details, see Rosenbaum and Rubin (1984, 1985).

When using this matching method, since we do not observe the actual propensity score, we need to estimate it. Researchers typically use a logistic or probit regression model to estimate the one-dimensional propensity score. In these models, the treatment status serves as the dependent variable ($y = 0$ for not treated, $y = 1$ for treated), and the independent variables are the covariates. The estimated propensity score (π) is the predicted value from this model, which represents the probability of an individual receiving treatment based on their observed covariates.

After estimating the propensity scores, the commonly used procedure for finding matched pairs of treated and control units is to identify a treated unit ($y = 1$) that has the same propensity score (π) as the control unit ($y = 0$). Alternatively, analysts may choose to relax the similarity requirement for propensity scores by bounding the difference with a caliper, or maximum distance.[5]

---

[5] In this context of propensity score matching or Mahalanobis distance matching (see Sect. 7.2.8 in this chapter), a caliper or maximum distance refers to a threshold that specifies the maximum distance between the scores or the estimated distance measure of a treated and control unit. If the distance between the propensity score of a treated and control unit is larger than the specified caliper, they cannot form a matched pair. The caliper size determines the trade-off between bias reduction and sample size. A smaller caliper will result in more similar matched pairs but reduce the sample size of matches, whereas a larger caliper will increase the number of matched pairs at the cost of balance between treated and control units.

7.2 Concepts and Examples

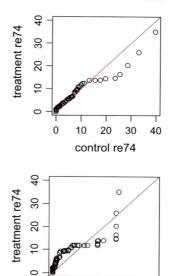

Fig. 7.3 Balance between treatment and control groups with respect to real earnings in 74 (re74) before matching. Points closer to equality line means more balance

Fig. 7.4 Balance between treatment and control groups with respect to real earnings in 74 (re74) after propensity score matching. Points are moving further away from the equality line after matching

The propensity score matching procedure simplifies the process of matching treated and control groups by reducing multiple covariates to a one-dimensional score (π). However, some critics argue that the primary objective of matching is to identify pairs of units that share similar values of the covariates themselves, not just predicted scores (King and Nielsen 2019). They highlight that pairs with the same propensity score might differ significantly in some or all their covariates. Additionally, Sekhon (2011, p. 3) notes that "A significant shortcoming of matching methods such as Mahalanobis distance and propensity score matching is that they may (and, in practice, frequently do) make balance worse, in practice … These limitations often surprise applied researchers."

Sekhon (2011) uses data from Dehejia and Wahba (1999) to demonstrate the limitations of propensity score matching. Figure 7.3 displays the balance on a single covariate, re74 (real earnings in 74), *before matching*. In the quantile-quantile plot, shown in the figure, the more the points away from the equality line (red), the greater the imbalance. However, when comparing Fig. 7.3 with Fig. 7.4, which displays the balance *after* propensity score matching, it becomes evident that balance was worse after matching than before. This finding highlights the need for caution when relying solely on propensity scores to create matched pairs.

Diamond and Sekhon (2013) proposed the genetic matching method to address the limitations evident in propensity score matching. This method uses an algorithm to improve the balance of covariates between the treated and control groups. However, before delving into genetic matching, we will discuss an intermediate step, Mahalanobis distance matching.

7.2.8 Mahalanobis Distance Matching

Mahalanobis distance is a statistical technique that is used to measure distances between units in a multidimensional setting. This approach was developed by P. C. Mahalanobis as a general way to measure distances between points in a multidimensional setting, as it is natural to think of units as possessing multiple attributes rather than just one. For example, if we only consider age to describe a person (ignoring all other attributes including gender), the distance between three unidimensional people (say A, B, and C) would be the difference in their ages. We would have three distance measures (A to B, B to C, and A to C), and we can select the two closest ones as the nearest neighbors or pairs. However, what if, in addition to age, we consider education to describe them? How do we determine the closest neighbor among the three?

Mahalanobis proposed a solution to this problem by standardizing the distribution of each attribute (e.g., age and education) and then calculating how many standard deviations each individual is from the mean for each attribute. This approach enables us to place all of the different covariates on the same scale and then calculate the distance between any two units.

Moreover, to create matched pairs that are similar, we can set a maximum distance in their Mahalanobis distances as a threshold for a match. This means that a treated person can only be matched with an untreated person if their Mahalanobis distance is below the threshold distance, sometimes called the caliper. Conversely, if the Mahalanobis distance between two individuals is above the set caliper, they cannot be paired. This helps to ensure that the matched individuals are similar in terms of their attributes, which is crucial for drawing valid causal inferences. However, setting this threshold involves making a bias-variance trade-off, as with other methods. Setting a small caliper improves the covariate balance but makes finding the matched pair less likely.

We now discuss the genetic matching method which uses a generalized version of Mahalanobis distance matching.

7.2.9 Genetic Matching

We turn our attention to an algorithmic matching method that builds on ideas from distance matching to generate balanced treatment and control groups through computation. The algorithmic method, called genetic matching, was developed by Diamond and Sekhon (2013) (hereafter DS), and offers improvements over propensity score or distance matching by optimizing the number of matched samples while considering the bias-variance trade-off.

DS point out that propensity score matching can achieve balance in observed covariates asymptotically (i.e., in very large samples), but the appropriate specification to estimate the propensity scores is generally unknown. If the analyst uses a misspecified model, the imbalance in observed variables could be worsened, which could increase bias.

7.2 Concepts and Examples

Rosenbaum and Rubin (1984) recommended researchers to iteratively examine the actual balance of the covariates between the treated and control groups after matching the propensity scores until the imbalance is minimized. However, the process of checking for balance and manually tweaking the model until the 'right' regression specification is found to minimize the imbalance is challenging. Consequently, researchers often fail to report the covariate balance. DS note that less than 50% of articles published in a reputed economics journal that use matching methods reported covariate balance after matching. Checking for balance is crucial because balance may worsen after matching (as we have highlighted in Figs. 7.3 and 7.4), which increases the chance of biased treatment estimates.

To address these limitations, DS propose an alternative genetic matching (Genmatch), which uses a generalized version of Mahalanobis distance matching (GMD) and algorithmically balances the treated and control groups. GenMatch automates the process of finding optimal balance and measuring the distance between observations in a multidimensional covariate space. The formula makes the GMD explicit:

$$GMD(X_i, X_j, W) = \sqrt{(X_i - X_j)^T (S^{-1/2})^T W S^{-1/2}(X_i - X_j)))}. \quad (7.1)$$

GenMatch builds on Mahalanobis distance by including W, which allows flexibility in adjusting the weights (W) to achieve balance in the covariates (Xs). The algorithm iteratively adjusts these weights to optimize the bias-variance trade-off, with the goal of improving balance while maximizing the number of matches. Although the details of the algorithm may be a black box for many of us, the key takeaway is that GenMatch automates the process of finding the covariate balance while increasing the sample size of the matched units. Analysts can include not only attributes of the units as covariates (Xs) in equation (1) but also the propensity scores directly as another covariate. For more information on the GenMatch algorithm, see DS.

☞ **Your turn**   Read DS and write a short note on how W makes the Genmatch more general compared to MDM.

DS conducted simulations to compare the performance of GenMatch to other matching methods (e.g., random forests, logistic regression, or simple difference in means). GenMatch performed well in its goal of trading off bias and covariate balance when compared to these other methods. Although the bias is never large compared to other methods, GenMatch generates the best matches in terms of covariate balance.

DS also ran simulations on the Lalonde (1986) data, which has discrete variables with skewed distributions. This dataset allowed DS to demonstrate the trade-off between bias and variance in matching. The results showed that, in small samples, matching can worsen bias even if it improves covariate balance. However, GenMatch outperformed the other methods even with small samples.[6],[7]

DS present a final empirical example using the same job training data that Lalonde (1986) and Dehejia and Wahba (1999) used to test the efficacy of the genetic matching estimator. The data was from the NSW program (discussed earlier in the chapter) and has been widely distributed in matching software. Lalonde (1986) compared results from observational data collected as part of the national program to the experimental data arising from the randomized job training treatment to a subgroup of participants. As we noted, Lalonde (1986) found a wide range of training 'impact' estimates from the observational data depending on the specifications used, in contrast to the relatively robust results from the experimental data.

DS highlight that the observational data that Lalonde (1986) used in the comparison differed substantially from the experimental data in terms of age, marital status, ethnicity, and preintervention earnings. Lalonde (1986) attempted to create subsets from the observational data to make it similar to the experimental data, but DS argue that the subsets remained dissimilar, leading to unbalanced treated and control groups. To test if the genetic matching method can find suitable matches, DS applied the method to the subsets and found that genetic matching balanced the covariates well and brought the treated and control groups closer to an apples-to-apples comparison. The corresponding estimates with genetic matching were closer to the experimental benchmark than Dehejia and Wahba (1999) estimate with propensity score matching, with some exceptions.

Sekhon (2011) has also demonstrated the superior balancing performance of genetic matching using data from Dehejia and Wahba (1999). Although the paper employed numerous balance statistics, Fig. 7.5 provides an intuitive illustration of the balance achieved between the treatment and control groups on real earnings in 1974 (re74) after using genetic matching. Upon comparing Fig. 7.5 with the pre-matching data (Fig. 7.3), it is evident that genetic matching has substantially improved balance.

DS developed the GenMatch method as an automated approach to optimize covariate balance. Unlike traditional methods where analysts manually adjust a model (e.g., tweaking specifications predicting propensity scores) to achieve similar covariate

---

[6] Genetic matching algorithm can accommodate both ellipsoidal (e.g., normal or t distributions) and non-ellipsoidal distributions (let's say, more funky distributions) for covariates, making it more flexible than other methods such as Mahalanobis distance matching or propensity score matching, which require covariates to have ellipsoidal distributions (Sekhon 2011). Sekhon (2011) notes that covariates rarely have such restrictive distribution properties, adding to the broader appeal of the genetic matching method.

[7] To further illustrate the advantages of Genmatch, DS use the distribution of covariates from the experimental sample of the Lalonde (1986) data based on Dehejia and Wahba's (1999) analysis. The dataset contains some discrete variables and skewed distributions, making the matching problem challenging, particularly given the small sample size of 185 treated and 260 control observations. Despite these difficulties, GenMatch performed admirably in terms of the bias and variance tradeoffs when compared to a range of estimators, including random forest and logit, even with small samples. However, all the estimators, including Genmatch, improved their performance, as the sample size increases.

7.2 Concepts and Examples

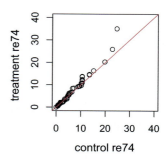

Fig. 7.5 Balance between treatment and control groups with respect to real earnings in 74 (re74) after genetic matching

distributions between treated and control groups, GenMatch automates this process. This frees researchers to focus on the substantive content of their research, such as selecting the most relevant variables to model relationships, while ensuring balance through automation.

7.2.10 Model Dependence and Cherry-Picking

As we conclude discussing the 'magic' of matching it would be remiss if we don't consider the robustness of estimates after matching. Those who have conducted regression analysis for research or writing a term paper would have likely encountered model dependence, where different models with varying specifications yield different results. For example, a model explaining the effect of education on wages may include age as a covariate, while another model may include both age and gender, and a third model may include age, gender, and age squared. These models may estimate different coefficients on the independent variable of interest, i.e., years of education, and the coefficient may even change signs between models. Researchers may be tempted to cherry-pick and present the model with the most favorable results for their hypothesis.

This selection process can be accentuated by publication bias. For example, if significant results (e.g., showing a difference in policy outcomes for women reservations) are published more frequently than null results (i.e., no difference in outcomes), researchers may be incentivized to present models with significant results, even if many of the models they ran showed insignificant effects. Similarly, the incentives for producing exciting and counterintuitive results may also motivate researchers to present some (surprising) results over others. Long story short, if the results are model-dependent, there is room for researcher discretion in choosing what to present.

To achieve better balance, researchers may choose to conduct a matching exercise before analyzing their data. Unlike regression models, where researchers may test various specifications and select what to report, matching restricts researcher discretion by preparing the data for analysis beforehand. As a result, the coefficients are typically more stable even when changing specifications. The matching process ensures that the results are less likely to be model-dependent, and honest researchers are bound by the data from the matching exercise, giving them less freedom to cherry-pick the results. In short, matching can help reduce model dependence and increase the reliability of the results.

We illustrate this reduction in model dependence with the analysis of the data related to the effect of village council management on forest cover.

We ran regressions without matching.

1. We regressed the outcome, crown cover, on the treatment, village forest dummy. The coefficient on the village forest dummy was −11.88, and the standard error was 2.05.
2. We regressed the outcome, crown cover, on the treatment, village forest dummy, and aspect, popdensity, and Nstock. The coefficient on the village forest dummy was −5.63, and the standard error was 1.85.
3. We regressed the outcome, crown cover, on the treatment, village forest dummy, and aspect, popdensity, Nstock, and popdsq. The coefficient on the village forest dummy was −1.94, and the standard error was 2.00.

We then ran regressions with the same specifications (1, 2, and 3 above) *after* matching, using the method of coarsened exact matching.

1. We regressed the outcome, crown cover, on the treatment, village forest dummy. The coefficient on the village forest dummy was −6.92, and the standard error was 2.06.
2. We regressed the outcome, crown cover, on the treatment, village forest dummy, and aspect, popdensity, and Nstock. The coefficient on the village forest dummy was −1.09, and the standard error was 2.59.
3. We regressed the outcome, crown cover, on the treatment, village forest dummy, and aspect, popdensity, Nstock, and popdsq. The coefficient on the village forest dummy was 0.39, and the standard error was 2.63.

We see that when the data analysis is done after matching, the results tend to be less model-dependent. Also, one can use multivariate regression after matching, since exact matching is not feasible, and some imbalance may remain.

7.3 R Code

7.3.1 Lalonde's Data

The papers by Diamond and Sekhon (2013) and Sekhon (2011) are comprehensive discussions of matching and the performance of the Genetic Matching algorithm. Here, we selectively draw on Sekhon (2011), to illustrate that simply using a propensity score model by itself may not be very productive in terms of improving balance, and also that the genetic matching algorithm will keep moving toward improving balance. Although the Matching package is designed to run very fast, because of the

7.3 R Code

algorithm it still takes time, and so we have suppressed the results here, and only present the code.

We load the Matching package (after installing it):

```
# first remove objects
rm(list = ls())
library(Matching)
library(tidyverse)
```

We use the Lalonde dataset that is provided by the Matching package:

```
data("lalonde")
attach(lalonde)
# rename data as Lal
Lal <- lalonde
rm(lalonde)
# can glimpse the data
#glimpse(Lal)
```

The Matching package requires the inputs in a certain format. The outcome Y is re78 (earnings) in the data. The treatment Tr is treat in the data:

```
# Outcome
Y <- Lal$re78
# Treatment
Tr <- Lal$treat
```

7.3.1.1 Propensity Scores

We first use propensity scores for matching. We don't know the true propensity score, but need to use a model to estimate the propensity score.

We can use the following model:

```
# propensity score model
ps_model <- glm(Tr ~ age + black + educ +
  hisp + married + nodegr + re74 + re75,
  family = binomial, data = Lal)
```

We can now match using the `Match` function, with fitted values from the propensity score model provided as inputs for X:

```
# match
Match1 <- Match(Y = Y, Tr = Tr,
        X = ps_model$fitted)
```

We can check the balance with the MatchBalance function, as below; we suppress the output since there are abundant balance-related statistics that are provided:

```
# check balance
MatchBalance(Tr ~ age + black + educ +
    hisp + married + nodegr + re74 + re75,
    match.out = Match1,
    nboots = 100, data = Lal, print.level = 1)
```

We will instead zoom in on just one variable, re74, and examine the balance visually with a quantile-quantile plot and with selected associated statistics:

```
# transform
Lal$re74thou <- Lal$re74/1000

# plot
qqplot(Lal$re74thou[treat == 0],
       Lal$re74thou[treat == 1],
       xlab = "control re74",
        ylab = "treatment re74",
       ylim = c(0,40),
       xlim = c(0, 40))
axis(1, at = seq(from = 0, to = 40, by = 10))
axis(2, at = seq(from = 0, to = 40, by = 10))
abline(coef = c(0,1), col = 2)

# statistics
qqstats(Lal$re74[treat == 0],
        Lal$re74[treat == 1])


qqplot(Lal$re74thou[Match1$index.control],
       Lal$re74thou[Match1$index.treated],
       xlab = "control re74",
        ylab = "treatment re74",
       ylim = c(0,40),
       xlim = c(0, 40))
axis(1, at = seq(from = 0, to = 40, by = 10))
axis(2, at = seq(from = 0, to = 40, by = 10))
abline(coef = c(0,1), col = 2)
qqstats(Lal$re74[Match1$index.control],
        Lal$re74[Match1$index.treated])
```

As noted earlier, in this case, remarkably, the balance with respect to re74 is worse after matching! It is possible to improve the propensity score model but this requires checking, then reformulation of the model.

7.3 R Code

7.3.1.2 Genetic Matching

We now use Genetic Matching, in which the algorithm powerfully moves toward better balance. We provide covariates X and BalanceMatrix, which includes functions of the covariates (squares, interactions, etc.):

```
X <- cbind(age, black, educ, hisp, married, nodegr, re74, u74, u75)
BalanceMatrix <- cbind(age, I(age^2), educ, I(educ^2), black, hisp,
       married, nodegr, re74, I(re74^2), re75, I(re75^2), u74, u75,
       I(re74*re75), I(age*nodegr), I(educ*re74), I(educ*re75))
genM <- GenMatch(Tr = Tr, X = X, BalanceMatrix = BalanceMatrix,
                 pop.size = 500, print.level = 0)
```

Ideally pop.size should be higher.[8] We now examine balance:

```
Mgen <- Match(Y = Y, Tr = Tr, X = X, Weight.matrix = genM)
qqplot(Lal$re74thou[Mgen$index.control],
       Lal$re74thou[Mgen$index.treated],
       xlab = "control re74",
        ylab = "treatment re74",
       ylim = c(0,40),
       xlim = c(0, 40))
axis(1, at = seq(from = 0, to = 40, by = 10))
axis(2, at = seq(from = 0, to = 40, by = 10))
abline(coef = c(0,1), col = 2)
qqstats(Lal$re74[Mgen$index.control],
        Lal$re74[Mgen$index.treated])


summary(Mgen)
```

We got an estimate of the ATT = 1661, with Abadie-Imbens standard error = 890.

7.3.2 Decentralized Forest Management

We read in the data. The data is available on the webpage of the paper, and can be downloaded:

```
library(tidyverse)
frd <- read_csv("cipfrfall_som.csv")
```

We follow the code provided by the authors (translating from STATA to R). Some work with the data is required.

---

[8] We have deliberately kept it low to keep the time for running low

Table 7.5 Sample of data

ccbl	vfdum	aspect	popdensity	Nstock
86.13	0	0.23	0.05	6.28
16.00	0	0.36	0.48	0.72
46.35	1	0.41	0.63	3.97
88.77	1	0.44	1.96	1.72
96.74	1	0.46	0.93	7.27
93.94	0	0.50	0.42	5.83
95.09	1	0.54	1.26	5.17
71.35	0	0.57	0.73	1.92
69.66	0	0.64	1.15	2.47
70.93	1	0.67	1.62	2.66

```
frd2 <- frd %>%
  filter(cidum == 0, blarea_ha > 0.25,
         Nstock > 0)
```

We create a new variable with mutate, then select key variables, and create variables with different names:

```
frd3 <- frd2 %>%
  mutate(popdcu = popdsq * popdensity) %>%
  select("ccbl", "rfdum", "blasp",
         "popdensity", "Nstock", "popdsq",
         "rdist") %>%
  na.omit() %>%
  mutate(vfdum = ifelse(rfdum == 1,0,1),
         aspect = blasp)
```

We look at a sample of the data, picking 10 rows at random (Table 7.5):

```
# showing sample of data
pick <- sample(x = nrow(frd3), 10, replace = F)
```

We now select key variables and display them in a table. The outcome is ccbl, crown cover, and the treatment if vfdum, village forest dummy = 1 for village council managed forests:

```
library(knitr)
frd3[pick,] %>%
  select("ccbl","vfdum","aspect",
         "popdensity", "Nstock") %>%
  arrange(aspect) %>%
  kable(digits = 2, format = "latex",
        caption = "Sample of data.", booktabs = TRUE)
```

7.3 R Code

Fig. 7.6 Balance plot

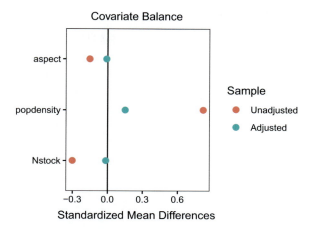

We now do matching using the MatchIt package, and use the coarsened exact matching technique.[9] We use the matchit function which requires the variables in the same syntax as used for regressions in R. We further use the match.data function to get the matched data:

```
library(MatchIt)

bl_match_cem <- matchit(vfdum ~ aspect +
        popdensity + Nstock,
        method = "cem",
        data = frd3)
matched_cem<- match.data(bl_match_cem)
```

We use the cobalt package for a plot of univariate balance before and after matching (Fig. 7.6). Figure 7.6 shows that matching has improved balance:

```
library(cobalt)
love.plot(bl_match_cem, drop.distance = TRUE)
```

We use matching to prune data to reduce extrapolation beyond support of data, model dependence. The coefficient of vfdum varies less across specifications with matched data (Models 3 and 4) than with unmatched data (Models 1 and 2) (Table 7.6):

```
library(texreg)

mod1 <- lm(ccbl ~ vfdum, data = frd3)
mod2 <- lm(ccbl ~ vfdum + aspect + popdensity + Nstock, data = frd3)
mod2B <- lm(ccbl ~ vfdum + aspect + popdensity + Nstock + popdsq, data = frd3)
mod3 <- lm(ccbl ~ vfdum , data = matched_cem)
mod4 <- lm(ccbl ~ vfdum + aspect + popdensity +
```

---

[9] See Iacus et al. (2012) and King and Nielsen (2019) on matching.

Table 7.6 Crown Cover

	Model 1	Model 2	Model 3	Model 4	Model 5	Model 6
(Intercept)	77.02	42.73	48.12	74.53	51.93	57.06
	(1.28)	(3.00)	(3.18)	(1.91)	(5.17)	(5.51)
vfdum	−11.88	−5.63	−1.94	−6.92	−1.09	0.39
	(2.05)	(1.85)	(2.00)	(2.96)	(2.59)	(2.63)
aspect		28.03	28.80		25.65	27.93
		(3.77)	(3.71)		(6.04)	(6.05)
popdensity		−2.49	−11.29		−10.32	−21.25
		(0.99)	(2.17)		(2.26)	(4.91)
Nstock		6.05	5.53		5.48	4.93
		(0.46)	(0.47)		(0.86)	(0.88)
popdsq			1.60			3.67
			(0.35)			(1.47)
Num. obs.	582	582	582	277	277	277

Standard errors in parentheses

```
        Nstock, data = matched_cem)
mod4B <- lm(ccbl~vfdum + aspect + popdensity + Nstock + popdsq, data = matched_cem)
texreg(list(mod1, mod2, mod2B, mod3, mod4,
         mod4B), include.rsquared = FALSE, include.adjrs = FALSE,
      caption = "Crown Cover",
      caption.above = TRUE,
      stars = numeric(0),
      include.ci = FALSE,
      custom.note = "Standard errors in parentheses.")
```

7.3.3 Your Turn, Compensation for Injury

☞ **Your turn** Try using matching with the following published example (Meyer et al. 1995). We provide some background and hints.

We now turn to a reanalysis of the original Meyer et al. (1995) (hereafter, Meyer et al. 1995) study of worker injury compensation laws. MVD 1995 used the difference-in-differences approach (which we revisit in our DD chapter) in studying the issue while Rosenbaum (2017) reanalyzes the policy with matching methods.

So, if you want to estimate the effect of being in a policy or program on your outcome, you need to know what the outcome would be if you are in the program and what the outcome would be if you are not in the program (the counterfactual outcome). Take the case of the effect of worker compensation laws on the duration that a worker was out of work following injury. Meyer et al. (1995) studied the case of Kentucky, where high-income workers injured after July 1980 were eligible for higher compensatory wages when they were out of work (recovery time). Did the

7.3 R Code

workers affected by the program stay longer out of work than those eligible for a lower compensation due to an injury before July 1980? With matching, one may find pairs of workers of the same gender, marital status, age, occupation, and injury type: one member from the pre-treatment and one from the post-treatment group. We can then compare their duration of stay out of work.

In an earlier section, we used the Matching package with the Lalonde data. Here, you can try to use the Matching package again, for the Rosenbaum (2017) analysis of the effect of worker compensation laws on duration that workers are out of work following injury. We have suppressed the output.

Load the data, which is in the wooldridge package:

```
library(wooldridge)
data(injury)
```

Load the tidyverse package:

```
library(tidyverse)
```

Remove observations with missing values:

```
injury <- injury %>%
  na.omit()
```

Create a subset, filtering for high earners (`highearn`) in Kentucky (`ky`):

```
inj_ky_high <- injury %>%
  filter(ky == 1, highearn == 1)
```

Create another subset, filtering for low earners in Kentucky:

```
inj_ky_low <- injury %>%
  filter(ky == 1, highearn == 0)
```

Load the Matching package:

```
library(Matching)
```

You need to provide the covariates as X, outcome as Y, and treatment as Tr:

```
injX <- inj_ky_high %>%
  dplyr::select(male, married, hosp, indust, injtype,
         age, lprewage) # used dplyr::
head(injX)

X <- cbind(injX)
dim(X)
Y <- inj_ky_high$ldurat
Tr <- inj_ky_high$afchnge
```

Use the GenMatch and Match functions:

```
gen1 <- GenMatch(Tr = Tr, X = X, print.level = 0, pop.size = 500)
mgen1 <- Match(Y = Y, Tr = Tr, X = X, Weight.matrix = gen1)
```

Get the output and interpret it:

```
summary(mgen1)
```

Now carry out the analysis for the low earners (`inj_ky_low`) in the same way. Read Rosenbaum's (2017) account of this study in his beautiful book *Observation and Experiment*.

7.4 Resources

7.4.1 For Better Understanding

Ho et al.'s (2007) paper on *Matching as Nonparametric Preprocessing for Reducing Model Dependence in Parametric Causal Inference*.

7.4.2 For Exploring Further

DS paper on *Genetic Matching for Estimating Causal Effects*.

Packages Used in This Chapter

The citations for the packages used in this chapter are[10]

```
## Greifer N (2022). _cobalt: Covariate Balance Tables and ##
Plots_. R package version 4.3.2, <URL: ##
https://CRAN.R-project.org/package=cobalt>.


## Ho DE, Imai K, King G, Stuart EA (2011). "MatchIt: ##
Nonparametric Preprocessing for Parametric Causal Inference." ##
_Journal of Statistical Software_, *42*(8), 1-28. doi: ##
10.18637/jss.v042.i08 (URL: ##
https://doi.org/10.18637/jss.v042.i08).


## Leifeld P (2013). "texreg: Conversion of Statistical Model ##
Output in R to LaTeX and HTML Tables." _Journal of Statistical ##
Software_, *55*(8), 1-24. <URL: ##
http://dx.doi.org/10.18637/jss.v055.i08>.
```

---

[10] The tidyverse package itself contains several packages.

```
## R Core Team (2021). _R: A Language and Environment for ##
Statistical Computing_. R Foundation for Statistical ## Computing,
Vienna, Austria. <URL: https://www.R-project.org/>.


## Sekhon JS (2011). "Multivariate and Propensity Score Matching
## Software with Automated Balance Optimization: The Matching
## Package for R." _Journal of Statistical Software_, *42*(7),
## 1-52. doi: 10.18637/jss.v042.i07 (URL:
## https://doi.org/10.18637/jss.v042.i07).
##
## Diamond A, Sekhon JS (2013). "Genetic Matching for Estimating
## Causal Effects: A General Multivariate Matching Method for
## Achieving Balance in Observational Studies." _Review of
## Economics and Statistics_, *95*(3), 932-945. <URL:
## http://sekhon.berkeley.edu/papers/GenMatch.pdf>.
##
## Sekhon JS, Grieve RD (2012). "A Matching Method For Improving
## Covariate Balance in Cost-Effectiveness Analyses." _Health
## Economics_, *21*(6), 695-714.


## Wickham H, Averick M, Bryan J, Chang W, McGowan LD, François ##
R, Grolemund G, Hayes A, Henry L, Hester J, Kuhn M, Pedersen ## TL,
Miller E, Bache SM, Müller K, Ooms J, Robinson D, Seidel ## DP,
Spinu V, Takahashi K, Vaughan D, Wilke C, Woo K, Yutani H ## (2019).
"Welcome to the tidyverse." _Journal of Open Source ## Software_,
*4*(43), 1686. doi: 10.21105/joss.01686 (URL: ##
https://doi.org/10.21105/joss.01686).


## Xie Y (2022). _knitr: A General-Purpose Package for Dynamic ##
Report Generation in R_. R package version 1.41, <URL: ##
https://yihui.org/knitr/>.


## Xie Y (2023). _formatR: Format R Code Automatically_. R ##
package version 1.14, <URL: ##
https://CRAN.R-project.org/package=formatR>.
```

References

Abadie, Alberto, and Guido W. Imbens. 2016. Matching on the Estimated Propensity Score. *Econometrica* 84 (2): 781–807. https://onlinelibrary.wiley.com/doi/pdf/10.3982/ECTA11293

Amel, Elise, Christie Manning, Britain Scott, and Susan Koger. 2017. Beyond the Roots of Human Inaction: Fostering Collective Effort Toward Ecosystem Conservation. *Science* 356: 275–279.

Centofanti, Tiziana, and Anand Murugesan. 2022. Leader and Citizens Participation for the Environment: Experimental Evidence from Eastern Europe. *Journal of Behavioral and Experimental Economics (formerly The Journal of Socio-Economics)*, 100(C). (Publisher: Elsevier).

Cunningham, Scott. 2021. *Causal Inference: The Mixtape*. New Haven; London: Yale University Press. (January 2021)

Dehejia, Rajeev H., and Sadek Wahba. 1999. Causal Effects in Nonexperimental Studies: Reevaluating the Evaluation of Training Programs. *Journal of the American Statistical Association* 94 (448): 1053–1062. https://www.tandfonline.com/doi/pdf/10.1080/01621459.1999.10473858. (December 1999. Publisher: Taylor & Francis).

Dehejia, Rajeev H., and Sadek Wahba. 2002. Propensity Score Matching Methods for Nonexperimental Causal Studies. *Review of Economics and Statistics* 84 (1): 151–161.

Diamond, Alexis, and Jasjeet S. Sekhon. 2013. Genetic Matching for Estimating Causal Effects: A General Multivariate Matching Method for Achieving Balance in Observational Studies. *The Review of Economics and Statistics* 95 (3): 932–945.

Ho, Daniel E., Kosuke Imai, Gary King, and Elizabeth A. Stuart. 2007. *Matching as Nonparametric Preprocessing for Reducing Model Dependence in Parametric Causal Inference*. *Political Analysis* 15 (3): 199–236. Publisher: Cambridge University Press.

Iacus, Stefano M., Gary King, and Giuseppe Porro. 2012. *Causal Inference Without Balance Checking: Coarsened Exact Matching*. *Political Analysis* 20 (1): 1–24. Publisher: Cambridge University Press.

King, Gary, and Richard Nielsen. 2019. Why Propensity Scores Should not be Used for Matching. *Political Analysis* 27 (4): 435–454. (October 2019. Publisher: Cambridge University Press).

Lalonde, Robert. 1986. Evaluating the Econometric Evaluations of Training Programs with Experiment Data. *American Economic Review* 76: 604–620.

Meyer, B.D., W.K. Viscusi, and D.L. Durbin. 1995. Workers' Compensation and Injury Duration: Evidence from a Natural Experiment. *The American Economic Review* 85 (3): 322–340.

Ostrom, Elinor. 1990. *Governing the Commons: The Evolution of Institutions for Collective Action*. Cambridge: Political Economy of Institutions and Decisions. Cambridge University Press.

Rosenbaum, Paul R., and Donald B. Rubin. 1984. Reducing Bias in Observational Studies Using Subclassification on the Propensity Score. *Journal of the American Statistical Association* 79 (387): 516–524. https://www.tandfonline.com/doi/pdf/10.1080/01621459.1984.10478078. (September 1984. Publisher: Taylor & Francis).

Rosenbaum, Paul. 2017. *Observation and Experiment: An Introduction to Causal Inference*. Illustrated edition. Massachusetts: Harvard University Press, Cambridge. (August 2017).

Rubin, Donald, and Paul Rosenbaum. Constructing a Control Group Using Multivariate Matched Sampling Methods that Incorporate the Propensity Score. *The American Statistician* 39. (February 1985).

Sekhon, Jasjeet S. 2011. Multivariate and Propensity Score Matching Software with Automated Balance Optimization: The Matching Package for R. *Journal of Statistical Software* 42: 1–52.

Smith, Jeffrey A., and Petra E. Todd. 2005. Does Matching Overcome LaLonde's Critique of Nonexperimental Estimators? *Journal of Econometrics* 125 (1): 305–353.

Somanathan, E., R. Prabhakar, and Bhupendra Singh Mehta. 2009. Decentralization for Cost-effective Conservation. *Proceedings of the National Academy of Sciences* 106 (11): 4143–4147. (March 2009. Publisher: Proceedings of the National Academy of Sciences).

Instrumental Variables

8.1 Introduction

Archimedes, famously said, "Give me a lever long enough and a fulcrum on which to place it, and I shall move the world."[1] These words resonate with empirical researchers who seek a lever of their own to causally influence the treatment variable without directly affecting the outcome of interest.

In this chapter, we will delve into the mechanics of instrumental variables—a lever used to identify causal relationships. Similar to Archimedes' requirements of a long lever and a stable fulcrum, researchers seek an instrumental variable that can partially manipulate the treatment while remaining unrelated to the outcome of interest. To develop a deeper understanding of instrumental variables, we begin with a simple example using causal graphs. Then, we will embark on a historical journey to find an instrument to investigate the causal impact of institutions on economic development. Moving forward in time, we will explore the causal relationship between globalization and Brexit in the twenty-first century. Lastly, we will discuss the intricate conditions that can build our confidence in the validity of an instrument, focusing on policies in the United States aimed at reducing tobacco consumption—a cancer causing agent. Brace up!

---

[1] The accuracy of this quote attributed to Archimedes is subject to debate. According to Ceccarelli (2014), there are records suggesting that while discussing lever mechanics, Archimedes is believed to have said, "Give me a place to stand, and I will move the earth."

8.2 Concepts and Examples

8.2.1 A Basic Example with an Encouragement Design

To better understand the mechanics of an instrumental variable, it is helpful to start with an example where treatment is not randomly assigned, but encouragement to get treated is randomized. In this case, the random assignment of encouragement serves as our lever to estimate the effect of the treatment on the outcome.

An educational television show for preschool-aged-children, Sesame Street, began to be telecast in 1969, in the United States. Children were randomly allocated into two major groups. In the first group, mothers or teachers were given persuasive arguments so that their children would be encouraged to view the show. In the other group, no such arguments were given. In other words, encouragement was randomly assigned: one group received encouragement, the other did not. The question of interest was the effect of the educational show (meant to be entertaining also), Sesame Street, on educational outcomes. Watching the educational show was not randomly assigned. In fact, children who were in the non-encouraged group also watched the show (Bogatz and Ball 1971). The Sesame Street was continuously analyzed over the years, and Gelman et al. (2020) present this case.

8.2.1.1 The Causal Graph View

We present a causal graph view for this example (Fig. 8.1). Because encouragement E was randomly assigned, there are no 'confounder' arrows into E. E is likely to affect watching Sesame Street (the treatment, X). Watching (X) is determined by both E and other variables S. Watching affects the educational outcome R, and R is also affected by S. By using encouragement as an instrumental variable, the researchers can randomly move the causal lever.

The assumptions underlying instrumental variables have been expressed in different ways, depending on the disciplinary background, such as potential outcomes, the language econometricians prefer, or using causal graphs. In earlier chapters, we

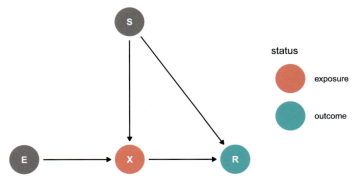

Fig. 8.1 Causal graph for the effect of watching (X) an educational television program on recognition (R) of letters. E denotes encouragement to watch

8.2 Concepts and Examples

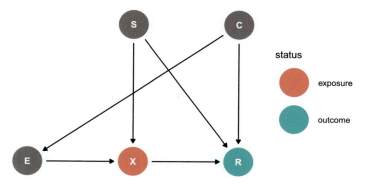

Fig. 8.2 Violation of assumption 2. There is a backdoor path $E <-C-> R$

have seen assumptions expressed in both the language of potential outcomes and through the use of causal graphs.

To get started, it is helpful to express the assumptions graphically (Glymour and Swanson 2021). The assumptions while using instrumental variables, in the context of this example, are as follows:

1. The instrument, E is associated with the treatment X.
2. There are no backdoor paths linking the instrument E and the outcome R.
3. The instrument E does not affect the outcome R through any other paths that do not pass through the treatment X.

Figure 8.2 presents a case where Assumption 2 is violated. There is a backdoor path $E \leftarrow C \rightarrow R$. This path is referred to as a backdoor path because it enters (points the arrow into) the instrumental variable, E. We can use E as an instrumental variable if we adjust for variable C in our analysis. Note that if E is an encouragement that is randomly assigned, we would not have any arrow pointing to E. In this case (no arrow pointing into E), we can rule out the violation of assumption 2.

Figure 8.3 depicts a case where Assumption 3 is violated. In this case, the instrument E not only influences the treatment X (which is acceptable), but it also has a direct effect on the outcome R (which violates the assumption); we can see this violation through the path $E \rightarrow R$. Even if E is randomly assigned, this violation demands careful consideration. Encouraged mothers and teachers may not only help children watch Sesame Street, but may also make other efforts to improve educational outcomes.

Following Angrist et al. (2015),

The effect of E on R = the effect of E on X × the effect of X on R.

So,

The effect of X on R = the effect of E on R/the effect of E on X.

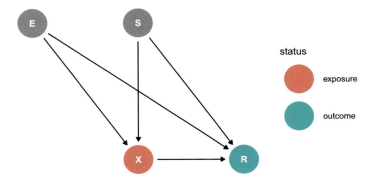

Fig. 8.3 Violation of assumption 3. E causes R directly, not only indirectly through X

We now use the data to estimate the above chain.

The effect of X on R approximately equals 2.876/0.3624 (we can get these values with regression), which equals about 7.9. The example illustrates the bare bones of instrumental variable estimation.

8.2.1.2 Heterogeneity of Effects

Different children may respond differently to encouragement. In our example, some may comply and watch the program if encouraged, while others may choose not to watch even if encouraged. Additionally, there may be children who watch the program regardless of whether they are encouraged or not. We assume that there are no 'defiers', i.e., those who watch if not encouraged and would not watch if encouraged.

In a well-known paper, Angrist et al. (1996, p. 444) showed that "under some simple and easily interpretable assumptions, the IV estimand is the average causal effect for a subgroup of units, the compliers." This implies that we obtain estimates of the local average treatment effect, as our estimates are only for a subgroup who are induced to watch the program through encouragement.

To illustrate this concept further, Steiner et al. (2017) present two causal graphs. Figure 8.4 shows the causal graph for the compliers, who always comply with the encouragement assignment. On the other hand, Fig. 8.5 shows the causal graph for the always-takers and never-takers, who are not affected by the encouragement assignment. Always-takers, take the treatment no matter what, and conversely, never-takers, do not take the treatment, regardless of encouragement.

8.2.1.3 Two-Stage Least Squares

We now present a commonly used approach for estimating causal effects using instrumental variables, known as the two-stage least squares (2SLS) method. As the name suggests, this method involves applying least squares in two stages as explained below:

8.2 Concepts and Examples

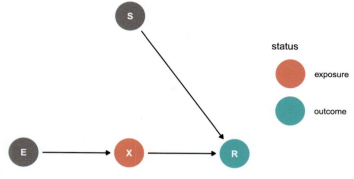

Fig. 8.4 Compliers

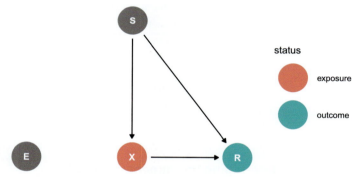

Fig. 8.5 Always-takers and never-takers

Stage 1. Regress the treatment variable (in this case, 'watched the program') on the instrument (in this case, 'encouraged'). This regression breaks the treatment (watched) into two parts: (1) the part that can be predicted by the instrument (encouraged) and (2) the problematic part that is correlated with the error term. From this regression, we obtain the predicted values of the treatment variable, referred to as 'predicted watched'

Stage 2. Regress the outcome ('letter recognition score') on the predicted treatment ('predicted watched'). Since the predicted treatment variable from the first stage has been purged of the problematic part, we can get a consistent estimate of the causal effect in this stage.

In Table 8.2, by using the 2SLS method, we get the same estimate as in Table 8.1. But the standard errors are not correct in Table 8.1 and are correct in Table 8.2.

We can use a computer package for the two-stage least squares estimate and the associated standard error, as seen in the R code section (see Table 8.2).

Table 8.1 Two stages of two-stage least squares

	Stage 1	Stage 2
(Intercept)	0.55	20.59
	(0.04)	(3.91)
Encouraged	0.36	
	(0.05)	
watched.hat		7.93
		(4.93)
R^2	0.17	0.01
Num. obs.	240	240

Standard errors in parentheses

Table 8.2 Two-stages least squares regression. Dependent variable is recognition of letters

	Model 1
(Intercept)	20.59
	(3.70)
Watched	7.93
	(4.64)
R^2	0.14
Num. obs.	240

Standard errors in parentheses

8.2.2 Prologue to Leveraging Instrumental Variables

To deepen our understanding, we will now explore three case studies. Our primary goal has been to ascertain the causal effect of the treatment variable (X) on the outcome variable (Y), rather than simply establishing an association between the two. Let's consider a scenario that has been of interest to scholars and enlightened policymakers: the impact of the rule of law (X) on economic development (Y). In this scenario, empirical researchers are concerned about confounders that exert influence on both the rule of law (the independent variable X) and economic development (the outcome variable Y), as indicated by the causal arrow originating from the confounder and pointing toward X and Y. Employing a simple regression in such a case would result in a biased estimate of the effect of X on Y, if we do not account for the confounder. If we can observe the confounding variable, we include it as a covariate in the regression to address the bias. However, there may be unobserved confounders, such as cultural factors, that remain unaccounted for. This presents us with a common problem, which we'll refer to as problem number one.

Alternatively, or in addition, there can be other sources of bias to consider. One could reasonably argue that it is not X that causes changes in Y but rather the reverse. It is not the quality of the rule of law that impacts economic development, but rather economic development ushers in improvements in the rule of law. Another critic may contend that there are indeed feedback or bidirectional effects, with each variable influencing the other in a mutually reinforcing manner. This familiar conundrum is

8.2 Concepts and Examples

often referred to as the *chicken and egg* problem. Addressing the issue of causal direction presents problem number two.

Furthermore, we tend to overlook the issue of measurement error. While measurement errors in the outcome variable Y can increase the standard error of the estimate, they do not necessarily introduce bias into the estimate itself. Instead, such errors result in lowered precision, rather than biasing the estimate. On the other hand, measurement errors in the treatment variable X can introduce a downward bias, known as attenuation bias, which presents problem number three.

To tackle these biases, scholars of causal inference have developed various techniques. One approach is to randomize the treatment (as discussed in Chap. 6 on Experiments). Alternatively, researchers can look for appropriate settings with arbitrary rules or thresholds above which the treatment is administered (see Chap. 9 on Regression Discontinuity Design). Another technique involves differencing with panel data to account for fixed effects, as discussed in Chap. 10 on Panel data and Chap. 11 on Differences-in-differences.

Economist Philip Wright and his polymath son, Sewall Wright, are credited with making a significant contribution to the arsenal of causal inference: the instrumental variables (IV) method (Stock and Trebbi, 2003). An instrumental variable, *when valid*, serves as an Archimedean lever, effectively addressing various biases that affect our causal estimates. However, the real challenge lies in finding a suitable IV that satisfies the validity assumptions. It is not uncommon for students and researchers to hastily assert cause and effect with their instrumental variable, only to discover upon scratching the surface, that their instrument fails to meet the conditions.

Stock and Watson (2017) highlight two main approaches to finding valid instruments: (1) theory-based and (2) exploiting exogenous source of variation in the independent variable X. The theory-based approach, exemplified by Wrights' instrument, is grounded in economic theory, which led them to an instrument that only shifted the supply side of the market, not the demand side (more on this in Sect. 8.2.5). However, Stock and Watson (2017, p. 449) emphasize that theories are "abstractions that often do not take into account the nuances and details necessary for analyzing a particular dataset. Thus this approach does not always work."

The second approach involves locating an exogenous source of variation in the independent variable, X. This source of variation should in essence be a random phenomenon that partially shifts the X. Some researchers have used unexpected factors like rainfall, weather shocks, or natural disasters as sources of variation, if they shift X. It is crucial to underscore the element of 'unexpectedness' or randomness in these cases.

In the two upcoming empirical case studies, we will explore contexts where the authors argue for the randomness in the lever originating from historical events such as colonial history or idiosyncratic occurrences in different parts of the world. Additionally, we will examine a third case where the authors rely on the theory-based approach to validate their instrument. Here we go on a brief journey through space and time to uncover and explore these instrumental levers of causal inference.

8.2.3 Colonial Origins of Economic Development

The quest to unravel the determinants of development stands as one of the most significant inquiries in the social sciences. Many factors have been put forth, including capital, geography, and natural endowments (Diamond 1997), ideas and technological innovation (Mc-Closkey 2016), and trade (Romer and Frankel 1999). Within this realm of unlocking the keys to development, Acemoglu, Johnson, and Robinson (2001) (hereafter, AJR) align themselves with the perspective of Douglass North, emphasizing the pivotal role of institutions in economic development and growth. Through their reliance on novel sources of data and innovative causal inference methods, coupled with a deep understanding of institutions, Acemoglu and his team have renewed the focus on the profound influence of institutions in shaping long-run outcomes.

Institutions can take on a formal nature, such as constitutions and the rule of law, or appear in informal guise, like cultural norms (North 1991). Whether independently or in combination, these formal and informal institutions arguably impact the development trajectories of countries. In their influential 2001 paper, "The Colonial Origins of Comparative Development," AJR delve into the role of formal institutions (X) in economic development (Y). To tackle the challenge of reverse causality, they use the variation in settler mortality rates upon arrival in colonies as a historical instrument to study the effect of institutions on economic performance. Their findings reveal a distinct negative relationship between settler mortality rates in the eighteenth and nineteenth centuries and levels of economic development (GDP per capita) observed over a century later.

Figure 8.6 presents this reduced-form relationship between AJR's proposed instrument, settler mortality in the past, and GDP per capita in 1995.

AJR argue that formal institutions, which safeguard property rights and reduce the risk of expropriation, will foster higher investment, greater returns, and overall economic growth. To empirically assess the quality of institutions, they use a proxy called the 'risk of appropriation' index, which quantifies the level of protection

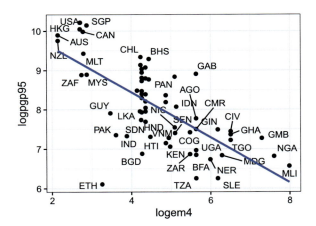

Fig. 8.6 Log of gdp per capita, 1995 is negatively associated with the log of settler mortality

8.2 Concepts and Examples

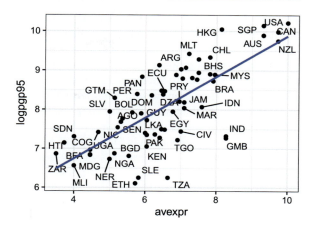

Fig. 8.7 Log of gdp per capita, 1995 is positively related to the average protection against expropriation risk

Table 8.3 OLS Regressions, Dependent variable is log GDP per capita in 1995

	Model 1	Model 2	Model 3
(Intercept)	4.66	4.73	5.74
	(0.41)	(0.40)	(0.40)
avexpr	0.52	0.47	0.40
	(0.06)	(0.06)	(0.06)
lat_abst		1.58	0.88
		(0.71)	(0.63)
Asia			−0.58
			(0.23)
Africa			−0.88
			(0.17)
Other			0.11
			(0.38)
R^2	0.54	0.57	0.71
Num. obs.	64	64	64

Standard errors in parentheses

individuals have against expropriation by the government or other entities. GDP per capita is used as their indicator of economic growth (p. 1370, AJR).

Figure 8.7 depicts the correlation between the average risk of expropriation index and economic performance, as measured by GDP per capita in 1995.

Table 8.3 presents the results from three ordinary least squares (OLS) regression models demonstrating a positive association between the quality of institutions (measured by the average risk of expropriation) and economic development (measured by GDP per capita). This relationship remains statistically significant even after accounting for other factors like geography (latitude) and continent dummies for Asia and Africa, as evidenced in models 2 and 3 in Table 8.3. However, AJR caution against drawing causal inferences based on this association due to the chicken and egg problem, or problem number two as discussed previously in the chapter: It is unclear whether better institutions lead to economic growth or if "rich economies may be able to afford, or perhaps prefer, better institutions" (AJR, p. 1379).

Furthermore, there may be other factors influencing income growth that are also correlated with institutional quality, introducing the issue of 'omitted variables,' or problem number one. To address these issues, AJR turned to history for a potential solution lever. They propose settler mortality (not native mortality) from the history of colonization, as the lever that they argue set the institutional ball rolling, shaping them for better or worse in present times.

Let's outline their argument in four steps, as depicted in their causal graph: (Potential) settler mortality → settlements → early institutions → current institutions → current performance.

Step one: (Potential) settler mortality → settlements

AJR put forth the argument that the European settlers *unexpectedly* encountered high-disease-environments in certain parts of the colonies, leading to their higher mortality rates. For instance, parts of Africa, India, and the Caribbean were prone to diseases like malaria and yellow fever, resulting in significant fatalities among European settlers. In contrast, the native population had developed relative immunity to these diseases due to early exposure. Consequently, regions with high settler mortality witnessed fewer settlements. Conversely, in colonies with favorable environments, such as New Zealand, European settlers were able to establish communities, raise families, and engage in farming.

Step two: Settlements → early institutions The variation in mortality in the colonies influenced where the Europeans settled down to engage in farming or other economic activities. The authors argue that the settlers established productive institutions that protected property rights in more conducive environments. In environments with higher mortality, the settlers were less incentivized to build long-term settlements and instead set up extractive institutions that facilitated resource extraction and exploitation for the benefit of their European homelands. This aligns with Mancur Olson's theory of roving and stationary bandits, where stationary bandits, who aim to maintain power over a longer period, invest in productive institutions that foster economic growth while roving bandits prioritize short-term gains through extractive institutions.

Step three: Early institutions → current institutions

The institutions established by the settlers, whether productive or extractive, often persisted even after the colonies gained independence, shaping current institutions. This path-dependence of institutions can be attributed, in part, to local elites who inherited power from the colonizers and benefited from the extractive institutions. AJR provide historical examples of the persistence of forced labor and slavery in South America, long after the end of colonial rule by Spain and Portugal. They generally argue that an enduring relationship exists between past and present institutions.

Step four: Current institutions → current performance

Finally, the last step is the causal relationship of interest, between current institutions and economic development, as measured by GDP. By using settler mortality as an instrument, AJR were able to focus on the part of current institutions which can be explained by those set-in motion by the past. If the historical lever is strong

8.2 Concepts and Examples

Table 8.4 First stage and IV regression, Dependent variable is Average protection against expropriation risk (First stage) and log GDP per capita in 1995 (IV)

	First stage	IV
(Intercept)	9.34	1.91
	(0.61)	(1.03)
logem4	−0.61	
	(0.13)	
avexpr		0.94
		(0.16)
Num. obs.	64	64

Standard errors in parentheses

Table 8.5 IV Regressions, Dependent variable is log GDP per capita in 1995

	Model 1	Model 2	Model 3
(Intercept)	1.91	1.69	1.44
	(1.03)	(1.29)	(2.84)
avexpr	0.94	1.00	1.11
	(0.16)	(0.22)	(0.46)
lat_abst		−0.65	−1.18
		(1.34)	(1.76)
Asia			−1.05
			(0.52)
Africa			−0.44
			(0.42)
Other			−0.99
			(1.00)
Num. obs.	64	64	64

Standard errors in parentheses

enough, it can provide the necessary first-stage correlation to draw causal inferences about how current institutions impact economic growth.

In summary, by advocating for settler mortality as a valid instrumental variable, AJR address the challenges of reverse causality and confounder bias, enabling them to identify a causal relationship between current institutions and economic development.

Table 8.4 presents the findings of both the first-stage regression and the instrumental variable (IV) regression for a straightforward specification. The first-stage results demonstrate a correlation between settler mortality and the measure of institutional quality, specifically the average protection against expropriation risk. Furthermore, the IV regression reveals a positive impact of current institutions on GDP per capita.

Table 8.5 presents the IV estimates of economic performance, employing settler mortality as an instrument for the current level of institutions. The IV estimates are higher than the OLS estimates (shown in Table 8.3), indicating that the relationship between institutional quality and economic performance may have been underestimated when relying on OLS regression. In addition to tackling confounder biases and the chicken and egg problem, a valid IV could also help mitigate biases arising from measurement errors.

AJR acknowledge that the average risk of expropriation index, used as a proxy for institutional quality, may be a coarse measure that fails to capture relevant aspects of institutional quality. This mismeasurement or noisy measure of the independent variable could be the cause of the attenuation bias in the OLS estimates.[2] Acemoglu et al. (2001, p. 1371) state the magnitude of their point estimate: "Our two-stage least squares estimate of the effect of institutions on performance is relatively precisely estimated and large. For example, it implies that improving Nigeria's institutions to the level of Chile could, in the long run, lead to as much as a 7-fold increase in Nigeria's income."

Recently, many scholars have turned to history for insights into the impact of institutions on economic development. AJR argue that variation in mortality rates among European settlers can partially explain the present quality of institutions, emphasizing the historical persistence that enables the fulfillment of the instrumental relevance condition. They further argue that settler mortality, as an instrumental variable, satisfies the exclusion restriction because historical settler mortality should not directly affect current economic performance. Moreover, if the mortality was random and unexpected, it would meet the exogeneity condition for an instrument. The authors contend that settler mortality meets all three conditions necessary for instrument validity, and therefore, provides a reliable estimate of current institutions on economic performance.

However, critics have raised concerns regarding the settler mortality instrument's ability to satisfy the exclusion restriction condition, as they argue that the past disease environments, which influenced the institutional setup, may have persisted and directly impacted current economic activity and performance. In response, AJR argue that they specifically use settler mortality, not overall mortality or native mortality, and that the natives were relatively immune to diseases that affected the settlers. Furthermore, advances in medicine and technology may have mitigated some of the remaining vulnerabilities, thereby strengthening the exclusion restriction condition.

All things considered, the work of AJR has served as a catalyst in the field of institutional economics, building upon the conceptual foundations laid by North, Weingast, and Williamson. With their careful empirical design, exhaustive data collection and extensive scholarship they have taken up the challenge of addressing big questions of development. Their work has paved the way for numerous studies in subsequent years, further advancing our understanding of institutions and their impact.

☞ **Discussion.** Provide cases or conditions where the exclusion restriction condition in AJR (2001) would not be met.

---

[2] Measurement bias is discussed in greater detail in Chap. 10.

Read Deaton (2010) and see what he has to say about the validity of instruments in papers such as AJR (2001).
Read the Albouy 2012 paper and summarize the merits of their criticism. Read the response by AJR 2012 and provide your thoughts on the debated topic.

8.2.4 Globalization, Voter Preferences, and Brexit

We now transport ourselves back to the twenty-first century to study the political implications of globalization, with a specific focus on the case of Brexit in 2016. The decision of the United Kingdom (UK) to leave the European Union (EU) in 2016 was a multi-faceted one with many complexities, and Colantone and Stanig (2018) (hereafter, CS 2018) explored the potential role of economic globalization as a contributing factor. Economic globalization, characterized by increased international trade and the displacement of manufacturing jobs, saw cheap labor from emerging economies like China and India substituting labor in advanced economies such as the US and UK. CS 2018 argue that this discontent stemming from economic globalization played a causal role in the Brexit vote. Their study of the UK's experience with Brexit serves as a captivating case study that sheds light on the political implications of globalization, while also highlighting a specific instrumental variable approach (shift-share) to identify causal effects.

In 2016, the UK held a referendum to decide whether to remain in or leave the European Union, with the 'leave' option securing a narrow victory by a margin of four percentage points. Subsequently, a substantial debate ensued regarding the causes of Brexit, including the impact of immigration, job losses in the manufacturing sector, and the rise in inequality and poverty in the UK. While evidence suggests that these factors are related to the vote share for Brexit, CS 2018 employ an instrumental variable approach to examine the issue causally.

CS 2018 direct their attention to the surge in Chinese imports, as China was the major importing country for the UK between the 1980s and the early 2000s, with an eight-fold growth in shares during this period. The growth in Chinese imports had differential effects on different sectors (such as textiles and plastics) and regions (like Leicester) within the UK, creating the necessary variation for their analysis. The authors construct an import shock variable that estimates the impact of increased Chinese imports on manufacturing employment within specific sectors and regions in the UK. For instance, when China increases its textile exports to the UK in a particular year, the shock will be stronger for regions like Leicester which historically had a higher proportion of textile manufacturing.

This approach, known as a shift-share or Bartik instrument, combines historical local industry shares with aggregate industry level shocks or growth rates to construct an instrument. Since the pioneering work of Bartik (1991), it has been widely used in many fields to identify causal effects. Goldsmith-Pinkham et al. (2020) emphasizes that the exogeneity condition for Bartik instruments can arise from either the variation in historical sector shares across regions or the shocks in aggregate growth

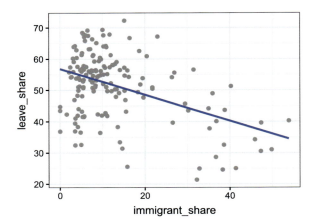

Fig. 8.8 Leave share versus immigrant share

rates within those sectors (see Borusyak and Kirill 2022 for further insights on the exogenous shock approach).

In CS 2018, the authors primarily rely on the shocks from Chinese imports to understand the causal influence of globalization on UK voter preferences. Their shift-share approach involves combining the annual variation in Chinese imports into the UK by sector with the historical variation in manufacturing sectors across UK regions to create an 'import shock' instrument. The remarkable growth of China's imports, they argue was largely unforeseen outside of China prior to the 1980s, and was driven by unique domestic 'idiosyncratic factors.' These factors enabled China to bridge the productivity gap and capitalize on its comparative advantage in manufacturing. To mitigate concerns regarding endogeneity between Chinese imports and UK politics, CS 2018 point out that trade policies are predominantly determined at the EU level. Moreover, their study period from 1990 to 2007 preceded the Brexit vote in 2016. Furthermore, in order to address endogeneity concerns more comprehensively, CS 2018 construct a second instrument called the 'instrumented import shock.' They achieve this by modifying their original 'import shock' instrument and using Chinese imports to the US instead of Chinese imports into the UK. This alternative instrument further strengthens their argument for the exclusion restriction.

After establishing the validity of their instrument, CS 2018 present an intriguing finding. They find an unexpected negative correlation between the share of immigrants in the UK's NUTS3 regions (the lowest level of official disaggregation in the EU) and the percentage of 'Leave' votes in the Brexit referendum, as depicted in Fig. 8.8. However, when the cosmopolitan megalopolis London is excluded from the data, no relationship emerges between the Brexit vote and the share of immigrants (non-UK-born residents).

In contrast, there is a positive relationship between import shock from China into the UK, as demonstrated in Fig. 8.9.

In Table 8.6, CS 2018 present their main results regarding the relationship between import shocks and the share of 'Leave' votes in the Brexit referendum. The results demonstrate that higher import shocks are associated with a greater proportion of

Fig. 8.9 Leave share versus import shock

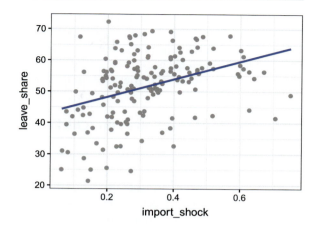

Table 8.6 Regional-level Results, Dependent Variable is Leave Share, NUTS fixed effects used in both regressions

	Linear	IV
import_shock	12.23	12.97
	(4.76)	(4.76)
R^2	0.57	0.57
Num. obs.	167	167
N Clusters	39	39

Standard errors in parentheses

'Leave' votes. Model 1 (in Table 8.6) shows the results from the specification with the import shock variable and model 2 with the instrumented import shock variable (constructed using Chinese imports to the US in the shift-share approach). Notably, both models yield similar results, indicating that the import shock variable was already devoid of endogeneity concerns, supporting the authors' arguments.

Furthermore, CS 2018 conducted an analysis using individual-level reported data on the voting intentions to further augment their findings and explore heterogeneity based on labor market status and occupation groups.[3] They found that regardless of occupation and labor market status, a stronger import shock leads to a higher intention to vote for leaving the EU. This suggests that individuals react to the socioeconomic conditions in their respective regions rather than the direct impact of globalization on their personal circumstances. CS 2018 interpret these results as evidence for the sociotropic reaction of voters, indicating that their voting decisions are influenced by broader social factors rather than narrow self-interest or economic considerations (termed as pocketbook voting).

---

[3] The individual-level results support the regional-level findings, also indicating that immigrant stock and flow do not have a direct influence on the Brexit vote.

It is worth noting that an unintended outcome of the UK's exit from the EU could be an increase in trade integration with China, resulting in a further influx of Chinese imports. This highlights the notion that political discontent can stem from economic factors, but the consequences, such as the rise of populism, may not effectively address the real concerns and grievances of those affected.

8.2.5 Wrights' Lever Solves the 'Chicken and Egg Problem'

In the 1920s, the economist Philip Wright faced the policy challenge of setting import tariffs for cooking oils, which were a major source of US tax revenue. To do so, Wright needed to estimate the demand and supply elasticity of demand for cooking oils by analyzing data by analyzing market data on prices and quantities. The elasticity of demand measures how the demand for any good changes in response to a price change of the good, while the elasticity of supply indicates how supply changes with a price change.

A fundamental principle in economics is that the demand for a good decreases as its price increases, represented by a downward-sloping demand curve. Conversely, a price increase provides an incentive for suppliers to increase their supply, resulting in an upward-sloping supply curve. The simultaneity problem arises when trying to estimate demand elasticity using market prices and quantities. It stems from the fact that any changes in price not only influence the quantity demanded (demand curve), but they also affect the quantity supplied (supply curve). The challenge for Wright was to account for the feedback effects between these two forces of demand and supply, as the two are interdependent through prices. This interdependence makes it difficult to separate the effect of price on quantity demanded from the effect of price on the quantity supplied.

Wright's insight was to recognize that in order to estimate the demand and supply curves, it was necessary to identify external factors that could influence demand conditions without affecting cost (or supply) conditions or which could affect supply conditions without impacting demand. These external factors could serve as instrumental variables to isolate the cause and effect in chicken and egg problems.

One such 'external factor' (the term Phillip Wright uses for exogenous) was below-average rainfall in regions that supplied dairy products. This would affect grazing conditions and therefore impact the cost of dairy production or the supply curve directly. However, this change in rainfall would not affect the demand curve, making it a suitable instrument to shift the supply curves. By observing the effects of shifting supply curves while holding demand constant, Wright could deduce the elasticity of demand (for an excellent graphical discussion on the topic, see Stock and Watson 2017).

For instance, if unfavorable rainfall conditions caused the supply curve to shift left, resulting in reduced supply and increased commodity prices, Wright could analyze whether the quantity demanded decreased significantly, indicating an elastic demand for the commodity. On the other hand, if the quantity demanded decreased only slightly, it would suggest inelastic demand. Commodities like rice, wheat, and

8.2 Concepts and Examples

essential items such as salt typically exhibit inelastic demand. Wright used his expertise in economic theory and knowledge of agricultural production, to argue that rainfall served as a potential instrumental variable (Z) that affected the price of dairy products (X) through reduced supply but did not directly impact the demand curve (Y).[4]

But can unexpected rainfall, or other natural events, be used as instruments for policy analysis? Yes, they can, as long as they meet two conditions to be considered valid instruments[5]:

(1) Instrument relevance: The instrument (Z) should significantly affect (or partially move) X, meaning that Z should be correlated with X. $Cov(Z, X) \neq 0$.

(2) Instrument exogeneity: The instrument should not be related to any other factors that affect the outcome being studied, meaning it should not be correlated with the error term. $Cov(Z, error) = 0$.

To test if rainfall or any other variable, is a suitable instrument, we need to empirically check if it satisfies the first condition. This involves regressing the price of dairy products (X) on the instrument (Z) and checking if the estimated coefficient is statistically significant and the sign of the coefficient is aligned with the theoretical prediction (positive or negative). Statistical tests such as the F statistic can be used, and a general guideline is that the F statistic should be above 10 (see Stock and Watson 2017).[6] Most statistical packages provide sophisticated statistical tests (e.g., Kleibergen-Paap weak instrument statistics) to determine the strength of the relationship between the instrument (e.g., rainfall) and the endogenous variable (e.g., price of dairy products). It is important to note that Z should be a strong predictor of X, as weak instruments can lead to unreliable estimates. In the case of weak instruments, *the cure (instrument) may be worse than the disease (endogeneity)*.

The second (exogeneity) condition cannot be directly tested using empirical methods. In cases where randomization of treatment has naturally occurred or can be feasibly conducted, as exemplified in our basic example (Sect. 8.2.1), the instrumental lever is considered exogenous. However, in many situations, assessing whether the instrument meets the two conditions requires a thorough understanding of relevant theories about the causal relationships in that context, logical reasoning and institutional knowledge. Such knowledge helps ensure that instrument E does not affect the outcome in any other channel except through the treatment (X).

---

[4] For many commodities, it is reasonable to assume that rainfall primarily affects supply and not demand. However, it's important to note that rain can also have an impact on the quantity demanded for some commodities. For example, during rainy days, there is often an increase in demand for hot beverages like coffee or tea as people seek warmth and comfort. It is crucial to exercise caution when selecting an instrument and making the case for its validity in instrumental variable analysis.

[5] Note that the econometricians Stock and Watson (2017) are stating the assumptions in a different way from the way the epidemiologists Glymour and Swanson (2021) state them.

[6] The F statistic is a statistical measure used to test the overall significance of a regression model. In the context of instrumental variables, the F statistic is used the assess the strength of the relationship between the instrument and the endogenous variable (X).

In (potentially) fortunate scenarios where two instruments are available for a single endogenous regressor, both instruments can be used to calculate two different estimators. If both instruments are valid, the resulting estimates should be similar.[7] On the other hand, if the estimates significantly differ, it suggests that one or both instruments may *not be valid*. Identifying which instrument poses a problem can be challenging, and it's possible that both instruments are unreliable. In such cases, theory and institutional knowledge are again needed to separate the wheat from the chaff.

Despite these challenges, instrumental variables have been a powerful tool for uncovering causal effects. IVs have also been used in conjunction with other methods as an independent lever. In later chapters, we explore how instrumental variables serve as a complementary tool for other methods. For instance, instrumental variables empowers regression discontinuity designs when the relationship between the treatment and the threshold is not sharp but rather 'fuzzy.' Similarly, when an encouragement design is employed (as in the basic example in Sect. 8.2.1 of this chapter), where only a subset of individuals exposed to the treatment actually undergoes the treatment, instrumental variables can be harnessed to find the treatment effects.

Finally, let's delve into a policy question similar to the one Wright faced: Can cigarette taxes effectively reduce the consumption of cigarettes?

8.2.6 Taxes and Consumption of Cigarettes

Cigarette smoking poses a significant public health concern in many countries, prompting policymakers to take measures to reduce both the private and public health externalities associated with smoking. One approach to achieve this is by implementing taxes on cigarettes. To assess the impact of taxes on cigarette consumption, analysts need to consider the demand elasticity of cigarettes. This raises a similar issue to what Wright encountered with the challenge of understanding the relationship between prices and quantities. In this case, we will use a panel dataset covering the period from 1985 to 1995, focusing on cigarette consumption in the United States, to estimate the price elasticity of demand for cigarettes.[8]

Stock and Watson (2017) propose using sales tax as an instrumental variable to estimate the impact of taxes on cigarette consumption. They argue that sales tax satisfies the relevance condition for instruments, because it increases the post-tax prices of cigarettes, and they find that the F statistic is well above the thumb rule of 10. Furthermore, they contend that sales tax is exogenous, meaning it is not related to the demand for cigarettes, and is chosen for a variety of other reasons. Sales tax is also not expected to directly affect cigarette demand, except through associated

---

[7] However, the argument does not hold the other way around. That is, if the estimates are similar, it doesn't guarantee the validity of the instruments, although it does increase our confidence in their validity (more details on this can be found in Sect. 8.2.7).

[8] Panel data refers to observing data on the same unit, such as states in the US, over multiple years. For further details, refer to Chap. 10.

8.2 Concepts and Examples

Table 8.7 Regression for dependent variable difference in log of quantity of cigarettes between 1995 and 1985

	OLS
(Intercept)	0.04
	(0.04)
Rpricediff	−1.07
	(0.17)
Incomediff	−0.28
	(0.09)
R^2	0.58
Num. obs.	48

Standard errors in parentheses

price increase.[9] Therefore, it can serve as a suitable instrument for estimating the effect of cigarette prices on consumption.

In addition to general sales tax, the authors also propose cigarette-specific taxes as a second instrument and evaluate the strengths and weaknesses of both instruments in meeting the conditions required for a valid instrument.

☞ **Discussion.** Take a moment to reflect on the two instruments and their strengths and weakness in meeting the conditions for a valid instrument. Can one of them be considered better than the other in terms of validity? Why?

Stock and Watson used data for only two years, 1985 and 1995, from the panel data. To estimate the effect of cigarette prices on cigarette consumption, they analyzed data on the demand for cigarette packs (the outcome variable), cigarette prices (the endogenous regressor), income (GDP per capita in the state, as it can influence consumption), general sales tax, and cigarette-specific tax (as two instruments).

In our replication in Table 8.7, we use the difference between the values for these variables between 1995 and 1985 and estimate a regression model where the demand for cigarette packs is regressed on the price of cigarettes (rpricediff, the independent variable of interest) with income as a covariate (incomediff). The results in Table 8.7 suggest that the price of cigarettes is negatively associated with demand for cigarettes.

We conducted a replication of the authors' analysis to assess the instrument relevance, and the results are presented in Table 8.8. We examined the first stage and observed a positive and statistically significant relationship between the general sales tax and cigarette prices in Model 1. Similarly, in Model 2, there was a positive association between the cigarette-specific tax and cigarette prices. Even when both instru-

---

[9] However, it is important to note that the behavioral economics literature on tax salience suggests that taxes and their framing can have direct effects on consumer behavior. If this is the case for the sales or cigarette taxes in this example, it may violate the exclusion restriction condition.

Table 8.8 First stage of IV regressions, dependent variable difference in log of price of cigarettes betwen 1995 and 1985

	Model 1	Model 2	Model 3
(Intercept)	0.13	0.16	0.13
	(0.02)	(0.01)	(0.01)
SalesTaxdiff	0.03		0.01
	(0.00)		(0.00)
Incomediff	0.11	−0.01	0.05
	(0.08)	(0.06)	(0.06)
CigTaxdiff		0.01	0.01
		(0.00)	(0.00)
R^2	0.52	0.68	0.78
Num. obs.	48	48	48

Standard errors in parentheses

Table 8.9 Instrumental variable estimates

	Model 1	Model 2	Model 3
(Intercept)	0.03	0.11	0.08
	(0.04)	(0.05)	(0.04)
Rpricediff	−1.01	−1.36	−1.24
	(0.20)	(0.25)	(0.21)
Incomediff	−0.28	−0.27	−0.27
	(0.09)	(0.09)	(0.09)
R^2	0.58	0.54	0.57
Num. obs.	48	48	48

Standard errors in parentheses

ments were included in the regression model (Model 3), the positive association with prices persisted.

The strength of the instrumental lever in the first stage can be evaluated by considering the F statistic of the regression, where the independent variable of interest is regressed on the instrument. As mentioned, the F statistic should exceed the thumb rule of 10. The first-stage F statistic is 35 for Model 1, 111.7 for Model 2, and 94.9 for Model 3 in Table 8.8. The instrument relevance condition is satisfied, as the F statistics surpass the threshold value.

Table 8.9 presents the key findings regarding the estimation of the demand elasticity of cigarettes using the instrumental variables method. The instruments used in the three models of Table 8.9 correspond to those used in the models presented in Table 8.8: Model 1 employs only the general sales tax as an instrument, Model 2 uses only the cigarette-specific tax as an instrument, and Model 3 includes both taxes as instruments.

Let's compare the estimates obtained from the three models: In Model 1, where the general sales tax is used as the instrument, the estimated demand elasticity is relatively lower compared to Model 2, where the cigarette-specific tax serves as

8.2 Concepts and Examples

the instrument. In Model 3, which incorporates both instruments, the estimate falls between the results of Models 1 and 2. These differences in estimates using different instruments lead us to infer that either one or both of these instruments may not be reliable. The question then arises: Which of the two instruments is unreliable, or could it be that both instruments are invalid?

Stock and Watson (2017) employ a J-overidentification test to assess the validity of their instruments. This test is possible when there are more instruments than endogenous regressors. In this study, the authors have two instruments and one endogenous regressor.[10]

In our replication of Stock and Watson (2017), we found a moderately small p-value from the overidentification test, 0.068. This suggests that at least one of the instruments is invalid. Stock and Watson (2017) argue that the general sales tax is a more valid instrument compared to cigarette-specific taxes and favor results from Model 1. They suggest that cigarette-specific taxes may not meet the exogeneity condition, for instance, "if tobacco farming and cigarette production are important industries in the state, then these industries can exert influence to keep cigarette-specific taxes low" (p. 356). On the other hand, the general sales tax is less likely to be affected by changes in cigarette demand, making it more likely to satisfy the exogeneity condition and provide a valid estimate of the effect of cigarette prices on demand. They, therefore, end up with an estimated price elasticity of about -1, which is somewhat elastic: an increase in the price of 1% is estimated to lead to a decrease in consumption of about 1%.

In the next section, we would like to highlight a cautionary note for students of causal inference regarding the limitations of certain statistical tests, including J-overidentification tests. It is important to recognize that these tests are useful and indicative in nature but do not provide conclusive evidence.

8.2.7 Overidentification Test is only Indicative of IV Validity

It is important to note that the overidentification tests are only indicative and not definitive tests of the validity of instrumental variables. Deaton (2010) wrote,

> because exogeneity is an identifying assumption that must be made prior to analysis of the data, empirical tests cannot settle the question. This does not prevent many attempts in the literature, often by misinterpreting a satisfactory overidentification test as evidence for

---

[10] The J-overidentification test is specifically designed for situations with multiple instruments and aims to evaluate their validity. It examines whether both instruments satisfy the criteria of being valid instruments, meaning they effectively move the endogenous regressor (price), are exogenous, and do not directly affect the outcome variable except through the treatment. If the two instruments yield similar estimates of the effect, the null hypothesis of the overidentification test is not rejected, which strengthens the credibility of the estimates. In such cases, we have increased confidence in the quality of the instrumental variable estimation, as the two instruments independently produced consistent results. However, if the estimates differ significantly, it suggests a more uncertain situation where one or both of the instruments may be invalid.

valid identification. Such tests can tell us whether estimates change when we select different subsets from a set of possible instruments. While the test is clearly useful and informative, acceptance is consistent with all of the instruments being invalid, while failure is consistent with a subset being correct.

We illustrate Deaton's statement with a simple simulated example.

Figure 8.10 shows the causal graph of the hypothetical example. We are interested in the effect of X on Y. An unobserved variable W is a common cause of X and Y. Z2 and Z1 both have an effect on X, while M is a direct cause of Z2, Z1 and Y (Fig. 8.10).

We can list out the paths:

```
paths(overid)
## $paths
## [1] "X -> Y"
## [2] "X <- W -> Y"
## [3] "X <- Z1 <- M -> Y"
## [4] "X <- Z2 <- M -> Y"
##
## $open
## [1] TRUE TRUE TRUE TRUE
```

We generate data consistent with the causal graph:

```
set.seed(43)
N <- 1000
w <- rnorm(N, 2)
m <- rnorm(N, 2)
z2 <- 2 * m + rnorm(N)
z1 <- 2 * m + rnorm(N)
x <- -4 * w + z1 + z2 + rnorm(N)
y <- 3 * x + 2 * w + 2 * m + rnorm(N)
```

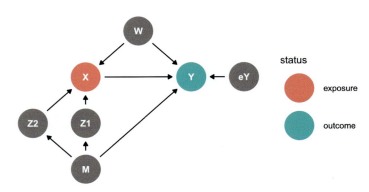

Fig. 8.10 Hypothetical causal graph

8.2 Concepts and Examples

Table 8.10 Regressions for dependent variable y (true effect of x is 3)

	OLS1	OLS2	IV	Correct IV
(Intercept)	0.52	−0.04	8.12	4.27
	(0.11)	(0.09)	(0.13)	(0.51)
x	2.58	3.01	3.52	3.07
	(0.01)	(0.02)	(0.03)	(0.06)
m	3.76	2.03		1.91
	(0.05)	(0.08)		(0.25)
w		2.01		
		(0.08)		
R^2	0.99	1.00	0.94	0.98
Num. obs.	1000	1000	1000	1000

Standard errors in parentheses

Note that the true causal effect of X on Y is 3.

If we regress Y on X and M, we get omitted variable bias from not including the unobserved variable W. We check that if we regress Y on X, W and M, we get an estimate that is close to the true effect (Table 8.10).

However, we assume that W is unobserved. We can use Z1 and Z2 as instruments and if we do so we need to adjust for M to block the paths from Z1 and Z2 to Y via M. We consider two cases:

Misspecified case   using Z1 and Z2 as instruments, but not adjusting for M.
Correctly specified case   using Z1 and Z2 as instruments, while adjusting for M.

We test for overidentification in both IV models:

```
##      value        df   p.value
## 0.4465662 1.0000000 0.5039701
##      value        df   p.value
## 0.2354988 1.0000000 0.6274762
```

We obtain a p-value from the overidentification test, 0.504 for the misspecified IV model. We obtain a p-value from the overidentification test, 0.627 for the correctly specified IV model. Thus, both the misspecified and correctly specified models 'pass' the overidentification test.

We now see how the results come out with a small sample size, which is the only thing we change while generating the data.

Instrumental variable regressions result in coefficients that are consistent in large samples. In small samples, given larger standard errors, the estimate may not be close to the true effect, even if correctly specified.

We obtain a p-value from the overidentification test, 0.524 for the misspecified IV model. We obtain a p-value from the overidentification test, 0.397 for the correctly specified IV model.

Table 8.11 Regressions for dependent variable y (true effect of x is 3, small sample size)

	OLS1	OLS2	IV	Correct IV
(Intercept)	0.14	0.09	8.09	5.09
	(0.79)	(0.53)	(0.83)	(3.50)
x	2.56	2.99	3.67	3.28
	(0.07)	(0.09)	(0.23)	(0.56)
m	4.11	1.85		1.55
	(0.39)	(0.46)		(1.79)
w		2.17		
		(0.36)		
R^2	0.99	1.00	0.92	0.96
Num. obs.	30	30	30	30

Standard errors in parentheses

☞ **Your turn.** Compare the point estimates for x in Tables 8.10 and 8.11. What do you conclude?

8.3 R Code

8.3.1 A Basic Example with an Encouragement Design

8.3.1.1 Causal Graph View

The code for the causal graph:

```
library(ggdag)
library(dagitty)
simple <- dagify(R ~ W, R ~ X, W ~ X, W ~
    E, exposure = "W", outcome = "R", coords = list(x = c(E = 1,
    W = 2, X = 2, R = 3), y = c(E = 1, W = 1,
    X = 1.5, R = 1)))
```

We display the causal graph:

```
ggdag_status(simple) + theme_dag()
```

We read in the data for Sesame Street. It is available from the website accompanying the book by Gelman et al. (2020):

```
library(readr)
sesame <- read_csv("sesame.csv")
```

We can implement the calculations thus:

8.3 R Code

```
lm(y ~ encouraged, data = sesame)
lm(watched ~ encouraged, data = sesame)
lm(y ~ encouraged, data = sesame)$coef[2]/lm(watched ~
    encouraged, data = sesame)$coef[2]
```

8.3.1.2 Heterogeneity of Effects
We set up the causal graph for the compliers:

```
compliers <- dagify(R ~ W, R ~ X, W ~ E,
    exposure = "W", outcome = "R", coords = list(x = c(E = 1,
        W = 2, X = 2, R = 3), y = c(E = 1,
        W = 1, X = 1.5, R = 1)))
```

We display the causal graph:

```
ggdag_status(compliers) + theme_dag()
```

We set up the causal graph:

```
alwaysNever <- dagify(E ~ E, R ~ X, W ~ X,
    R ~ W, exposure = "W", outcome = "R",
    coords = list(x = c(E = 1, W = 2, X = 2,
        R = 3), y = c(E = 1, W = 1, X = 1.5,
        R = 1)))
```

We display the causal graph:

```
ggdag_status(alwaysNever) + theme_dag()
```

8.3.1.3 Two-Stage Least Squares
We can implement the two stages, stage by stage with the following code:

```
library(texreg)
stage1 <- lm(watched ~ encouraged, data = sesame)
stage1
watched.hat <- stage1$fitted
stage2 <- lm(y ~ watched.hat, data = sesame)
stage2
texreg(list(stage1, stage2))
```

We can use the `iv_robust` function in the `estimatr` package to get the two-stage least squares estimate:

```
library(estimatr)
modB <- iv_robust(y ~ watched | encouraged,
    data = sesame)
texreg(list(modB))
```

8.3.2 Colonial Origins of Economic Development

We first load the data:

```
library(tidyverse)
ajr <- read_csv("complete.data.iv.csv")
```

The base sample data used by AJR is a subset, so we filter the complete data:

```
ajrb <- ajr %>%
    filter(baseco == 1)
```

We now will make a scatter plot of log GDP per capita, PPP, 1995 versus log of settler mortality:

```
library(ggrepel)
ggplot(ajrb, aes(x = logem4, y = logpgp95,
    label = shortnam)) + geom_text_repel(size = 3) +
    geom_point() + geom_smooth(method = "lm",
    se = F) + theme_bw()
```

We estimate with OLS:

```
library(texreg)
ol1 <- lm(logpgp95 ~ avexpr, data = ajrb)
ol2 <- lm(logpgp95 ~ avexpr + lat_abst, data = ajrb)
ol3 <- lm(logpgp95 ~ avexpr + lat_abst +
    asia + africa + other, data = ajrb)
texreg(list(ol1, ol2, ol3), caption = "OLS Regressions,
 Dependent variable           is log GDP per capita in 1995",
    caption.above = TRUE, include.adjrs = FALSE,
    include.rmse = FALSE, stars = 0)
```

We now make a scatter plot of log gdp per capita, PPP, 1995 versus Average protection against expropriation risk, 1985–1995:

```
ggplot(ajrb, aes(x = avexpr, y = logpgp95,
    label = shortnam)) + geom_text_repel(size = 3) +
    geom_point() + geom_smooth(method = "lm",
    se = F) + theme_bw()
```

8.3 R Code

AJR estimate the effect of protection against expropriation on income by using settler mortality as an instrument. We now replicate their Fig. 8.3:

```
ggplot(ajrb, aes(x = logem4, y = avexpr,
    label = shortnam)) + geom_text_repel(size = 3) +
    geom_point() + geom_smooth(method = "lm",
    se = F) + theme_bw()
```

We use the AER package to carry out IV regressions with the `ivreg` function. We first estimate the first stage and IV for a simple specification:

```
library(AER)
mod1 <- lm(avexpr ~ logem4, data = ajrb)
mod2 <- ivreg(logpgp95 ~ avexpr | logem4,
    data = ajrb)
texreg(list(mod1, mod2), caption = "First stage (Model 1) and IV regression (Model 2),
Dependent variable is Average protection against expropriation
risk (Model 1) and log GDP per capita in 1995 (Model 2).",
    caption.above = TRUE, include.rsq = FALSE,
    include.adjrs = FALSE, include.rmse = FALSE,
    stars = 0, custom.note = "Standard errors in parentheses.")
```

More specifications:

```
library(AER)
mod1 <- ivreg(logpgp95 ~ avexpr | logem4,
    data = ajrb)
mod2 <- ivreg(logpgp95 ~ avexpr + lat_abst |
    logem4 + lat_abst, data = ajrb)
mod3 <- ivreg(logpgp95 ~ avexpr + lat_abst +
    asia + africa + other | logem4 + lat_abst +
    asia + africa + other, data = ajrb)
texreg(list(mod1, mod2, mod3), caption = "IV Regressions, Dependent variable is log
GDP per capita in 1995",
    caption.above = TRUE, include.rsq = FALSE,
    include.adjrs = FALSE, include.rmse = FALSE,
    stars = 0, custom.note = "Standard errors in parentheses.")
```

Table 8.3 corresponds to Table 8.4 of their paper, columns 1, 2, and 8.

8.3.3 Globalization, Voter Preferences, and Brexit

We load packages:

```
library(estimatr)
library(haven)
library(texreg)
library(tidyverse)
```

We read in the data. The data is available from the journal website:

```
data_reg <- read_dta("Replication_DB_Regional.dta")
```

We make scatter plots:

```
ggplot(data_reg, aes(x = immigrant_share,
    y = leave_share)) + geom_point() + geom_smooth(method = "lm",
    se = F)


ggplot(data_reg, aes(x = import_shock, y = leave_share)) +
    geom_point() + geom_smooth(method = "lm",
    se = F)
```

We estimate effects:

```
mod1 <- lm_robust(leave_share ~ import_shock +
    factor(nuts1), data = data_reg, clusters = nuts2,
    se_type = "stata")
mod2 <- iv_robust(leave_share ~ import_shock +
    factor(nuts1) | instrument_for_shock +
    factor(nuts1), data = data_reg, clusters = nuts2,
    se_type = "stata")

texreg(list(mod1, mod2))
```

8.3.4 Taxes on Consumption of Cigarettes

☞ **Your turn.** Analyze the data, using the code provided below.

We load packages and data:

```
library(tidyverse)
library(AER)
data("CigarettesSW")
Cig <- CigarettesSW
```

We convert to real terms by dividing by the cpi:

```
Cig <- Cig %>%
    mutate(rprice = price/cpi, rincome = income/cpi,
        rtaxs = (taxs - tax)/cpi, rtax = tax/cpi)
```

We filter out for the years 1985 and 1995:

```
Cig85 <- Cig %>%
    filter(year == 1985)
Cig95 <- Cig %>%
    filter(year == 1995)
```

We create new variables:

8.3 R Code

```
Cig85 <- Cig85 %>%
    mutate(pack85 = log(packs), logRprice85 = log(rprice),
        logIncome85 = log(rincome), SalesTax85 = rtaxs,
        CigTax85 = rtax) %>%
    select(pack85, logRprice85, logIncome85,
        SalesTax85, CigTax85)


Cig95 <- Cig95 %>%
    mutate(pack95 = log(packs), logRprice95 = log(rprice),
        logIncome95 = log(rincome), SalesTax95 = rtaxs,
        CigTax95 = rtax) %>%
    select(pack95, logRprice95, logIncome95,
        SalesTax95, CigTax95)
```

We now take differences between variables for years 1995 and 1985:

```
pack_diff <- Cig95[, 1] - Cig85[, 1]
rpricediff <- Cig95[, 2] - Cig85[, 2]
incomediff <- Cig95[, 3] - Cig85[, 3]
SalesTaxdiff <- Cig95[, 4] - Cig85[, 4]
CigTaxdiff <- Cig95[, 5] - Cig85[, 5]
```

We use the estimatr package.
We use texreg for display:

```
mod1 <- iv_robust(pack_diff ~ rpricediff +
    incomediff | incomediff + SalesTaxdiff,
    diagnostics = TRUE)
mod2 <- iv_robust(pack_diff ~ rpricediff +
    incomediff | incomediff + CigTaxdiff,
    diagnostics = TRUE)
mod3 <- iv_robust(pack_diff ~ rpricediff +
    incomediff | incomediff + SalesTaxdiff +
    CigTaxdiff, diagnostics = TRUE)
```

We get the diagnostics for first stage:

```
summary(mod1)$diagnostic_first_stage_fstatistic[1]
summary(mod2)$diagnostic_first_stage_fstatistic[1]
summary(mod3)$diagnostic_first_stage_fstatistic[1]
```

We display results:

```
texreg(list(mod1, mod2, mod3), caption = "Instrumental variable estimates",
    caption.above = TRUE, custom.note = "Standard errors in parentheses.")
```

Overidentification test diagnostics:

```
summary(mod3)$diagnostic_overid_test
##         value         df    p.value
## 3.33247808 1.00000000 0.06792446
```

8.3.5 Overidentification is Only Indicative of IV Validity

We set up the causal graph and plot it with ggdag:

```
library(ggdag)
library(dagitty)
overid <- dagify(X ~ W + Z1 + Z2, Y ~ X +
    W + eY + M, Z2 ~ M, Z1 ~ M, exposure = "X",
    outcome = "Y", coords = list(x = c(Z2 = 0,
        M = 1, X = 1, Z1 = 1, W = 2, Y = 3,
        eY = 4), y = c(M = 0, Z2 = 1, Z1 = 1,
        X = 2, Y = 2, eY = 2, W = 3)))

ggdag_status(overid) + theme_dag()
```

We get the paths:

```
paths(overid)
```

We generate data consistent with the causal graph:

```
set.seed(43)
N <- 1000
w <- rnorm(N, 2)
m <- rnorm(N, 2)
z2 <- 2 * m + rnorm(N)
z1 <- 2 * m + rnorm(N)
x <- -4 * w + z1 + z2 + rnorm(N)
y <- 3 * x + 2 * w + 2 * m + rnorm(N)
```

Note that the true causal effect of X on Y is 3:
We use lm:

```
modlm <- lm(y ~ x + w + m)
```

For the IV regressions, we use estimatr:

```
library(estimatr)
modMisspecified <- iv_robust(y ~ x | z1 +
    z2, diagnostics = TRUE)
```

We use texreg to display the results:

8.4 Resources

```
modCorrectlyspecified <- iv_robust(y ~ x +
    m | m + z1 + z2, diagnostics = TRUE)
# summary(modCorrectlyspecified)
library(texreg)
texreg(list(modlm, modMisspecified, modCorrectlyspecified),
    custom.model.names = c("OLS", "IV", "Correct IV"),
    caption = "Regressions for dependent variable y (true effect of x is 3).",
    caption.above = TRUE, stars = numeric(0),
    include.ci = FALSE, include.adjrs = FALSE,
    include.rmse = FALSE, custom.note = "Standard errors in parentheses.")
```

We test for overidentification in both IV models:

```
summary(modMisspecified)$diagnostic_overid_test
summary(modCorrectlyspecified)$diagnostic_overid_test
```

We now see how are results come out with a small sample size. We only change N to 30:

```
N <- 30
w <- rnorm(N, 2)
m <- rnorm(N, 2)
z2 <- 2 * m + rnorm(N)
z1 <- 2 * m + rnorm(N)
x <- -4 * w + z1 + z2 + rnorm(N)
y <- 3 * x + 2 * w + 2 * m + rnorm(N)
modlm2 <- lm(y ~ x + w + m)
modMisspecified2 <- iv_robust(y ~ x | z1 +
    z2, diagnostics = TRUE)
modCorrectlyspecified2 <- iv_robust(y ~ x +
    m | m + z1 + z2, diagnostics = TRUE)
texreg(list(modlm2, modMisspecified2, modCorrectlyspecified2),
    custom.model.names = c("OLS", "IV", "Correct IV"),
    caption = "Regressions for dependent variable y (true effect of x is 3).",
    caption.above = TRUE, stars = numeric(0),
    include.ci = FALSE, include.adjrs = FALSE,
    include.rmse = FALSE, custom.note = "Standard errors in parentheses.")
```

```
summary(modMisspecified2)$diagnostic_overid_test
summary(modCorrectlyspecified2)$diagnostic_overid_test
```

8.4 Resources

8.4.1 For Better Understanding

Chapter by Angrist et al. (2015) in their book *Mastering Metrics*.

8.4.2 For Going Further

Deaton's (2010) paper on Instruments, Randomization, and Learning about Development.

Packages Used in This Chapter

The citations for the packages used in this chapter are[11]:

```
## Barrett M (2021). _ggdag: Analyze and Create Elegant Directed
## Acyclic Graphs_. R package version 0.2.4, <URL:
## https://CRAN.R-project.org/package=ggdag>.


## Blair G, Cooper J, Coppock A, Humphreys M, Sonnet L (2022).
## _estimatr: Fast Estimators for Design-Based Inference_. R
## package version 1.0.0, <URL:
## https://CRAN.R-project.org/package=estimatr>.


## Fox J, Weisberg S (2019). _An R Companion to Applied
## Regression_, Third edition. Sage, Thousand Oaks CA. <URL:
## https://socialsciences.mcmaster.ca/jfox/Books/Companion/>.


## Fox J, Weisberg S, Price B (2022). _carData: Companion to
## Applied Regression Data Sets_. R package version 3.0-5, <URL:
## https://CRAN.R-project.org/package=carData>.


## Kleiber C, Zeileis A (2008). _Applied Econometrics with R_.
## Springer-Verlag, New York. ISBN 978-0-387-77316-2, <URL:
## https://CRAN.R-project.org/package=AER>.


## Leifeld P (2013). "texreg: Conversion of Statistical Model
## Output in R to LaTeX and HTML Tables." _Journal of Statistical
## Software_, *55*(8), 1-24. <URL:
## http://dx.doi.org/10.18637/jss.v055.i08>.


## Slowikowski K (2021). _ggrepel: Automatically Position
## Non-Overlapping Text Labels with 'ggplot2'_. R package version
## 0.9.1, <URL: https://CRAN.R-project.org/package=ggrepel>.
```

---

[11] The tidyverse package itself contains several packages.

8.4 Resources

```
## Textor J, van der Zander B, Gilthorpe MS, Liskiewicz M, ##
Ellison GT (2016). "Robust causal inference using directed ##
acyclic graphs: the R package 'dagitty'." _International ## Journal
of Epidemiology_, *45*(6), 1887-1894. doi: ## 10.1093/ije/dyw341
(URL: https://doi.org/10.1093/ije/dyw341).


print(citation("tidyverse"), style = "text") ## Wickham H, Averick
M, Bryan J, Chang W, McGowan LD, François ## R, Grolemund G, Hayes
A, Henry L, Hester J, Kuhn M, Pedersen ## TL, Miller E, Bache SM,
Müller K, Ooms J, Robinson D, Seidel ## DP, Spinu V, Takahashi K,
Vaughan D, Wilke C, Woo K, Yutani H ## (2019). "Welcome to the
tidyverse." _Journal of Open Source ## Software_, *4*(43), 1686.
doi: 10.21105/joss.01686 (URL: ##
https://doi.org/10.21105/joss.01686).


print(citation("knitr")[[1]], style = "text")
## Xie Y (2022). _knitr: A General-Purpose Package for Dynamic
## Report Generation in R_. R package version 1.41, <URL:
## https://yihui.org/knitr/>.


print(citation("formatR"), style = "text")
## Xie Y (2023). _formatR: Format R Code Automatically_. R
## package version 1.14, <URL:
## https://CRAN.R-project.org/package=formatR>.


## Zeileis A, Grothendieck G (2005). "zoo: S3 Infrastructure for
## Regular and Irregular Time Series." _Journal of Statistical
## Software_, *14*(6), 1-27. doi: 10.18637/jss.v014.i06 (URL:
## https://doi.org/10.18637/jss.v014.i06).


## Zeileis A, Hothorn T (2002). "Diagnostic Checking in
## Regression Relationships." _R News_, *2*(3), 7-10. <URL:
## https://CRAN.R-project.org/doc/Rnews/>.


## Zeileis A, Köll S, Graham N (2020). "Various Versatile
## Variances: An Object-Oriented Implementation of Clustered
## Covariances in R." _Journal of Statistical Software_, *95*(1),
## 1-36. doi: 10.18637/jss.v095.i01 (URL:
## https://doi.org/10.18637/jss.v095.i01).
##
## Zeileis A (2004). "Econometric Computing with HC and HAC
## Covariance Matrix Estimators." _Journal of Statistical
## Software_, *11*(10), 1-17. doi: 10.18637/jss.v011.i10 (URL:
## https://doi.org/10.18637/jss.v011.i10).
##
## Zeileis A (2006). "Object-Oriented Computation of Sandwich
## Estimators." _Journal of Statistical Software_, *16*(9), 1-16.
```

```
## doi: 10.18637/jss.v016.i09 (URL:
## https://doi.org/10.18637/jss.v016.i09).
```

References

Acemoglu, Daron, Simon Johnson, and James A. Robinson. 2001. The colonial origins of comparative development: an empirical investigation. *American Economic Review* 91 (5): 1369–1401.

Acemoglu, Daron, Simon Johnson, and James A. Robinson. 2012. The colonial origins of comparative development: an empirical investigation: reply. *American Economic Review* 102 (6): 3077–3110.

Albouy, David Y. 2012. The colonial origins of comparative development: an empirical investigation: comment. *American Economic Review* 102 (6): 3059–3076.

Angrist, Joshua D., Jörn.-steffen Pischke, and Jorn-steffen Pischke. 2015. *Mastering 'Metrics*. Princeton; Oxford: Princeton University Press. (with french flaps edition).

Angrist, Joshua D., Guido W. Imbens, and Donald B. Rubin. 1996. Identification of Causal Effects Using Instrumental Variables. *Journal of the American Statistical Association* 91 (434): 444–455.

Bartik, Timothy J. 1991. *Who Benefits from State and Local Economic Development Policies?* Kalamazoo, MI: W.E. Upjohn Institute.

Borusyak, Kirill, Peter Hull, and Xavier Jaravel. 2022. Quasi-experimental shift-share research designs. *The Review of Economic Studies* 89 (1): 181–213.

Ceccarelli, Marco. 2014. Contributions of Archimedes on mechanics and design of mechanisms. *Mechanism and Machine Theory* 72: 86–93.

Colantone, Italo, and Piero Stanig. 2018. Global competition and brexit. *American Political Science Review* 112 (2): 201–218. (May 2018. Publisher: Cambridge University Press).

Deaton, Angus. 2010. Instruments, randomization, and learning about development. *Journal of Economic Literature* 48 (2): 424–455.

Gerry Ann Bogatz and Samuel Ball. 1971. *The Second Year of Sesame Street: A Continuing Evaluation*. Princeton, N.J.: Educational Testing Service.

Gelman, Andrew, Jennifer Hill, and Aki Vehtari. 2020. *Regression and Other Stories*. Cambridge New York, NY Port Melbourne, VIC New Delhi Singapore: Cambridge University Press.

Goldsmith-Pinkham, Paul, Isaac Sorkin, and Henry Swift. 2020. Bartik instruments: what, when, why, and how. *American Economic Review* 110 (8): 2586–2624.

Glymour, Maria M., and Sonja A Swanson. 2021. Instrumental variables and quasi-experimental approaches. In *Modern Epidemiology*, eds. Timothy L Lash, Tyler J Vanderweele, Sebastien Haneuse, and Kenneth J Rothman.

Diamond, Jared. 1997. *Guns, Germs, and Steel: The Fates of Human Societies*. New York: Norton and Company.

Mc-Closkey, D.N. 2016. *Bourgeois equality: How ideas, not capital or institutions, enriched the world*. University of Chicago Press.

North, Douglass C. 1991. Institutions. *Journal of Economic Perspectives* 5 (1): 97–112.

Romer D.H.., and Frankel, J.A. 1999. Does Trade Cause Growth? *American Economic Review* 89 (3): 379–399.

Steiner, Peter M., Yongnam Kim, Courtney E. Hall, and Dan Su. 2017. Graphical Models for Quasi-experimental Designs. *Sociological Methods & Research* 46 (2): 155–188. (March 2017. Publisher: SAGE Publications Inc.).

Stock, James H., and Mark W. Watson. 2017. *Introduction to Econometrics* (3rd ed.) By Pearson. Pearson Education. (October 2017).

Stock, James H., and Francesco Trebbi. 2003. Retrospectives: Who invented instrumental variable regression? *Journal of Economic Perspectives* 17 (3): 177–194.

Regression Discontinuity Design 9

9.1 Introduction

Consider two students, one scoring 89 and the other scoring 90 on a causal inference course. Are they so different after all? Our hunch is they are not so different as the slight difference in their score could be due to random error or temporary factors like fatigue or fever during the exam. However, in many universities, a student with a score of 89 would receive a B plus, while a score of 90 would secure an A. This one-point difference resulting in an A or B can have real-world consequences, as it can be a deciding factor for scholarship eligibility or admission to a university. In such scenarios, the Regression Discontinuity Design (RDD) method comes into play.

The RDD method leverages arbitrary cutoffs, such as the distinct difference in letter grades between a B and an A, resulting from a small score change (e.g., 89–90) to estimate the causal effect of a treatment on various outcomes of interest. These outcomes can encompass both short-term achievements like receiving a scholarship or securing a coveted internship, as well as long-term outcomes such as job placements and wage levels. Despite the similarities between students, the use of these score cutoffs for determining distinctly different treatments is at the heart of the RDD method. Achieving an A likely opens more doors and opportunities for the treated students, despite their similarity to students just short of an A. In this example, we can use the jump in the treatment status for students between 89 and 90 to analyze the impact of obtaining an A on their short and longterm outcomes.

The apparent arbitrariness of these cutoffs provides a setting for an apples-to-apples comparison between the treated and control groups around the cutoff, where they receive different treatments based on a small numerical difference in their score. RDD has emerged as a popular and credible design for evaluating policies in diverse contexts, including assessing the effectiveness of educational programs and evaluating the impact of environmental policies (Lee and Lemieux 2010; Cattaneo et al. 2019).

Let's consider the example of age-based eligibility as a means to evaluate effects of policies. Certain policies, such as pension and alcohol consumption regulations, employ age-based cutoffs. These thresholds (cutoffs and thresholds are often used interchangeably in the RDD literature) can be used to study how policy changes impact individuals' lives.

Take the case of pension eligibility, where individuals in many countries become eligible at age 65 despite the continuous aging process. Researchers have used this age cutoff to investigate the welfare implications of pension policies. By comparing individuals who have recently turned 65 and started receiving pensions with those who are slightly under 65 and have not yet qualified, we can access the welfare effects of the pension.

To ensure a fairly balanced apples-to-apples comparison, it is important to have treated and control groups similar in all aspects except for the treatment they receive. RDD banks on having enough individuals close to the cutoff, on either side, while also observing a discontinuous jump in treatment at the cutoff. This jump in treatment allows us to estimate the effect of the treatment on our outcomes of interest.

As mentioned, these outcomes can vary, such as comparing job placement rates between students who receive A's (scoring 90) and those who receive B's (scoring 89) or examining the health of pensioners who are a few months older than 65 compared to those who are a few months younger than 64 years of age. To illustrate the concept, we first examine the adverse outcome of traffic fatalities among young adults who gain legal access to alcohol at the age of 21 in the United States compared to those slightly younger by a few days or months. We then delve into the effect of political term limits on politician performance in Brazil, followed by an investigation into the surprisingly unremarkable impact of rural roads in India, relying on specific discontinuous treatments at arbitrary thresholds.

9.2 Concepts and Examples

9.2.1 Minimum Legal Drinking Age and Fatalities in the US

In the United States, the minimum legal drinking age is 21, which means individuals under the age of 21 are not legally allowed to purchase or consume alcohol. The minimum legal drinking age (MLDA) law creates a clear cutoff point where one day a person is prohibited from drinking, and the next they become eligible to drink. Carpenter et al. (2009) use this sudden jump in alcohol access at the age of 21 to investigate the adverse effects of alcohol on young adults.

In the chapter on panel data (Chap. 10), we explore an alternative method to estimate the impact of alcohol access by examining variations in minimum legal drinking age policies and beer taxes across different states in the US. However, one challenging issue arises when comparing states with different policies or taxes and attempting to estimate causal effects with fixed effects models (as discussed in Chap. 10 on Panel

9.2 Concepts and Examples

data). The issue lies in the selection of states that implement these policies. States with distinct cultural attitudes may have varying attitudes toward drinking, leading to differences in the timing of policy adoption. This endogeneity issue can affect both the policy adoption and the outcome, such as alcohol-related traffic fatalities.[1] Panel data can only account for these selection issues if the unobserved factors affecting the selection of policies are fixed over time within the states. The panel data fixed effects models would be unable to address biases if the unobserved factors vary over time within states.

To address this concern, researchers can rely on the arbitrary cutoff-based jump in treatment provided by RDD as an alternative method to study the issue. The RDD approach brings us closer to a randomized setup as it allows for the comparison of similar individuals just before and after they turn 21, enabling (nearly) an apples-to-apples comparison.

Consider the scenario of an individual in the US who has recently turned 21. With this milestone, they gain the legal privilege to purchase alcohol. Carpenter et al. (2009) (CD, hereafter) investigate the impact of this sudden and unrestricted access to alcohol on young adults. They explore various adverse outcomes such as traffic fatalities, suicides, and other related consequences. Additionally, CD also examine outcomes that should remain unaffected by alcohol access, serving as placebo outcomes to reinforce their findings that the observed effects are indeed attributable to alcohol consumption and not affected by other confounding factors.

CD uses the abrupt and sharp change in access to alcohol on either side of age 21 as the lever to study the effect of alcohol and address concerns regarding the selection effect. CD focus on individuals who are near the age cutoff, just days or months before and after turning 21, and observe a significant increase in alcohol-related deaths among those who have recently reached the legal drinking age. To provide a comparative view, they also examine age cutoffs around 20 (where there is no change in legal access to alcohol) and around 22 (where there is already legal access to alcohol) and find no significant changes in those outcomes around these age cutoffs. The authors emphasize that the key distinction between individuals who have just turned 21 and those who are exactly one year younger or older is the discontinuous change in their legal access to alcohol, which serves as the treatment variable. This discontinuity in treatment at the age threshold is a fundamental requirement for applying the RDD method.[2]

---

[1] Endogeneity is a term used to indicate that two variables may be related or correlated but inferring if there is a causal relationship is not straightforward. Income and education may be causally related, but education is an endogenous independent variable since they could be positively affected by the individual's ability, which also directly affects income.

[2] An alternative, technical assumption is made to estimate the treatment effect with RDD. Abadie and Cattaneo (2018, p. 492) state this precisely: "if the regression functions $E[Y_1|X = x]$ and $E[Y_0|X = x]$ are continuous at $x = c$ then τ_{SRD} is nonparametrically identified." Here, Y_1 and Y_0 are the potential outcomes, X is the running variable, and τ_{SRD} is the sharp regression discontinuity treatment effect. With this assumption, the gap between the two regression functions at the cutoff gives us the treatment effect.

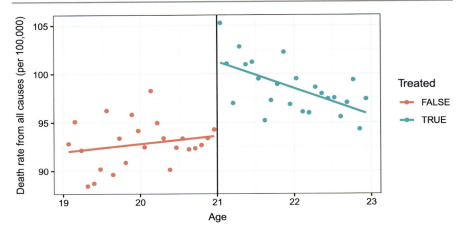

Fig. 9.1 Death rate from all causes (per 100,000) versus Age in years

A morbid pattern becomes evident at the age of 21 when compared to the immediate years before and after 21 (Fig. 9.1). As individuals can only legally access alcohol at the age of 21, there is a sudden change in treatment at 21. The authors attribute the increase in adverse outcomes at the cutoff to the change in alcohol access, assuming that all other factors are (nearly) equal around the cutoff.[3]

In this case, age serves as the **'running' variable,** while legal alcohol access is considered the **treatment variable**, that is activated discontinuously at the **threshold** or **cutoff** age of 21 in the US. Any change in the outcome can be causally attributed to the corresponding change in treatment at age 21.

It is crucial to stay near the cutoff to ensure balanced comparisons. While someone who is a day or a week older than 21 may be similar to someone who is a few days younger than 21, as we move further along the age spectrum (the running variable), the ability to make apples-to-apples comparison diminishes. For instance, comparing the death rates of individuals aged 25 to those aged 16 would not provide a balanced comparison, as numerous other factors come into play during those years. Similarly, comparing individuals who scored 89 and 90 may yield a balanced comparison, but comparing those who scored 97 and 79 not, as they are likely different in many characteristics. These large differences confound the estimation of causal effects, as factors such as work ethic can influence scores and job placements, as hard-working individuals will diligently pursue tasks and opportunities. By staying close to the cutoff, we minimize confounding factors that can affect our causal inferences.

On the one hand, when the bandwidth of comparison is larger, such as including students who scored between 78 and 100 rather than a narrow bandwidth of 86

---

[3] We use the word 'nearly' as there is a slight difference in the age between the treated and control groups, ranging from a few hours to days or weeks. If this minor age difference can be considered negligible and can be ignored, we achieve an apples-to-apples comparison rather than a nearly apples-to-apples comparison.

9.2 Concepts and Examples

to 92, with the cutoff at 90 for the treatment with an A grade, we have a larger pool of students for analysis. However, as we move away from the cutoff, we gain more observations for making comparisons, but at the cost of reducing balance and introducing bias. More data provides more information but also adds more bias, thereby worsening balance and amplifying selection effects. This tradeoff is known as the bias-variance tradeoff.

In Fig. 9.1, the control group observations are represented on the left (in red), while the treated observations are on the right (in blue). Each dot represents the (binned) average number of monthly deaths, with twelve dots for each year (on the X-axis). The cutoff age of 21 is depicted by the vertical black line, which signifies the abrupt change in alcohol access. The vertical distance between the fitted line on the left and the right at the cutoff indicates the effect size.

RDD is one of the most visual causal inference designs where the treatment effects can be depicted in visually stark forms, even allowing one to eyeball the effects. In Fig. 9.1, we can see that the blue line intersects the cutoff at just over 100, while the red line is below 95. This suggests that the estimated fatality rate is 9.595 higher when alcohol access is allowed. The R code for this analysis will be provided in a later section.

Next, we will discuss how imposing term limits on holding political office can have unintended negative consequences using a regression discontinuity design approach.

9.2.2 Term Limits and Politician Performance in Brazil

Term limits for incumbents in office are a common mechanism employed to curb the power of politicians in democratic systems. However, these limits may have some unintended drawbacks. One potential downside is that politicians may not be motivated to perform well, such as providing good governance and public goods, particularly in their last term in office. In light of this, Klašnja and Titiunik (2017) (hereafter, KT (2017)) studied whether term limits actually result in a decline in political performance. They compared the performance of political parties in constituencies where representatives were subject to term limits with those where re-election incentives remained.

However, comparing party performance in constituencies that are political strongholds of a particular party or politician does not enable a fair apples-to-apples comparison. To address this issue, KT adopted a RDD approach. They limited their study sample to constituencies where the winning margin in the previous election was narrow and then compared the party wins in the subsequent election between term-limited constituencies and those where incumbents were not term-limited. By employing this design, the authors achieved a balance between the treated and control groups, enhancing the credibility of the findings.

Despite the potential loss of incentive for term-limited politicians to perform, political parties still have a strong motivation to win elections. They can counterbalance this by effectively disciplining their term-limited politicians, mitigating the risk of nonperformance. However, to isolate the specific effect of term limits, it is important to study a setting where there is little to no party pressure on term-limited politicians to perform.

KT highlights the weak party system in the Brazilian municipal elections as a context for isolating the effect of term limits. They discovered that many politicians in Brazil changed parties after completing their term, providing further evidence of the country's weak party system. Furthermore, Brazil being an expansive country with competitive municipality-level elections, offered an ideal setting for RDD analysis. The large and competitive setting provided them with a substantial sample size of municipalities where candidates won or lost by narrow margins, enabling them to investigate the impact of term limits on politicians in a context where political parties lacked the ability to effectively discipline their representatives.

In these Brazilian municipal elections, a substantial number of candidates win by small margins. This abundance of data around the cutoff (a tie) allows a thorough statistical analysis. If the margin is positive, the candidate has received more votes and emerges as the winner. In a system where politicians are limited to two terms, it is anticipated that they will exert significant effort in their first term to secure re-election for a second term. However, once elected for a second term, they become ineligible for re-election and may no longer possess instrumental incentives to perform their duties effectively, although intrinsic motivations may still be present.

In their study, KT evaluated politicians' performance by examining their party's success in the constituency and measuring the provision of public goods as another direct indicator of performance. This approach allowed them to assess whether term limits had a negative impact on politician's performance.

To conduct the RDD analysis, KT (2017) recorded party performance in terms of scores. A positive score represented the margin of victory over the strongest opponent, while scores below the cutoff of zero indicated a loss. A zero score at the cutoff of zero indicated an unlikely tie. In this study, the treatment variable was a victory in the elections in period T (or the previous election), and the outcome variable was the party's performance (win or loss) in the current period (time $T + 1$). The authors specifically examined the party's election win in time $T + 1$ within a subset of data where the party had narrowly won or lost the elections in the constituency in the previous election (T). This approach ensured a balanced comparison between the treated and control groups.

The treatment group comprised municipalities where the party had narrowly won the election at time T, while the control group consisted of the municipalities where the party had narrowly lost at time T. The RDD estimate provided the local average treatment effect, specifically examining how barely winning the election influenced the party's performance in the subsequent period. We use the term 'local average' since RDD estimates can reliably measure the treatment effect only for parties winning or losing by small margins. However, extrapolating these results to larger wins would be challenging as they would no longer be an apples-to-apples comparison.

While RDD offers reasonable internal validity in terms of its results, it does not guarantee external validity. In other words, while RDD provides insights into the treatment's effect, its findings may not be applicable to other contexts. In this regard, RDD is often considered similar to an experiment. Sekhon and Titiunik (2017, p.

9.2 Concepts and Examples

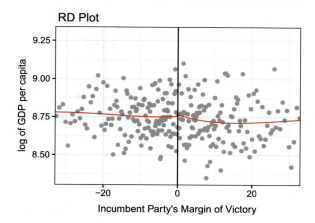

Fig. 9.2 No change (jump) in the log of GDP per capita across the cutoff

175) take a qualified stance on making inferences based on RDD: "In our view, RD designs are best conceived as non-experimental designs or observational studies—i.e., studies where the goal is to learn about the causal effects of a treatment, but the similarity or comparability of subjects receiving different treatments cannot be ensured by construction. Interpreting RD designs as observational studies implies that their credibility must necessarily rank below that of experiments. This, however, does not mean that RD designs are without special merit. Among observational studies, RD designs are one of the most credible alternatives because important features of the treatment assignment mechanism are known and empirically testable under reasonable assumptions."

Cattaneo et al. (2019) have made significant contributions to advancing the RDD design, from concept to estimation. RDD estimation using the rdrobust package is akin to a surgeon's skilled use of a scalpel. The package implements (Cattaneo et al. 2019, p. 35) "linear regression fits using only observations near the cutoff point, separately for control and treatment units. Specifically, this approach uses only observations between $c - h$ and $c + h$, where $h > 0$, is a so-called bandwidth that determines the size of the neighborhood around the cutoff where the empirical RD analysis is conducted." Cattaneo et al. (2019) provide an excellent step-by-step explanation (See also Imbens and Kalyanaraman 2012; Calonico et al. 2014).

Cattaneo et al. (2020) illustrate RDD methods by re-analyzing the data in Klašnja and Titiunik (2017) and conducting falsification tests, which help improve the validity of the findings. The authors check if the covariates at the margin of victory are not jumping, suggesting that the treated and control groups are otherwise balanced. For instance, the log of GDP is balanced at the cutoff, as seen in Fig. 9.2, so that there are no jumps.

Figure 9.3 presents the main result of the paper graphically. The horizontal axis (x-axis) represents the margin of victory in the previous elections (T), while the vertical axis (y-axis) displays the outcome, the margin of victory in the current polls (period T+1). A clear jump can be observed at the cutoff point. The effect was estimated using the rddrobust package, with the point estimate of -6.281.

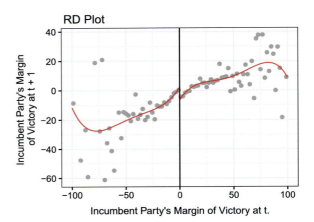

Fig. 9.3 Effect of victory at t on Vote Margin at t + 1, Incumbent Party, Brazilian Mayoral Elections 1996–2012

The authors' finding of a 6% loss is surprising because incumbents typically enjoy an 'incumbency advantage.' Incumbent politicians have the advantage of using their position of power to strategically allocate resources on hand to increase their chances of winning in future elections (Hicken 2011; Murugesan 2020). The results from KT (2017) are in stark contrast to this expectation, which further strengthens their findings regarding the unintended effect of term limits.

9.2.3 Rural Roads and Economic Development in India

Road infrastructure plays a critical role in connecting markets and providing opportunities for those living in remote areas far from major cities. Approximately, a billion people reside at least two kilometers away from paved roads, and a third of those billion live in India, the world's most populous country. In their study, Asher and Novosad (2020) focus on India to examine the impact of expanding road infrastructure on rural economic development. During the early 2000s, India embarked on substantial investments in road infrastructure with the goal of reducing poverty by integrating rural markets and creating more employment opportunities.

While multiple studies have demonstrated a positive correlation between road connectivity, rural economic growth, and poverty reduction, establishing a causal effect is challenging. This challenge arises from the presence of various confounding factors, both observable and unobservable, that can influence both road connectivity and economic outcomes in villages.

However, Asher and Novosad cleverly address this challenge by using a specific setting that helps overcome it. They focus on a program that determined the construction of rural roads based on village population thresholds. Specifically, villages with populations of at least 500 or 1000 were eligible for road construction under this program. The authors found that villages located just above these population thresholds had a 22% higher likelihood of receiving a road from the program on average. This unique setting raises the question of whether it is an ideal fit for the regression discontinuity design approach.

Fig. 9.4 Estimated density of the running variable

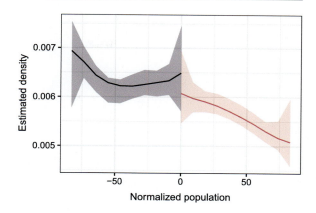

☞ **Discussion** Before reading further, take a moment to consider the distinction between this setting and the previous RDD cases where the policy abruptly changed the treatment status. What is different?

In simple terms, the answer is yes, the RDD approach is still applicable. However, unlike the 'sharp' RDD case studies we discussed previously, in this particular setting, the running variable going past the cutoff does not result in a 100% treatment rate. For example, in the minimum legal drinking age, everyone above 21 gains legal alcohol access, while in the case of elections, those with a positive victory margin win the elections in time T. The control groups in both cases do not receive the treatment.

In contrast, meeting the population threshold does not guarantee that *all* the villages will receive the treatment (as previously noted, there is an average increase of 22% in treatment at the cutoff). When treatment compliance is imperfect or 'fuzzy,' we can still employ the RDD approach with the help of an additional method: instrumental variables (which we discussed in Chap. 8). As Nobel Laureate in Economics, Joshua Angrist and his co-author Jorn-Steffen Pischke (2015, p. 169) point out, 'Fuzzy RD is IV.'

In order for RDD to be valid, it is important to ensure that the jump, if any, occurs in the outcome variable, at the cutoff for treatment status, while also checking that other variables do not exhibit significant differences at the cutoff.

Figure 9.4 presents the density plot of the running variable, which represents the population of villages. This figure, along with other pieces of evidence, is used by the authors to support the validity of the RDD design. The plot indicates that there is no notable difference in the distribution of the village population at the thresholds, as the confidence intervals of the treated and control groups overlap significantly. This finding suggests that villages located just above and just below the population threshold, which determines eligibility for road construction, share similar population characteristics.

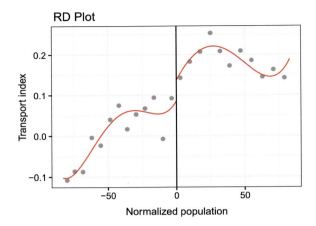

Fig. 9.5 Effect on transport index

Figure 9.5 showcases one of the many estimated effects examined by Asher and Novosad (2020) in their study. The authors found that the construction of roads had a positive impact on transportation as depicted in Fig. 9.5. Additionally, they find a significant labor shift away from agriculture, which may indicate increased opportunities for non-farm employment or migration to urban areas. However, in terms of reducing poverty through infrastructure investments, the study did not find any substantial changes in economic development measures such as increases in farm activity, agricultural production, or household consumption. Therefore, it remains unclear whether road investments will lead to substantial improvements in assets or income for rural communities in the short or medium run. Further research is needed to evaluate the long-term effects of road investments on rural economic growth and poverty reduction.

☞ **Discussion**   Read the results section of the Asher and Novosad paper and take note of the outcomes where the authors identify a positive, negative or no changes. Consider these findings in the context of the policymakers' goal of promoting rural economic development and reducing poverty.

Before we conclude, we must highlight that RDD has become a widely used method for policy evaluation, when there are opportune settings specifying rules, laws, or eligibility criteria that define cutoffs for receiving treatment. This is why the word 'setting' appears several times in this chapter, and having institutional knowledge about the setting greatly enhances the quality and reliability of the policy inferences made.

Like randomized controlled trials (RCTs), RDD estimates are often regarded to have higher internal validity. However, their external validity and generalizability are subject to scrutiny. As Abadie and Cattaneo (2018) point out, RDD "often provides highly credible and robust results for the local subpopulation of units whose scores

9.3 R Code

are near or at the cutoff, but it may not offer informative insights about the effects at score values far from the cutoff."

In conclusion, while RDD offers valuable insights for policy evaluation within specific settings, it is crucial to exercise caution when generalizing the findings beyond the immediate context of the cutoff. Additional considerations are necessary when going from an RDD estimate to a policy decision, just as with other methods, in order to account for methodological limitations, treatment heterogeneity, and other complexities and dynamics in the real world.

9.3 R Code

9.3.1 Minimum Legal Drinking Age and Fatalities in the US

We load the packages and the data. The data is available in the mastering metrics package:

```
library(tidyverse)
library(masteringmetrics)
data("mlda")
library(rdrobust)
```

The variable all in the data is the death rate from all causes. We create a variable called Treated if someone is over the minimum legal drinking age of 21. We create a binary variable Treat if someone is or is not over 21:

```
mlda$Treated <- mlda$agecell >= 21
mlda$Treat <- ifelse(mlda$agecell >= 21,
    1, 0)
```

We plot the data:

```
ggplot(mlda, aes(x = agecell, y = all, colour = Treated)) +
    geom_point() + geom_vline(xintercept = 21) +
    geom_smooth(method = "lm", se = F) +
    labs(y = "Death rate from all causes (per 100,000)",
        x = "Age") + theme_bw()
```

We can quickly estimate the effect with a regression of the variable all on the cutoff age and Treat:

```
mlda$agecut <- mlda$agecell - 20
mlda$Treat <- ifelse(mlda$agecell >= 21,
    1, 0)
lm(all ~ agecut + Treat, data = mlda)
##
## Call:
```

```
## lm(formula = all ~ agecut + Treat, data = mlda)
## 
## Coefficients:
## (Intercept)       agecut        Treat
##     92.8161      -0.9747       7.6627
```

We can use a more sophisticated estimation method available in the rdrobust package—the rdrobust function:

```
Y <- mlda$all
X <- mlda$agecell


rdr <- rdrobust(Y, X, c = 21)
summary(rdr)
## Call: rdrobust
## 
## Number of Obs.                 48
## BW type                     mserd
## Kernel                 Triangular
## VCE method                     NN
## 
## Number of Obs.                 24              24
## Eff. Number of Obs.             6               6
## Order est. (p)                  1               1
## Order bias  (q)                 2               2
## BW est. (h)                 0.493           0.493
## BW bias (b)                 0.780           0.780
## rho (h/b)                   0.632           0.632
## Unique Obs.                    24              24
## 
## =============================================================
##         Method     Coef. Std. Err.      z    P>|z|    [ 95% C.I. ]
## =============================================================
##   Conventional    9.595     3.591    2.672   0.008   [2.557 , 16.633]
##         Robust        -         -    2.205   0.027   [1.077 , 18.300]
## =============================================================
```

We can check the plausibility of drinking causing mortality by examining the effect of the minimum legal drinking age on motor vehicle-related fatalities (mva), which are known to be caused by drinking (Fig. 9.6):

```
ggplot(mlda, aes(x = agecell, y = mva, colour = Treated)) +
    geom_point() + geom_vline(xintercept = 21) +
    geom_smooth(method = "lm", se = F) +
    labs(y = "Death rate from motor vehicle fatalities (per 100,000)",
         x = "Age") + theme_bw()
```

☞ **Your turn.** Do you expect the minimum legal drinking age to affect the deaths due to internal causes (`internal`)? Use the code above to plot internal causes versus age as in the previous figure. What do you observe?

9.3 R Code

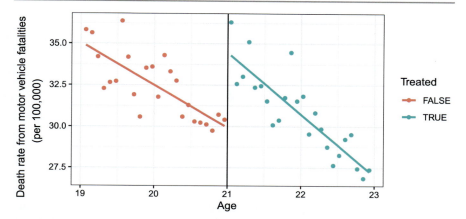

Fig. 9.6 Death rate from motor vehicle accidents (per 100,000) versus Age in years

9.3.2 Term Limits and Politician Performance in Brazil

Klašnja and Titiunik (2017) studied incumbency in Brazil. Cattaneo et al. (2020) illustrate RD methods by re-analyzing the data in Klasnja and Titiunik (2017). The variables used by Cattaneo et al. (2020) are different from those used in Klasnja and Titiunik, but illustrate the steps needed to carry out the analysis in Klasnja and Titiunik. Cattaneo et al. (2019) is an excellent resource in which the authors both explain fundamental ideas in regression discontinuity estimation and also the rdrobust package. The rdrobust package provides the state-of-the-art functions to carry out regression discontinuity analysis.

Note that the website https://rdpackages.github.io/ has links to papers, data, and software for regression discontinuity.

We first install and load the rdrobust and rdddensity packages:

```
rm(list = ls())
library(rdrobust)
library(rddensity)
```

We read in the data:

```
library(tidyverse)
data <- read.csv("CTV_2020_Sage.csv")
```

The variables are defined as follows. To use the packages, Y will be used for the outcome and X for the score variable:

```
Y <- data$mv_incpartyfor1
X <- data$mv_incparty
```

Next, we create a vector for the covariates:

```
covs <- data[, c("pibpc", "population", "numpar_candidates_eff",
    "party_DEM_wonlag1_b1", "party_PSDB_wonlag1_b1",
    "party_PT_wonlag1_b1", "party_PMDB_wonlag1_b1")]
covsnm <- c("GDP per capita", "Population",
    "No. Effective Parties", "DEM Victory t-1",
    "PSDB Victory t-1", "PT Victory t-1",
    "PMDB Victory t-1")
```

9.3.2.1 Falsification

We need to first do some checks. We check whether the density of X changes over the threshold; it should not. A local polynomial density estimator is used. The rddensity function is used:

```
rddens <- rddensity(X, bino = F)
summary(rddens)
##
## Manipulation testing using local polynomial density estimation.
##
## Number of obs       =    13308
## Model =                  unrestricted
## Kernel =                 triangular
## BW method =              estimated
## VCE method =             jackknife
##
## c = 0                    Left of c          Right of c
## Number of obs            6088               7220
## Eff. Number of obs       3852               3590
## Order est. (p)           2                  2
## Order bias (q)           3                  3
## BW est. (h)              15.493             13.392
##
## Method                   T                  P > |T|
## Robust                   -0.0757            0.9397
```

The value of the statistic is −0.076 and associated p-value is 0.94. We fail to reject the null hypothesis of no difference in the density of treated and control observations at the cutoff:

```
denplot <- rdplotdensity(rddens, X = data$mv_incparty[!is.na(data$mv_incparty)],
    xlab = "Incumbent Party's Margin of Victory at t",
    ylab = "Estimated density")

rm(denplot)
```

The density of the running variable does not change abruptly at the threshold (Fig. 9.7).

9.3 R Code

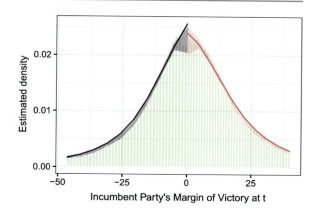

Fig. 9.7 Estimated density of running variable

We check whether covariates determined before the treatment change over the threshold graphically; they should not. RD effects on GDP per capita are shown graphically in Fig. 9.2:

```
summary(rdrobust(data$pibpc, X))
rdplot(log(data$pibpc), X, y.label = "log of GDP per capita",
    x.label = "Incumbent Party's Margin of Victory",
    x.lim = c(-30, 30), binselect = "qsmv",
    col.dots = "grey60")
```

We have suppressed the output, but we can carry out the tests for all covariates with the following code:

```
for (c in 1:ncol(covs)) {
    summary(rdrobust(covs[, c], X))
    rdplot(covs[, c], X, y.label = covsnm[c],
        x.label = "Incumbent Party's Margin of Victory",
        x.lim = c(-30, 30), binselect = "qsmv")
}
```

9.3.2.2 Outcome Analysis

We now produce the key figure, a plot of Y versus X, shown earlier in the chapter:

```
rdplot(Y, X, y.label = "Incumbent Party's Margin \nof Victory at t + 1",
    x.label = "Incumbent Party's Margin of Victory at t.",
    col.dots = "grey60")
```

We estimate the effect using local polynomial methods and with an optimal bandwidth ($p = 1$). We get a point estimate of -6.28 with a 95% robust bias-corrected confidence interval of -10.62 to -2.9:

```
rdr <- rdrobust(Y, X)
summary(rdr)
## Call: rdrobust
##
## Number of Obs.                 5463
## BW type                       mserd
## Kernel                   Triangular
## VCE method                       NN
##
## Number of Obs.                 2220        3243
## Eff. Number of Obs.            1533        1740
## Order est. (p)                    1           1
## Order bias  (q)                   2           2
## BW est. (h)                  15.291      15.291
## BW bias (b)                  27.509      27.509
## rho (h/b)                     0.556       0.556
## Unique Obs.                    2213        3119
##
## =====================================================================
##         Method     Coef.  Std. Err.       z    P>|z|    [ 95% C.I. ]
## =====================================================================
##   Conventional    -6.281      1.601  -3.924    0.000  [-9.419 , -3.144]
##         Robust         -          -  -3.545    0.000  [-10.223 , -2.944]
## =====================================================================
```

9.3.3 Rural Roads and Economic Development in India

We load:

```
library(haven)
library(tidyverse)
```

We do some preliminary work with the data downloaded from the journal website, and then work with a smaller version which has selected variables.

The code for the preliminary step (not run here):

```
data1 = read_dta("pmgsy_working_aer1.dta")

data1 %>%
    filter(mainsample == 1) %>%
    ggplot(aes(x = v_pop, y = r2012, col = factor(t))) +
    geom_smooth(method = "lm")

library(rddtools)

data2 <- data1 %>%
    filter(mainsample == 1) %>%
    select("transport_index_andrsn", "v_pop",
        "r2012", "occupation_index_andrsn",
        "firms_index_andrsn", "agriculture_index_andrsn",
        "consumption_index_andrsn", "t") %>%
    na.omit()
```

9.3 R Code

```
library(readr)

write_csv(data2, "Asher_Novosad_data2.csv")
```

We now read in the smaller file we had saved:

```
rm(list = ls())
library(rdrobust)
library(rddensity)

library(readr)
data2 <- read_csv("Asher_Novosad_data2.csv")
# rm(data1)
data2$factor_t <- factor(data2$t)
```

We use a density plot as a check for abrupt changes in the running variable (Fig. 9.4):

```
rddens <- rddensity(data2$v_pop, bino = F)
denplot <- rdplotdensity(rddens, X = data2$v_pop,
    hist = F, xlab = "Normalized population",
    ylab = "Estimated density")
rm(denplot)
```

We now examine the effect on an index of transportation, (see p. 811 in the paper). The replication here can be considered broadly illustrative, and is limited to the index of transportation. The paper has a lot of results:

```
m <- rdrobust(y = data2$transport_index_andrsn,
    x = data2$v_pop, fuzzy = data2$r2012,
    kernel = "triangular", p = 1, bwselect = "mserd")
summary(m)   # see Table 3, col 4 p. 811
rdplot(y = data2$transport_index_andrsn,
    x = data2$v_pop, binselect = "qs", y.label = "Transport index",
    x.label = "Normalized population", col.dots = "grey60")
```

We can put in other index variables instead of the transport index to get the other results on p. 811, and that is left as an exercise. The results we get vary with choice of bandwidth, etc. We have not included covariates, which would if included would be expected to ideally improve precision.

9.3.4 Simple Example with Simulation

We begin with the simplest case to illustrate RDD. We have a variable X, which we call the running variable. If $X > 0$, then a unit receives treatment. If $X < 0$, then a unit does not receive treatment. We say that 0 is the cutoff value. Let Y be the outcome variable. The value of Y for a unit depends on the value of X as well as whether the unit is treated or not.

We will generate some synthetic data for the treated group, Xt is X for the treated group and Yt is Y for the treated group. runif is a function to get random variables from a uniform distribution and rnorm is a function to get random variables from a normal distribution:

```
# Data for treated group
set.seed(124)
Xt <- runif(100, min = 0, max = 50)
Yt <- 20 + 0.3 * Xt + rnorm(100)
```

We now generate data for the control group, and here Xc and Yc denote values for the control group:

```
# Data for control group
Xc <- runif(100, min = -50, max = 0)
Yc <- 10 + 0.3 * Xc + rnorm(100)
```

Note that the average treatment effect by construction is $20 - 10 = 10$.

We now put the data into a dataframe and stack the values for the treatment and control groups:

```
X <- c(Xt, Xc)
# W is treatment indicator
W <- c(rep("T", 100), rep("C", 100))
Y <- c(Yt, Yc)
# dataframe below
datRD <- data.frame(X, W, Y)
# top observations
head(datRD)
##          X W        Y
## 1  4.150772 T 20.78318
## 2 20.439733 T 25.90682
## 3 25.764250 T 26.88283
## 4 19.844117 T 26.02628
## 5 11.136135 T 23.06580
## 6 14.617482 T 23.99882
# bottom observations
tail(datRD)
##             X W         Y
## 195  -7.327217 C  9.768123
## 196 -46.560303 C -5.239721
## 197 -47.962981 C -4.295843
## 198  -5.145477 C  8.763419
## 199  -2.079401 C  9.385712
## 200  -6.218773 C  7.438999
```

9.3 R Code

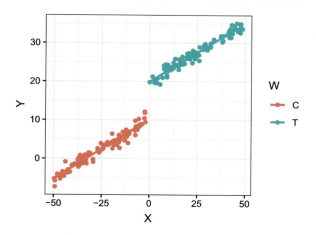

Fig. 9.8 RDD numerical example with synthetic data. C is control, T is treatment. The jump in the line at $X = 0$ gives us the treatment effect, which is 10 by construction

We now run a regression of Y on X and W:

```
lm(Y ~ X + W)
## 
## Call:
## lm(formula = Y ~ X + W)
## 
## Coefficients:
## (Intercept)            X           WT
##     10.1088       0.3058       9.7573
```

The estimated coefficient on W equals our true effect, 10.

We now generate a figure to illustrate the data and the regression fits (Fig. 9.8). The red points are the control observations, the turquoise points are the treatment observations. The jump between the lines at the cutoff value, i.e., $X = 0$ gives us the treatment effect.

☞ **Your turn**   Modify the code above by generating data consistent with an average treatment effect of -10.

```
library(tidyverse)
ggplot(datRD, aes(x = X, y = Y, col = W)) +
    geom_point() + geom_smooth(method = "lm",
    se = F) + theme_bw()
```

We now introduce just one complication; the relationship between Y and X is slightly nonlinear. We add a quadratic term (X^2). However, the treatment effect is still $20 - 10 = 10$:

```
# Data for treated group
Xt <- runif(100, min = 0, max = 50)
Yt <- 20 + 0.3*Xt + 0.02*(Xt^2) +   # quadratic term
   rnorm(100)
# Data for control group
Xc <- runif(100, min = -50, max = 0)
Yc <- 10 + 0.3*Xc + 0.02*(Xc^2)  +  # quadratic term
   rnorm(100)
# pulling data together
X <- c(Xt, Xc)
W <- c(rep("T", 100), rep("C",100))
Y <- c(Yt, Yc)
datRD <- data.frame(X, W, Y)
```

The regression of Y on X and W does not fit the data very well, and the estimate of the treatment effect is biased. We are just lucky here that the extent of bias is low.

```
lm(Y ~ X + W, data = datRD)
##
## Call:
## lm(formula = Y ~ X + W, data = datRD)
##
## Coefficients:
## (Intercept)            X           WT
##     26.2614       0.2824      11.5889
```

We generate values of Y consistent with the regression of Y on X and W above:

```
Xmodel <- seq(from = -50, to = 50, length = 100)
Wmodel <- c(rep(0, 50), rep(1, 50))
Ymodel <- 26.3 + 0.28 * Xmodel + 11.5 * Wmodel
datmodel <- data.frame(Ymodel, Xmodel, Wmodel)
```

We plot the data and the line of fit from the model (Fig. 9.9):

```
ggplot() + geom_point(data = datRD, aes(x = X,
    y = Y, col = W)) + geom_line(data = datmodel,
    aes(x = Xmodel, y = Ymodel)) + theme_bw()
```

We now regress Y on X and X squared and also interact W with X:

```
lm(Y ~ X + I(X^2) + W + W * X)   # regression with quadratic term
##
## Call:
## lm(formula = Y ~ X + I(X^2) + W + W * X)
##
## Coefficients:
```

9.3 R Code

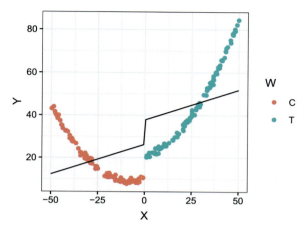

Fig. 9.9 RDD numerical example with synthetic data. C is control, T is treatment. Regression of Y on X and W does not fit the data well

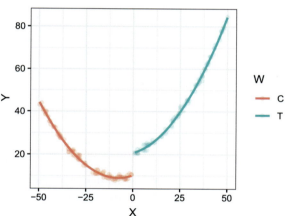

Fig. 9.10 RDD numerical example with synthetic data. C is control, T is treatment. The quadratic specification helps the model fit the data well

```
## (Intercept)            X        I(X^2)
##    10.34313      0.32485       0.02030
##          WT         X:WT
##    10.17091     -0.06002
```

We get an estimate which is close to the true effect (Fig. 9.10):

```
ggplot(datRD, aes(x = X, y = Y, col = W)) +
    geom_point(alpha = 0.2) + geom_smooth(method = "lm",
    se = F, formula = y ~ poly(x, 2, raw = TRUE)) +
    theme_bw()
```

We now fit a more local regression, so we take values of X that are less than 10 units away in absolute magnitude on either side of the cutoff:

Fig. 9.11 RDD numerical example with synthetic data. C is control, T is treatment. A more local regression (X lies between −10 and 10) fits the data well

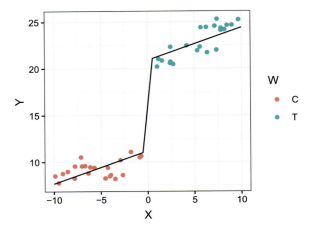

```
datRDlocal <- datRD %>%
    filter(X > -10, X < 10)
lm(Y ~ X + W, data = datRDlocal)
##
## Call:
## lm(formula = Y ~ X + W, data = datRDlocal)
##
## Coefficients:
## (Intercept)            X           WT
##     11.1845       0.3549       9.7221
```

We generate values of Y consistent with the local linear model. Once again the estimated effect is close to the true effect:

```
Xmodlocal <- seq(from = -10, to = 10, length = 20)
Wmodlocal <- c(rep(0, 10), rep(1, 10))
Ymodlocal <- 11.18 + 0.35 * Xmodlocal + 9.72 *
    Wmodlocal
datmodlocal <- data.frame(Ymodlocal, Xmodlocal,
    Wmodlocal)
```

We plot the data and the line of fit (Fig. 9.11):

```
ggplot() + geom_point(data = datRDlocal,
    aes(x = X, y = Y, col = W)) + geom_line(data = datmodlocal,
    aes(x = Xmodlocal, y = Ymodlocal)) +
    theme_bw()
```

The basic idea of RDD is simple, but to get as accurate results as possible we use sophisticated methods that are built into packages like `rdrobust`.

9.4 Resources

9.4.1 For Better Understanding

Paper by Cattaneo et al. (2020), *The Regression Discontinuity Design.*

9.4.2 For Going Further

Monograph by Cattaneo et al. (2019), *A Practical Introduction to Regression Discontinuity Designs: Foundations.*

Packages Used in This Chapter

The citations for the packages used in this chapter are:

```
print(citation("masteringmetrics"), style = "text")
## Arnold J (2022). _masteringmetrics: Datasets for Mastering
## 'Metrics_. R package version 0.1, <URL:
## https://github.com/jrnold/masteringmetrics>.


print(citation("rdrobust"), style = "text")
## Calonico S, Cattaneo MD, Farrell MH, Titiunik R (2021).
## _rdrobust: Robust Data-Driven Statistical Inference in
## Regression-Discontinuity Designs_. R package version 1.0.8,
## <URL: https://CRAN.R-project.org/package=rdrobust>.


print(citation("rddensity"), style = "text")
## Cattaneo MD, Jansson M, Ma X (2021). _rddensity: Manipulation
## Testing Based on Density Discontinuity_. R package version
## 2.2, <URL: https://CRAN.R-project.org/package=rddensity>.


print(citation("knitr")[[1]], style = "text")
## Xie Y (2022). _knitr: A General-Purpose Package for Dynamic
## Report Generation in R_. R package version 1.41, <URL:
## https://yihui.org/knitr/>.


print(citation("formatR"), style = "text")
## Xie Y (2023). _formatR: Format R Code Automatically_. R
## package version 1.14, <URL:
## https://CRAN.R-project.org/package=formatR>.
```

```
print(citation("tidyverse"), style = "text")
## Wickham H, Averick M, Bryan J, Chang W, McGowan LD, FranÃ§ois
## R, Grolemund G, Hayes A, Henry L, Hester J, Kuhn M, Pedersen
## TL, Miller E, Bache SM, MÃ¼ller K, Ooms J, Robinson D, Seidel
## DP, Spinu V, Takahashi K, Vaughan D, Wilke C, Woo K, Yutani H
## (2019). "Welcome to the tidyverse." _Journal of Open Source
## Software_, *4*(43), 1686. doi: 10.21105/joss.01686 (URL:
## https://doi.org/10.21105/joss.01686).
```

References

Abadie, Alberto and Matias D. Cattaneo. 2018. Econometric Methods for Program Evaluation. *Annual Review of Economics*, 10(1): 465–503. _eprint: https://doi.org/10.1146/annurev-economics-080217-053402.

Angrist, Joshua D., and Jörn-steffen Pischke. 2015. *Mastering 'Metrics*. Princeton; Oxford: Princeton University Press. with french flaps edition edition.

Asher, Sam, and Paul Novosad. 2020. Rural Roads and Local Economic Development. *American Economic Review* 110 (3): 797–823.

Calonico, S., M.D. Cattaneo, and R. Titiunik. 2014. Robust Nonparametric Confidence Intervals for Regression Discontinuity Designs. *Econometrica* 82 (6): 2295–2326.

Carpenter, Christopher, and Carlos Dobkin. 2009. The Effect of Alcohol Consumption on Mortality: Regression Discontinuity Evidence from the Minimum Drinking Age. *American Economic Journal: Applied Economics* 1 (1): 164–182.

Cattaneo, Matias D., Nicolás Idrobo, and Rocío Titiunik. 2019. A Practical Introduction to Regression Discontinuity Designs: Foundations. *Elements in Quantitative and Computational Methods for the Social Sciences*. ISBN: 9781108684606 9781108710206. Cambridge University Press.

Cattaneo, M.D., O. Titiunik, and G. Vazquez-Bare. 2020. The Regression Discontinuity Design. In *The SAGE Handbook of Research Methods in Political Science and International Relations*, ed. Luigi Curini and Robert Franzese. New York: SAGE Publications Ltd.

Hicken, Allen. Clientelism. *Annual Review of Political Science* 14 (1): 289–310. _eprint: https://doi.org/10.1146/annurev.polisci.031908.220508.

Imbens, G., and K. Kalyanaraman. 2012. Optimal Bandwidth Choice for the Regression Discontinuity Estimator. *The Review of Economic Studies* 79 (3): 933–959.

Klašnja, Marko, and Rocío Titiunik. 2017. The Incumbency Curse: Weak Parties, Term Limits, and Unfulfilled Accountability. *American Political Science Review* 111(1): 129–148. Cambridge University Press.

Lee, David S., and Thomas Lemieux. 2010. Regression Discontinuity Designs in Economics. *Journal of Economic Literature* 48 (2): 281–355.

Murugesan, Anand. 2020. Electoral Clientelism and Vote Buying. ISBN: 9780190228637.

Sekhon, Jasjeet S., and Rocío Titiunik. 2017. Understanding Regression Discontinuity Designs As Observational Studies. *Observational Studies* 3(2):174–182. University of Pennsylvania Press.

Panel Data and Fixed Effects 10

10.1 Introduction

We are all familiar with the aphorism, "The whole is greater than the sum of the parts," and this principle aptly applies to panel data. In this context, panel data refers to the whole, while its two components, cross-sectional data and time-series data, form the parts. By having access to panel data, analysts gain the ability to tackle issues that cannot be achieved by using the two parts separately. In this chapter, we explore the capabilities of panel data in mitigating unobservable confounders, which often present challenges when addressing causal questions.

Let's start with basic definitions. Panel data refers to a collection of data where the same units are observed over time. For example, we can collect information on beer taxes and traffic fatalities for all the states in the United States over time, such as several months or years. In this case, the units are the individual states, and we observe the data on beer taxes and fatalities over multiple time periods to form a panel dataset. On the other hand, cross-sectional data is a subset of panel data where we observe the units only at a single point in time. For instance, we could gather data on beer taxes and traffic fatalities across all the states in the US for the year 1990, with the states being the unit of analysis. Unlike panel data, cross-sectional data does not involve tracking changes over time. Conversely, time-series data involves collecting data at different points in time for the same unit. To illustrate this, using our previous example, we could focus on collecting data on beer taxes and traffic fatalities specifically for the state of California over a number of years. In time-series data, the unit of analysis remains the same, but we track changes for that unit over time.

Panel data is highly valuable because it combines the strengths of cross-sectional and time-series data enabling us to mitigate unobservable confounder bias that manifests in two distinct ways. The first scenario involves unobservable effects that remain constant over time for individual units. The second scenario pertains to unobservable effects that vary over time but are common for all units. Neither cross-sectional nor time-series data alone can tackle these two types of confounders. However, panel data offers a solution by utilizing the two-way fixed effects model, which enables us to adequately address these two confounder biases.

In this chapter, we explain the mechanics of fixed effects through a case study involving identical twins. Through this case, we gain insights into how panel data can address fixed effects. Furthermore, we showcase the strength of panel data in tackling two-way fixed effects using another case study that explores the impact of beer taxes on traffic fatalities in the US. By employing panel data methods, we get more credible results than when we used cross-section data. Finally, we reevaluate the robust positive association observed between income and the level of democracy across countries. Once again, employing panel data methods allows us to mitigate confounder biases and reveal a different story.

10.2 Concepts and Examples

10.2.1 Schooling and Wages

Education is a critical policy issue worldwide, and policymakers must grapple with difficult decisions about how much to invest in it at different levels. As many countries enforce mandated and free education for the early years of their citizens lives, governments seek to understand the benefits of schooling at both individual and social levels. A crucial query for policy arises: Do higher levels of schooling lead to higher wages?

To explore this question, we begin by comparing the wages of people with varying levels of schooling, employing the following regression equation:

$$Wages_i = \alpha + \beta \text{ Schooling Years}_i + \epsilon_i.$$

To investigate whether the estimated β would provide an unbiased estimate of schooling years, we must consider both observable and unobservable confounding factors that could impact both schooling and wages. One such confounding factor is the individual's innate ability, which may influence their education attainment and subsequent wages. Individuals with a higher innate ability may find schooling easier, and this ability will also lead them to jobs with higher wages. However, measuring innate ability or intelligence accurately is challenging with standardized tests. Standardized tests may only capture certain dimensions of ability, potentially missing nuances of an individual's ability that could affect both schooling and wages.

$$W_i = \alpha + \beta \text{ Schooling Years}_i + \gamma \text{ Ability}_i + \epsilon_i.$$

While random assignment of schooling years to individuals would be an ideal solution to address the confounding problem, practical and ethical considerations often limit its feasibility (as discussed in Chap. 6). However, researchers have developed alternative methods, some of which we have discussed in previous chapters.

10.2 Concepts and Examples

These methods may involve clever strategies, methods, or design elements. Let's discuss a study employing one such design.

Ashenfelter and Krueger (1994) (hereafter, AK) came up with an ingenious solution to estimate the effect of schooling on wages. They used a unique setting by attending the annual Twinsburg Festival in Ohio and finding pairs of identical twins to address the problem of unobserved ability confounding this estimation. Identical twins, also known as monozygotic twins (as the fertilized egg splits into two), are genetically identical, which provides a reasonable basis for assuming that innate ability is also identical between the twins. Moreover, identical twins typically grow up in nearly identical environments, residing under the same roof, having access to the same resources, networks, and experiences at the same age. Therefore, if AK were fortunate enough to find twins with different levels of schooling, it would create an ideal setting for studying the effect of schooling on wages while effectively addressing the issue of unobservable confounding.

AK capitalized on the inherent similarities between identical twins in terms of their genetic makeup (nature, which includes ability) and shared environment (nurture) to cancel out the common factors and estimate the impact of schooling years on wages, by comparing twins who had different levels of schooling. To do so, AK interviewed about 300 identical twins using a survey, with similar questions as those in the Current Population Survey (CPS), a general survey that is periodically conducted in the US. In these interviews, separately with each of the twin, they collected information on various socio-demographic characteristics, educational attainment, and the number of schooling years for each twin. Additionally, AK asked about the education years of the twin's sibling.

Subsequently, Ashenfelter et al. (1998) (hereafter, AR), built upon AK's work by analyzing data from subsequent years of the annual Twinsburg Festival in Ohio. We use both studies in our discussion of schooling on wages.

AK recognized that the Twinsburg Festival, being a celebration of similarities, might attract a higher proportion of similar twins than average. The excessive similarity of twins is ideal for making an apples-to-apples comparison, which naturally reduces a host of biases that would otherwise be present in such comparisons. However, AK cautioned against generalizing their findings if there were significant differences between the descriptive statistics of the twins and those of the general population. To evaluate this, AK compared the descriptive statistics of identical twins and fraternal twins in their study, with the CPS data on the general population.

When comparing the surveyed twins to the general population in the USA, AK found that the twins reported higher levels of education and earned higher wages. Notably, identical twins were more likely to have the same levels of education (49%) compared to fraternal twins (43%) and more likely to study together (74% vs. 38%, respectively). Despite being born at the same time, a significantly higher proportion (36% higher) of identical twins compared to fraternal twins reported studying simultaneously . However, only slightly over half of the identical twins (51%) reported having different years of education, suggesting that the similarity of identical twins extends to their educational choices.

With this backdrop, let's recall that we are interested in estimating the effect of schooling years on earnings. Two equations capture the earnings and schooling years of twin 1 (Eq. 10.1) and twin 2 (Eq. 10.2):

$$W_1 = \alpha + \beta \text{ Schooling Years}_1 + \gamma \text{ Ability}_1 + \epsilon_1 \qquad (10.1)$$

$$W_2 = \alpha + \beta \text{ Schooling Years}_2 + \gamma \text{ Ability}_2 + \epsilon_2. \qquad (10.2)$$

If we now difference Eq. 10.1 from Eq. 10.2, we get

$$\Delta W = \beta \Delta \text{ Schooling Years} + \epsilon_2 - \epsilon_1. \qquad (10.3)$$

What happens to ability in Eq. 10.3? As we mentioned, by assumption, the genetically identical twins have the same ability (so, $\text{Ability}_1 = \text{Ability}_2$). If this is the case, taking the difference between (10.1) and (10.2) will cancel out the effect of ability (as well as the constant term). AK addressed the issue of the fixed unobservable ability issue by leveraging the nature of identical twins, who share identical attributes and characteristics, and which therefore can be mathematically differenced out. The data and assumption about the identical nature of the twins allowed them to difference out time-invariant fixed effects. This indeed is the fundamental principle behind panel data methods. Panel data involves observing the same unit at different points in time, such as observing California in 1990 and 1991, allowing us to difference out the time-invariant unobservable fixed effects. While AK used twins simultaneously to achieve this, panel data methods utilize identical units observed at different times.

In essence, the AK design and panel data methods both aim to difference out fixed effects, whether through twins or through repeated observations of the same unit over time. The bottomline: anel data allows us to observe the same unit (e.g., state) over multiple periods, offering the opportunity to gather and throw out the unobserved fixed confounders, if any, that may influence the treatment and the outcome. These fixed effects, if left unaddressed, can introduce bias in estimating the treatment effects.

In order to determine the impact of schooling years on wages using the Twins study data, AK employed a regression approach that involved calculating the difference between the twins' wages (as the dependent variable) and the difference between their schooling years (as the independent variable of interest). This differencing allowed them to eliminate the influence of common unobservable factors, such as ability, as it was assumed to be identical between the twins. Moreover, AK recognized the potential for measurement error in the reported schooling years, which could introduce bias into the findings.

Measurement error refers to the discrepancy between the observed and actual values of a variable.[1] In surveys, measurement error can occur due to various factors

---

[1] Measurement error is due to random variation but should be differentiated from intentional overreporting or underreporting. For example, one may overreport or inflate one's education or wages

10.2 Concepts and Examples

such as forgetfulness, and adds noise or random variation to the true levels of a variable. When the dependent variable (Y) has measurement error, it increases the standard errors, but the estimates are usually unbiased. However, if the independent variable of interest (X) has measurement error, it can lead to a downward bias in the estimates, especially in large samples.[2] AK were concerned that reporting errors in schooling years could result in attenuation or a downward bias in their estimate of the effect of education on wages. In other words, if there are measurement errors in the reported years of schooling, this could lead to an underestimation of the effect of education on earnings.

To provide further clarification, differencing out unobserved fixed effects like ability can mitigate one source of bias. However, it can inadvertently amplify another source of bias if there is misreporting of schooling years, resulting in measurement error. While differencing helps address confounder bias stemming from unobserved ability, it can lead to attenuation bias. Out of the frying pan but into the fire! AK had anticipated this issue and used a solution lever: an instrumental variable (as discussed in Chap. 8).

AK (being masters of causal inference) thought a few steps ahead and had collected survey data not only on each twin's own years of schooling years but also on their report of their twins' years of schooling. They proposed using the twin's reported schooling years of their schooling as an instrument for their own reported schooling years. To illustrate, we borrow the names of exemplary twins, Donald and Ronald from Angrist et al. (2015).[3] Ronald's report of Donald's schooling years is used as the instrument for Donald's own reported schooling years. AK made the assumption that the reports provided by Donald and Ronald were independent of each other (they conducted their surveys in different booths). This assumption ensures that any misreporting errors are exogenous. Moreover, Donald's (mis)reporting of Ronald's schooling years should not directly impact Ronald's wages, satisfying the exclusion restriction condition. However, Donald's report of Ronald's schooling years should be positively correlated with Ronald's own reported schooling years (as both are associated with actual schooling years), making the instrument relevant.

The results of our replication (of AR) are presented in Table 10.1. In Model 1, which does not involve any differencing, we find a schooling return of approximately 11%. Model 2, which includes simple differencing, yields an estimate of around 6%. However, when we use both differencing and an instrumental variable, we once again arrive at a schooling return of approximately 11%. In this study, if we assume that the instrumental variables' estimate (in Model 3) is reliable, it suggests that the biases stemming from measurement error (in Model 2) are much worse than confounder biases (Model 1).

---

due to social desirability bias or underreport illicit behavior. In contrast, measurement error is just random noise in either direction.

[2] When the sample size is small, the measurement error on X could even lead to inflated effect sizes (see Loken and Gelman 2017).

[3] For the rest of this case and the data, we follow Chap. 6 of Angrist and Pischke 2015, who discuss both Ashenfelter and Krueger (1994) and Ashenfelter et al. (1998).

Table 10.1 Regressions for effect of education on wages

	Model 1	Model 2	Model 3
(Intercept)	1.18	0.03	0.03
	(0.16)	(0.03)	(0.03)
educ	0.11		
	(0.01)		
poly(age, 2)1	4.96		
	(0.58)		
poly(age, 2)2	−4.30		
	(0.60)		
female	−0.32		
	(0.04)		
white	−0.10		
	(0.07)		
deduc		0.06	0.11
		(0.02)	(0.03)
R^2	0.34	0.03	0.01
Num. obs.	680	340	340

Standard errors in parentheses

The case study emphasizes the importance of exercising caution when using methods to address specific issues. While attempting to tackle one problem, we may unknowingly introduce other biases. The policy analyst should carefully consider the potential consequences of chosen methods to gather reliable information about impacts.

10.2.2 Alcohol Policies and Traffic Fatalities

Now, let's shift our attention to another long-standing policy concern: the impact of alcohol-related policies on traffic deaths. In the United States, driving under the influence of alcohol contributes to half of all the traffic deaths among individuals under 40, with alcohol-related collisions accounting for approximately one-third of total traffic deaths (Ruhm and Christopher 1996). In response to this issue, policymakers have introduced several measures aimed at regulating access to alcohol, including laws such as the minimum legal drinking age of 21 in the US or other administrative laws to restrict the supply of alcohol.

Despite the implementation of stringent laws, traffic fatalities remained a persistent issue throughout the 1980s in the United States (Ruhm and Christopher 1996). Ruhm and Christopher (1996) highlighted that even as administrative regulations were in place, there was a steady decline in the price of beer, which was a popular beverage among younger folk in the US. This decline in beer prices, driven by decreasing taxes, may have resulted in increased consumption, particularly among the younger population who are more sensitive to price changes.

10.2 Concepts and Examples

Fig. 10.1 Positive relationship between fatality rate and beer taxes for the year 1982

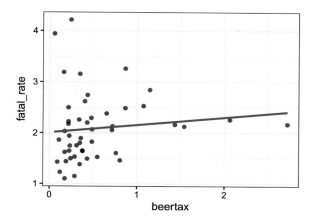

While variations in legislation and beer prices can explain some differences in traffic fatalities among states, they may not account for certain unobservable factors that vary across states. Factors such as road conditions or cultural attitudes toward drinking can differ from state to state and can influence traffic fatalities. For instance, the intensity of lobbying activities by associations like Mothers Against Drunk Driving (MADD) may vary depending on cultural attitudes toward drinking in a particular state. This can affect the advocacy efforts for policies like beer taxes or changes in driving under the influence (DUI) laws as well as directly affect drinking-related fatalities. These unobserved differences can introduce biases that cannot be fully eliminated even when including a rich set of observed variables as covariates.

Ruhm and Christopher (1996) propose using panel data to identify and account for these unobserved differences across regions. By employing panel data, we can difference out state-fixed effects. This approach enables us to improve our estimates of changes in alcohol policies on traffic deaths, by controlling for state-level variations that could otherwise confound the error terms and lead to biased estimates.

Ruhm chooses to focus on beer taxes instead of the price of beer directly for several reasons. Firstly, changes in prices can be influenced by both demand and supply factors. Estimating the price elasticity of demand requires isolating changes in prices that are driven by supply-side variations in costs rather than changes in prices caused by shifts in demand. By examining beer taxes, which are directly imposed by the government and (presumably) not subject to demand fluctuations, Ruhm can capture the supply-side changes affecting beer prices more accurately.

We follow the excellent discussion and analysis of this case in Stock James and Watson Mark (2017), who use the same data. Figure 10.1 illustrates the simple cross-sectional relationship between fatality rates and beer taxes for the year 1982. This graph surprisingly shows a positive slope between fatality rate and beer taxes, which contradicts our expectation. We would typically anticipate that as the price of beer increases, people would consume less of it, resulting in lower fatality rates in those states with higher beer prices. This is not what we see in Fig. 10.1.

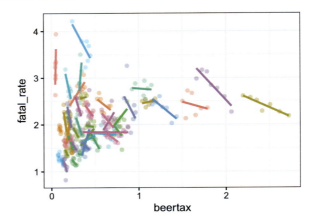

Fig. 10.2 Fatality rate and beer tax by state for several years

However, the figure does not account for the observed and unobserved differences across states that can influence the relationship between fatality rates and beer taxes. These differences, if any, can confound the picture we see in Fig. 10.1.

Figure 10.2 plots the fatality rates and beer taxes for multiple years with panel data by each state. Unlike Fig. 10.1, which only showed the relationship for a single year, Fig. 10.2 provides a more comprehensive, even if not clear, view. We now see that the relationship is positive for some states, negative for some, and shows little relation for others.

Panel data fixed effect models, as we know, allows us to account for these time-invariant differences in states. For example, cultural attitudes toward drinking are unlikely to change quickly over time within a state, which would be considered time-invariant in this context. Fixed effects models with panel data estimate coefficients capturing the average differences for each state in the dependent variable. By explicitly estimating the average difference for each state, they disentangle the time-invariant heterogeneity in the states, which can lead to biased estimates if unaddressed. In the case of Fig. 10.1, where a counterintuitive positive relationship between beer taxes and fatality rates was observed in 1982, the presence of unobserved heterogeneity across states likely influenced the results.

State-level fixed effects effectively account for unobserved time-invariant heterogeneity across states in panel data analysis. However, we also need to consider time-varying factors that may uniformly affect all states, such as improvements in car safety or road conditions. Thankfully, panel data can handle these pesky time-varying but inter-state-constant fixed effects as well.

To estimate both the time-invariant state-fixed effects (one for each state) and time-varying but state-constant time-fixed effects (one for each year), we can include dummy variables for each state (excluding one baseline state) and for each year (excluding one baseline year) in the regression specification. This allows us to capture the effects of these time-varying factors on the dependent variable while also accounting for state-specific time-invariant differences. Fortunately, most statistical software have in-built packages to estimate the two-way fixed-effects (state and time)

10.2 Concepts and Examples

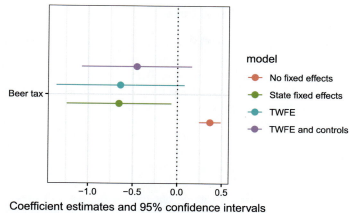

Fig. 10.3 Model results

by simply specifying the variables that indicate state and time identifiers in the panel data.

In this example analyzing beer taxes on fatality rates in the 48 contiguous US states over a period of 7 years, we would estimate 47 state-fixed effects and 6 year-fixed effects based on the available data. Figure 10.3 shows how models that include fixed effects can help us get more plausible results (see the later section for the R code).

We begin with our first model, without fixed effects, where we simply regress fatality rates (i.e., fatality cases/population * 1000) on beer taxes. This model shows a positive association between beer taxes and fatality rates (as depicted in Fig. 10.1). However, this estimate is biased since it fails to account for differences between states. To address this, in our second model, we incorporate state-level fixed effects, which effectively reverses the direction of the association between beer taxes and fatality rates, revealing a more intuitive negative relationship.

To account for both time-invariant state-fixed effects and time-varying but inter-state-constant fixed effects, we employ the TWFE model in our third model. In this model, the relationship between beer taxes and fatality rates remains negative, but is less precise. The TWFE model estimates are also different from the simple regression estimate, which indicated a positive relationship between beer taxes and traffic fatalities.

The TWFE model estimate provides valuable information. By considering state- and time-fixed effects, we identified a generally negative relationship between beer taxes and fatality rates. This is more compelling than the positive association finding in the model without fixed-effects. Researchers and policymakers need to dig deeper to get closer to the truth. For instance, it is possible that beer taxes have heterogenous treatment effects for different groups, such as young adults experiencing a stronger negative impact from beer taxes compared to older adults.

10.2.3 Causal Graphs for Panel Data

Panel data methods provide us with the means to address certain types of unobserved confounders. However, it is crucial to emphasize that making causal interpretations of TWFE estimates necessitates assumptions. Before we discuss the last case study on the relationship between income and democracy, let us take a quick detour to examine the assumptions associated with panel data methods.

Indeed, panel data allow us to adjust for unobserved time-invariant confounders at the unit level, whether the unit is individuals (as in the twins), states (as in beer taxes), or countries (as in the last case study). These time-invariant hidden (unobservable) factors can be differenced out or computed using panel data fixed effects methods. In this section, we look under the hood, at the assumptions necessary for estimating causal effects with panel data. To guide our discussion, we will draw upon the excellent work of Imai and Kim (2019), who provide a technically thorough treatment of these issues. Our focus will be solely on the one-way or unit-level fixed effects, and we use simplified versions of their causal graphs. To generate and work with these causal graphs, we use the ggdag package in R, which we introduced in Chap. 5. In a later section, we provide the R code, enabling the reader to further improve their skills and utilize this package for thinking about causal issues.

Imai and Kim (2019) bring out key assumptions and features of widely used panel data methods. The authors write (p. 467), "Unit fixed effects regression models are widely used for causal inference with longitudinal or panel data in the social sciences … Many researchers use these models to adjust for unobserved, unit-specific and time-invariant confounders when estimating causal effects from observational data. In spite of this widespread practice, much methodological discussion of unit fixed effects models in political science has taken place from model-based perspectives (often assuming linearity), with little attention to the causal identification assumptions … In contrast, our work builds upon a small literature on the use of linear fixed effects models for causal inference with longitudinal data in econometrics and statistics …".

10.2.3.1 Simple Case

Figure 10.4 displays the causal graph for a simple panel one-way fixed effects model (Imai and Kim 2019). The treatment or exposure variable is x, the outcome variable is y, e represents errors, the time periods are 1 and 2, and u is an unobserved variable. The causal graph shows that the past treatment x affects the current treatment, e.g., $x_1 \to x_2$. The current treatment then affects the current outcome, e.g., $x_2 \to y_2$. The unobservable time-invariant fixed effect (u) influences the treatments and outcomes every period, and thus acts as a confounder. However, since it is time-invariant, we can either difference it out or estimate it as an average effect for every unit. This requires assuming linearity and additivity. The causal graph provides a basic understanding of the panel data setup necessary for estimating causal effects with unit fixed effects.

Note that there are strong assumptions encoded in this causal graph (the missing arrows in Fig. 10.4), which Imai and Kim (p. 470) list:

10.2 Concepts and Examples

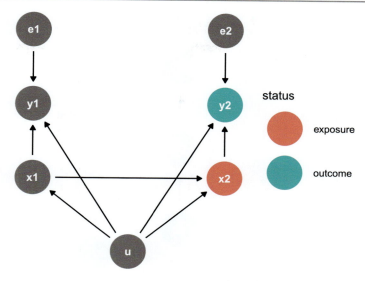

Fig. 10.4 Simple case: causal graph for regression models with unit fixed effects based on two time periods

1. There is no unobserved time-varying confounder.
2. The past outcome does not directly affect the current outcome.
3. The past outcome does not directly affect the current treatment.
4. The past treatment does not directly affect the current outcome.

We list all the paths and adjustment sets:

```
paths(case1)
## $paths
## [1] "x2 -> y2"
## [2] "x2 <- u -> y2"
## [3] "x2 <- x1 -> y1 <- u -> y2"
## [4] "x2 <- x1 <- u -> y2"
##
## $open
## [1]   TRUE   TRUE  FALSE   TRUE
adjustmentSets(case1)
## { u }
```

We have to adjust for u to identify the effect of x2 on y2. We plot the graph with the adjustments and see how this blocks the non-causal paths (the grayed out paths in Fig. 10.5).

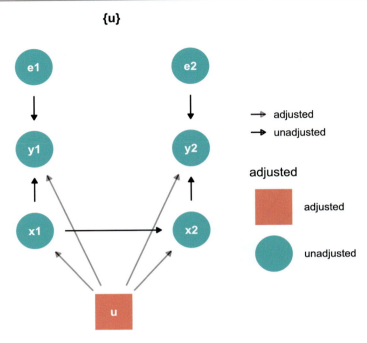

Fig. 10.5 Simple case: adjustment set and blocking of non-causal paths. We have to adjust for u which is not observed

The structural equations in Fig. 10.4 are

$$y_1 = \beta x_1 + u + e_1. \tag{10.4}$$

$$y_2 = \beta x_2 + u + e_2. \tag{10.5}$$

Equations 10.5–10.4 give us

$$(y_2 - y_1) = \beta(x_2 - x_1) + (e_2 - e_1). \tag{10.6}$$

We show you the simple algebra to spotlight the central concept of how panel data allows us to difference or cancel out the fixed effects. We see that u, the time-invariant fixed effect, drops out, and we can proceed with estimation. In a later Sect. 10.3, We simulate data and illustrate this.

10.2.3.2 Case Where Past Treatment Affects Current Outcome

Now, let's consider a setting where past treatments can influence current outcomes. Take, for example, the case of someone who took the first two doses of the COVID-19 MRNA vaccine. It is possible that the first COVID-19 MRNA vaccine may impact the current outcome, which is measured after the second MRNA shot, as depicted

10.2 Concepts and Examples

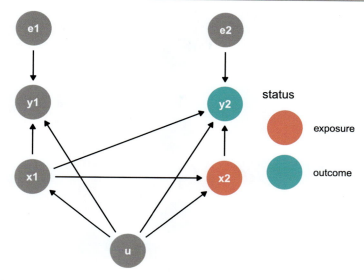

Fig. 10.6 Case where past treatment affects current outcome

in the causal graph (Fig. 10.6). This is a violation of assumption 4. But don't worry, rescue is close at hand if you pay attention to whether the confounders and past treatments are observable or unobservable. Since past treatments are observable, we can account for them by including lagged treatments in our estimation. For instance, if a previous MRNA shot has a direct effect on the outcome as well as determines the current outcome, we can include the current and earlier treatments in the regression specification. Phew! However, this reveals that using fixed effects alone would not have been sufficient.

We get the paths and adjustment set:

```
paths(case2b)
## $paths
## [1] "x2 -> y2"
## [2] "x2 <- u -> x1 -> y2"
## [3] "x2 <- u -> y1 <- x1 -> y2"
## [4] "x2 <- u -> y2"
## [5] "x2 <- x1 -> y1 <- u -> y2"
## [6] "x2 <- x1 -> y2"
## [7] "x2 <- x1 <- u -> y2"
##
## $open
## [1]  TRUE  TRUE FALSE  TRUE FALSE  TRUE  TRUE
adjustmentSets(case2b)
## { u, x1 }
```

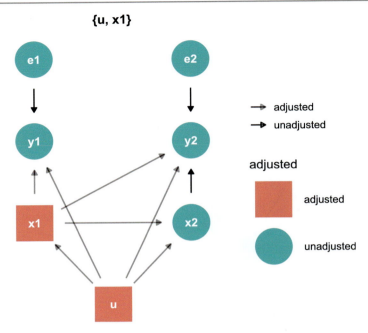

Fig. 10.7 Case where past treatment affects current outcome and current treatment: adjustment set and blocking of non-causal paths. We have to adjust for u, which is not observed, and x1, which is observed

We have to adjust for u and x1 to identify the effect of x2 on y2. We plot the graph with the adjustments and see how this blocks the non-causal paths (the grayed out paths in Fig. 10.7).

The structural equations in Fig. 10.6 are

$$y_1 = \beta x_1 + u + e_1. \tag{10.7}$$

$$y_2 = \beta x_2 + \gamma x_1 + u + e_2. \tag{10.8}$$

Equations 10.8–10.7 give us

$$(y_2 - y_1) = \beta(x_2 - x_1) + \gamma x_1 + (e_2 - e_1). \tag{10.9}$$

Notice that now we have x_1 remaining in Eq. 10.9, but which we can include as a covariate as it is observed. In a later section, we carry out a simulation.

10.2.3.3 Case Where Past Outcome Affects Both Current Treatment and Current Outcome

Now, let's consider a more complex situation where the past outcome affects both the current treatment and the current outcome. According to Imai and Kim (2019),

10.2 Concepts and Examples

this scenario poses a challenge for fixed-effect models, as we can no longer directly adjust the specification to address both the unit-level unobserved confounders and past outcomes as confounders. The bias stemming from this situation cannot be dealt with using fixed-effect models alone.

```
paths(case2d)
## $paths
##    [1]  "x2 -> y2"
##    [2]  "x2 <- u -> x1 -> y1 -> y2"
##    [3]  "x2 <- u -> y1 -> y2"
##    [4]  "x2 <- u -> y2"
##    [5]  "x2 <- x1 -> y1 -> y2"
##    [6]  "x2 <- x1 -> y1 <- u -> y2"
##    [7]  "x2 <- x1 <- u -> y1 -> y2"
##    [8]  "x2 <- x1 <- u -> y2"
##    [9]  "x2 <- y1 -> y2"
##   [10]  "x2 <- y1 <- u -> y2"
##   [11]  "x2 <- y1 <- x1 <- u -> y2"
##
## $open
##    [1]    TRUE    TRUE    TRUE    TRUE    TRUE   FALSE    TRUE
##    [8]    TRUE    TRUE    TRUE    TRUE
adjustmentSets(case2d)
## { u, y1 }
```

We need to adjust for both y1 and u. The problem is that u is unobserved, so we have to rely on differencing it out (see Fig. 10.9).

The structural equations in Fig. 10.8 are

$$y_1 = \beta x_1 + u + e_1. \qquad (10.10)$$

$$y_2 = \beta x_2 + \theta y_1 + u + e_2. \qquad (10.11)$$

Equations 10.11–10.10 give us

$$(y_2 - y_1) = \beta(x_2 - x_1) + \theta y_1 + (e_2 - e_1). \qquad (10.12)$$

You may have noticed that in Eq. 10.12, we now have y_1 on the right-hand side. This introduces an issue as y_1, a regressor, will be correlated with the error. To address this issue, we need to employ a method like the Arellano and Bond estimator (1991). This estimator takes into account the need to difference out the unobserved fixed effect and address the correlation between the past outcome and the error. The Arellano and Bond estimator uses lagged levels of the outcome variable as instruments. However, there is a risk of misspecification, and tests are only indicative and do not guarantee us knowing if a model is correctly specified. Verbeek writes

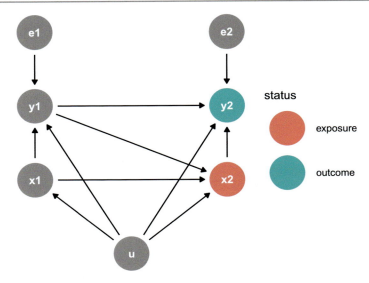

Fig. 10.8 Case where past outcome affects current treatment and current outcome

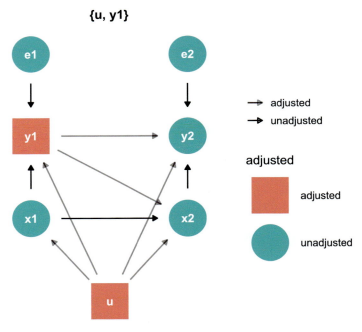

Fig. 10.9 Case where past outcome affects current outcome and current treatment: adjustment set and blocking of non-causal paths. We have to adjust for u and y1

(2022, p. 137), "If the model is misspecified, for example, due to the presence of an unobserved time-varying variable affecting both the dependent and endogenous explanatory variables, the GMM estimator will be biased. Nevertheless, it is possible that the test for serial correlation and the Sargan-Hansen test 'pass' at conventional levels. For example, the Sargan-Hansen test will have low power when the instruments are weak." Since different methods make different assumptions, analysts may present results using multiple methods to assess robustness.

10.2.4 Income and Democracy

The relationship between democracy and economic growth is a topic of great interest among scholars in both economics and political science. In these disciplines, there was a broad belief, although not without debate, that improvements in living standards are conducive to the development of democratic institutions. Several researchers have found evidence of a positive relationship between the quality of democracy and incomes. As a result, they have advocated economic growth to usher in democratic institutions.

Figure 10.10 illustrates this relationship with panel data from 1950 to 2004, dividing it into smaller five-year panels. It shows a consistent and clear positive association between an index of democracy and income. Acemoglu et al. (2008, p. 808) (hereafter, AJRY 2008) describe the relationship between income per capita and democracy as "one of the most notable empirical regularities."

Does the positive correlation imply that economic growth will affect the onset or revival of democratic institutions? An astute student of causal inference would caution against drawing such a conclusion, as correlation between the two does not imply that one causes the other, for at least two reasons. Firstly, we may be inverting the true causal relationship: it may not be economic growth ushering in better democratic institutions, but rather democracy fostering economic growth. Secondly, we should be aware of the possibility of omitted variable bias, where a confounding factor affects both democratic processes and economic development. AJRY 2008 unravel this puzzle through rigorous panel data analysis to unravel the underlying dynamics.

> **Discussion.** What possible confounding factor (a panacea for a liberal policymaker) can usher in both higher levels of democracy and economic development?

AJRY (2008) emphasize that such complex relationships evolve over the medium and long terms and therefore can only be accurately studied with panel data with a sufficient number of years. They use two-way fixed effects (TWFE) analysis on long-term income and democratic growth data, acknowledging that while TWFE models cannot address all types of omitted variable biases, they can address time-invariant country fixed effects.

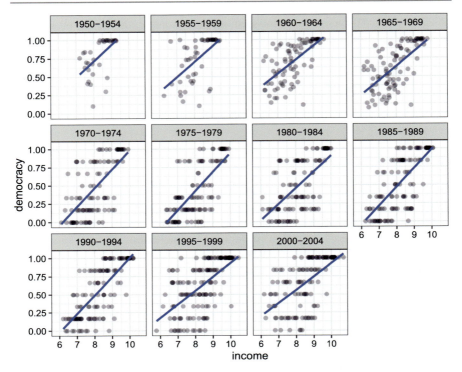

Fig. 10.10 Democracy versus income

To investigate this relationship, the authors employ a dynamic econometric model, as discussed in the previous section, and as specified in the equation below. They examine data on per capita GDP growth (y) and the quality of democratic institutions (d), measured by Freedom House Political Rights Index, across 124 countries from the post-World War II years:

$$d_{it} = \alpha d_{it-1} + \gamma y_{it-1} + X_{it-1}^T \beta + \mu_t + \delta_i + u_{it}, \tag{10.13}$$

where d_{it} is the democracy score of country i in period t. The effect of the lagged value of log income per capita, y_{it}, is the main quantity of interest.

AJRY (2008) present a striking finding when they examine and compare the coefficients in the three specifications. They emphasize that after accounting for fixed effects (in columns 2 and 3 of Table 10.2), the effect of income on democracy is vastly reduced in the five-year data. This finding challenges the long-held belief that economic growth directly leads to an improvement in the quality of democracy. The authors proceed to provide potential explanations for why the cross-sectional data exhibited the strong positive correlations depicted in Fig. 10.10.

10.2 Concepts and Examples

Table 10.2 Results using Freedom House measure of democracy

	Pooled	Fixed effects	Arellano-Bond
lag(democracy)	0.704	0.359	0.500
	(0.026)	(0.037)	(0.092)
lag(income)	0.069	−0.005	−0.197
	(0.009)	(0.031)	(0.126)
R^2	0.722	0.123	
Num. obs.	827	827	1369
n			195
T			9
Num. obs. used			691
Sargan Test: chisq			43.841
Sargan Test: df			27.000
Sargan Test: p-value			0.021
Wald Test Coefficients: chisq			38.698
Wald Test Coefficients: df			2
Wald Test Coefficients: p-value			0.000
Wald Test Time Dummies: chisq			35.907
Wald Test Time Dummies: df			7
Wald Test Time Dummies: p-value			0.000

☞ **Discussion.** Read the relevant sections of the paper and discuss why the positive correlations in the cross-sectional data are misleading.

Table 10.2 displays three specifications from the AJRY (2008) study. In the first model, they employ a pooled OLS and find a strong and positive association between the lagged income (income from the previous year), and democracy (the dependent variable). They also include the lagged value of the democracy index as an additional covariate in the regression "to capture persistence in democracy and also potentially mean-reverting dynamics (p. 815)." By including this covariate, they try to account for the tendency of the democracy score to return to some equilibrium value for the country.

When comparing the coefficients in the first specification with the other two, a striking difference emerges (Fig. 10.11). While the first model exhibits a strong and positive association, the second and third models paint a different picture. The use of TWFE in the second column and a dynamic panel data model (specifically,

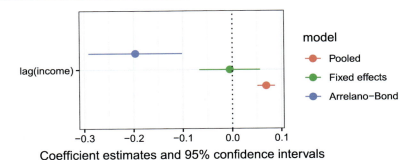

Fig. 10.11 Results using Freedom House measure of democracy

the Arrelano-Bond estimator) in the third column eliminate the previously observed positive relationship between income and democracy. These results show how panel data methods can be used to address specific confounding factors. Furthermore, the case highlights that the relationship between income and democracy is more complex than initially thought and warrants a deeper, long-run analysis.

☞ Discussion. Read section B of the AJRY (2008) paper when they take a longer run view (500 years) to examine the relationship between income and democracy. Do the authors suggest that the countries have a choice among the divergent paths of development?

We conclude by quoting AJRY (2008, p. 808), who write, "Existing studies establish a strong cross-country correlation between income and democracy but do not control for factors that simultaneously affect both variables. We show that controlling for such factors by including country fixed effects removes the statistical association between income per capita and various measures of democracy." AJRY thus provide evidence for a null result between income and democracy. The authors further argue that this lack of a causal relationship is consistent across different lengths of time, including long-term data spanning up to 500 years, and "the cross-country correlation between income and democracy can be largely accounted by ... divergent development paths."

10.3 R Code

10.3.1 Schooling and Wages

Here, we draw on code provided by Jeff Arnold for the section in the book Mastering Metrics by Angrist et al. (2015) related to estimating the effect of education on wages from data on twins. The data can be got from the following:

10.3 R Code

Fig. 10.12 Log wages against education

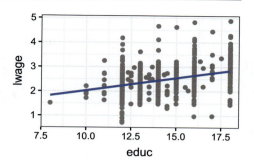

```
#devtools::install_github("jrnold/masteringmetrics",
#subdir = "masteringmetrics")
```

We load the data:

```
data("pubtwins", package = "masteringmetrics")
```

We load tidyverse and look at the data:

```
library(tidyverse)
pubtwins[,1:6]
## # A tibble: 680 x 6
##     first  educ educt hrwage lwage   age
##     <dbl> <dbl> <dbl>  <dbl> <dbl> <dbl>
##  1      1    16    16  11.9   2.48  33.3
##  2     NA    16    16   9.21  2.22  33.3
##  3     NA    12    16   9.28  2.23  43.6
##  4      1    18    12  19.1   2.95  43.6
##  5     NA    12    12  15.4   2.73  31.0
##  6      1    12    12  17.4   2.86  31.0
##  7     NA    14    14  19.3   2.89  35.2
##  8      1    14  14.3  16.7   2.81  35.2
##  9     NA    15    13   8.09  2.09  35.0
## 10      1    13    15  37.1   3.61  35.0
## # ... with 670 more rows
```

We make a scatter plot for log wages against education (Fig. 10.12):

```
ggplot(pubtwins, aes(x = educ, y = lwage)) +
  geom_point(col = "grey50") +
  geom_smooth(method = "lm", se = F) +
  theme_bw()
```

Now we will look at differences in log wages (between twins) versus differences in education. We need to filter the data before plotting (Fig. 10.13):

Fig. 10.13 Difference in log wages against difference in education, message = F

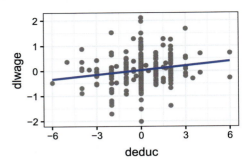

```
pubtwins2 <- pubtwins %>%
  filter(first == 1)

ggplot(pubtwins2, aes(x = deduc, y = dlwage)) +
  geom_point(col = "grey50") +
  geom_smooth(method = "lm", se = F) +
  theme_bw()
## `geom_smooth()` using formula = 'y ~ x'
```

We now will replicate Table 6.2 of Mastering Metrics. We use the estimatr package. The package provides a range of commonly used linear estimators, and is fast and convenient. The package helps us get robust standard errors. We use the `lm_robust` and `iv_robust` functions. The syntax is similar to the `lm` function:

```
library(estimatr)
mod1 <- lm_robust(lwage ~ educ + poly(age, 2) +
                     female + white, data = pubtwins)
mod2 <- lm_robust(dlwage ~ deduc, data = pubtwins2)
mod3 <- iv_robust(lwage ~ educ | educt, data = pubtwins)
mod4 <- iv_robust(dlwage ~ deduc | deduct, data = pubtwins2)
```

We now use texreg to produce a table of results. This table was displayed earlier in the chapter:

```
library(texreg)
texreg(list(mod1, mod2, mod3, mod4))
```

10.3.2 Alcohol Policies and Traffic Fatalities

We load the AER package, and load the Fatalities data. The AER package has several datasets:

10.3 R Code

```
library(AER)
data(Fatalities)
dim(Fatalities)
## [1] 336  34
```

We create a new variable, the fatality rate:

```
Fatalities2 <- Fatalities %>%
  mutate(fatal_rate = fatal / pop * 10000)
```

The code for the figures in an earlier section is below. We can use a filter to get values for 1982. Note that we can link the filtering process with the plotting process with the pipe operator %>%:

```
Fatalities2 %>%
  filter(year == "1982") %>%
  ggplot(aes(x = beertax, y = fatal_rate)) +
    geom_point(alpha = 0.5) +
    geom_smooth(method = "lm", se = F) +
  theme_bw()
```

To get state-wise plots, we use the col = state option:

```
ggplot(Fatalities2, aes(x = beertax, y = fatal_rate,
          col = state)) +
  geom_point(alpha = 0.4) +
  geom_smooth(method = "lm", se = F) +
  guides(col = FALSE) +
  theme_bw()
```

We load the modelsummary and fixest packages.

☞ **Your turn.** Look up the modelsummary and fixest packages online.

```
library(modelsummary)
library(fixest)
library(texreg)
```

We estimate some models and put the results together (Table 10.3):

```
mod1 <- lm(fatal_rate ~ beertax, data = Fatalities2)

mod2 <- feols(fatal_rate ~ beertax | state,
          data = Fatalities2)
```

Table 10.3 Regressions for traffic fatalities

	Model 1	Model 2	Model 3	Model 4
(Intercept)	1.85 (0.04)			
beertax	0.36 (0.06)	−0.66 (0.29)	−0.64 (0.36)	−0.46 (0.31)
drinkage				−0.00 (0.02)
jailyes				0.04 (0.10)
miles				0.00 (0.00)
unemp				−0.06 (0.01)
log(income)				1.79 (0.64)
R^2	0.09			
Num. obs.	336	336	336	335
Num. groups: state		48	48	48
R^2 (full model)		0.91	0.91	0.94
R^2 (proj model)		0.04	0.04	0.36
Num. groups: year			7	7

Standard errors in parentheses

```
mod3 <- feols(fatal_rate ~ beertax | state + year,
              data = Fatalities2)

mod4 <- feols(fatal_rate ~ beertax + drinkage +
                jail + miles + unemp + log(income) |
                state + year,
              data = Fatalities2)
texreg(list(mod1, mod2, mod3, mod4),
       caption = "Regressions for traffic fatalities",
       caption.above = TRUE,
       stars = numeric(0),
       include.ci = FALSE,
       include.adjrs = FALSE,
       custom.note = "Standard errors in parentheses.")
```

We use the modeplot function in the modelsummary package to plot confidence intervals. The code for the figure in an earlier section:

10.3 R Code

```
models <- list("No fixed effects" = mod1,
               "State fixed effects" = mod2,
               "TWFE" = mod3,
               "TWFE and controls" = mod4)
cm <- c('beertax' = 'Beer tax')
modelplot(models, coef_map = cm, fatten = 4) +
  geom_vline(xintercept = 0, linetype = "dotted") +
  theme_bw()
```

10.3.3 Causal Graphs for Panel Data

We load the ggdag and dagitty libraries:

```
library(ggdag)
library(dagitty)
```

10.3.3.1 Simple Case
We first consider the simple case. We provide the names of the variables, their relationships, and the coordinate information:

```
#Case 1
case1 <- dagify(y1 ~ x1 + u + e1,
                y2 ~ x2 + u + e2,
                x1 ~ u,
                x2 ~ u + x1,
                exposure = "x2",
                outcome = "y2",
        coords = list(x = c(x1 = 0, y1 = 0, e1 = 0,
                u = 1, x2 = 2, y2 = 2, e2 = 2),
                y = c(u = 0, x1 = 1, x2 = 1,
                y1 = 2, y2 = 2, e1 = 3, e2 = 3)))
```

We now plot the causal graph:

```
ggdag_status(case1) +
  theme_dag()
```

We list all the paths, and adjustment sets:

```
paths(case1)
adjustmentSets(case1)
```

The code for the graph of the adjustment:

```
ggdag_adjustment_set(case1, shadow = TRUE) +
  theme_dag()
```

We now simulate:

```
N <- 1000

b <- 2
e1 <- rnorm(N)
e2 <- rnorm(N)
u <- rnorm(N, mean = 2)
x1 <- u + rnorm(N)
y1 <- b*x1 + e1 + u
x2 <- u + rnorm(N) + x1
y2 <- b*x2 + e2 + u

mod1A <- lm(y2 ~ x2)
mod1B <- lm(I(y2 - y1) ~ I(x2 - x1))

library(texreg)
texreg(list(mod1A, mod1B),
       caption = "Simple case, true effect is 2",
       caption.above = TRUE,
       stars = numeric(0),
       include.ci = FALSE,
       include.adjrs = FALSE,
       custom.note = "Standard errors in parentheses.")
```

Regressing y2 on x2 gives us a biased estimate. But regressing the difference of y2 and y1 on the difference of x2 and x1 provides us with an estimate close to the true value of 2 (Table 10.4).

10.3.3.2 Case Where Past Treatment Affects Current Outcome

The code is similar to that used above:

```
case2b <- dagify(y1 ~ x1 + u + e1,
                 y2 ~ x2 + u + e2 + x1,
                 x1 ~ u,
                 x2 ~ u + x1,
```

10.3 R Code

Table 10.4 Simple case, true effect is 2

	Model 1	Model 2
(Intercept)	0.64	0.07
	(0.07)	(0.08)
x2	2.35	
	(0.01)	
x2–x1		2.02
		(0.03)
R^2	0.96	0.80
Num. obs.	1000	1000

Standard errors in parentheses

```
                     exposure = "x2",
                     outcome = "y2",
         coords = list(x = c(x1 = 0, y1 = 0, e1 = 0,
                      u = 1, x2 = 2, y2 = 2, e2 = 2),
                      y = c(u = 0, x1 = 1, x2 = 1,
                      y1 = 2, y2 = 2, e1 = 3, e2 = 3)))

ggdag_status(case2b) +
  theme_dag()

paths(case2b)

adjustmentSets(case2b)
ggdag_adjustment_set(case2b, shadow = TRUE) +
  theme_dag()
```

We now simulate:

```
b <- 2
m <- 0.5
k <- 0.3
e1 <- rnorm(N)
e2 <- rnorm(N)
u <- rnorm(N, mean = 2)
x1 <- u + rnorm(N)
y1 <- b*x1 + e1 + u
x2 <- u + rnorm(N) + m*x1
y2 <- b*x2 + e2 + u + k*x1

mod2A <- lm(y2 ~ x2)
mod2B <- lm(I(y2 - y1) ~ I(x2 - x1))
mod2C <- lm(I(y2 - y1) ~ I(x2 - x1) + x1)
```

Table 10.5 Past treatment affects current outcome, true effect is 2

	Model 1	Model 2	Model 3
(Intercept)	0.76	0.61	−0.01
	(0.08)	(0.06)	(0.09)
x2	2.60		
	(0.02)		
x2–x1		1.95	1.98
		(0.04)	(0.04)
x1			0.32
			(0.03)
R^2	0.93	0.71	0.73
Num. obs.	1000	1000	1000

Standard errors in parentheses

```
library(texreg)
texreg(list(mod2A, mod2B, mod2C),
       caption = "Past treatment affects current outcome, true effect is 2",
       caption.above = TRUE,
       stars = numeric(0),
       include.ci = FALSE,
       include.adjrs = FALSE,
       custom.note = "Standard errors in parentheses.")
```

☞ **Your turn**   Interpret the results in Table 10.5.

10.3.3.3 Case Where Past Outcome Affects Both Current Treatment and Current Outcome

We now consider the second case:

```
#Case 2d

case2d <- dagify(y1 ~ x1 + u + e1,
                 y2 ~ x2 + u + e2 + y1,
                 x1 ~ u,
                 x2 ~ u + x1 + y1,
                 exposure = "x2",
                 outcome = "y2",
           coords = list(x = c(x1 = 0, y1 = 0, e1 = 0,
                   u = 1, x2 = 2, y2 = 2, e2 = 2),
                  y = c(u = 0, x1 = 1, x2 = 1,
                  y1 = 2, y2 = 2, e1 = 3, e2 = 3)))

ggdag_status(case2d) +
  theme_dag()
```

10.3 R Code

```
paths(case2d)

adjustmentSets(case2d)
ggdag_adjustment_set(case2d, shadow = TRUE) +
  theme_dag()
instrumentalVariables(case2d)
```

We now simulate:

```
N <- 1000

b <- 2
m <- 0.5
e1 <- rnorm(N)
e2 <- rnorm(N)
u <- rnorm(N, mean = 2)
x1 <- u + rnorm(N)
y1 <- b*x1 + e1 + u
x2 <- u + rnorm(N) + y1
y2 <- b*x2 + e2 + u + m*y1

mod3A <- lm(y2 ~ x2)
mod3B <- lm(I(y2 - y1) ~ I(x2 - x1))
mod3C <- lm(I(y2 - y1) ~ I(x2 - x1) + y1)


library(texreg)
texreg(list(mod3A, mod3B, mod3C),
       caption = "Past outcome affects both current treatment and current outcome,
true effect is 2",
       caption.above = TRUE,
       stars = numeric(0),
       include.ci = FALSE,
       include.adjrs = FALSE,
       custom.note = "Standard errors in parentheses.")
```

☞ **Your turn**   Interpret the results in Table 10.6.

10.3.4 Income and Democracy

The data for the paper is linked to the paper online. The pder package in R has a subset of the data used in the paper. The pder package accompanies the book Panel Data Econometrics with R. We load the package and read in the data:

Table 10.6 Past outcome affects both current treatment and current outcome, true effect is 2

	Model 1	Model 2	Model 3
(Intercept)	0.54	0.57	0.55
	(0.08)	(0.10)	(0.09)
x2	2.56		
	(0.01)		
x2–x1		2.41	1.98
		(0.01)	(0.03)
y1			0.44
			(0.03)
R^2	0.99	0.97	0.97
Num. obs.	1000	1000	1000

Standard errors in parentheses

```
library(tidyverse)
library(pder)
data("DemocracyIncome")
```

The online journal paper website provides links to data to replicate the figures in the paper. Here, we use the data we have to plot the strong correlation that the authors note between democracy and income (shown in an earlier section):

```
DemocracyIncome %>%
  ggplot(aes(x = income, y = democracy #,
             #col = year
             )) +
  geom_point(alpha = 0.2) +
  facet_wrap(~ year) +
  geom_smooth(method = "lm", se = F) +
  theme_bw()
detach("package:tidyverse", unload=TRUE)
```

We use the plm package for our estimation, since it can also do dynamic panel estimation. The plm package has helpful vignettes.

☞ Your turn. Look up the plm package online.

deflist

```
library(plm)
```

We create a panel dataframe:

10.3 R Code

```
Democ <- DemocracyIncome %>%
    filter(sample == 1)
Democ2 <- pdata.frame(Democ,
                    index = c("country", "year"))
```

We replicate a few of the estimations reported in Table 10.2. We use the `plm` and the `pgmm` functions:

```
# Pooled OLS
modT2C1 <- plm(democracy ~ lag(democracy) + lag(income) + year - 1,
            Democ2, model = "pooling")


# Fixed effects OLS
modTC2 <- plm(democracy ~ lag(democracy) + lag(income),
        Democ2, effect = "twoways")


# Arellano-Bond GMM
modTC4 <- pgmm(democracy ~ lag(democracy) + lag(income) |
                lag(democracy, 2:99)| lag(income, 2),
                Democ2, model="onestep", effect="twoways")

library(texreg)
texreg(list(modT2C1, modTC2, modTC4),
        omit.coef = "year",
        custom.model.names = c("Pooled OLS", "Fixed Effects OLS", "Arellano-Bond GMM"),
        caption = "Fixed Effects Results using Freedom House measure of democracy",
        caption.above = TRUE, digits = 3)
```

10.4 Resources

10.4.1 For Better Understanding

Chapter on Panel Data in the book by Stock James and Watson Mark (2017), *Introduction to Econometrics*.

10.4.2 For Going Further

Paper by Imai and Kim (2019), *When Should We use Unit Fixed Effects?*

Packages Used in This Chapter

The citations for the packages used in this chapter are[4]

---

[4] The tidyverse package itself contains several packages.

```
## Arel-Bundock V (2022). "modelsummary: Data and Model Summaries
## in R." _Journal of Statistical Software_, *103*(1), 1-23. doi:
## 10.18637/jss.v103.i01 (URL:
## https://doi.org/10.18637/jss.v103.i01).


## Barrett M (2021). _ggdag: Analyze and Create Elegant Directed
## Acyclic Graphs_. R package version 0.2.4, <URL:
## https://CRAN.R-project.org/package=ggdag>.


## Bergé L (2018). "Efficient estimation of maximum likelihood
## models with multiple fixed-effects: the R package FENmlm."
## _CREA Discussion Papers_.


## Croissant Y, Millo G (2018). _Panel Data Econometrics with R_.
## Wiley.
##
## Croissant Y, Millo G (2008). "Panel Data Econometrics in R:
## The plm Package." _Journal of Statistical Software_, *27*(2),
## 1-43. doi: 10.18637/jss.v027.i02 (URL:
## https://doi.org/10.18637/jss.v027.i02).
##
## Millo G (2017). "Robust Standard Error Estimators for Panel
## Models: A Unifying Approach." _Journal of Statistical
## Software_, *82*(3), 1-27. doi: 10.18637/jss.v082.i03 (URL:
## https://doi.org/10.18637/jss.v082.i03).


## Croissant Y, Millo G (2022). _pder: Panel Data Econometrics
## with R_. R package version 1.0-2, <URL:
## https://CRAN.R-project.org/package=pder>.


## Fox J, Weisberg S (2019). _An R Companion to Applied
## Regression_, Third edition. Sage, Thousand Oaks CA. <URL:
## https://socialsciences.mcmaster.ca/jfox/Books/Companion/>.


## Fox J, Weisberg S, Price B (2022). _carData: Companion to
## Applied Regression Data Sets_. R package version 3.0-5, <URL:
## https://CRAN.R-project.org/package=carData>.


## Kleiber C, Zeileis A (2008). _Applied Econometrics with R_.
## Springer-Verlag, New York. ISBN 978-0-387-77316-2, <URL:
## https://CRAN.R-project.org/package=AER>.
```

10.4 Resources

```
## Leifeld P (2013). "texreg: Conversion of Statistical Model
## Output in R to LaTeX and HTML Tables." _Journal of Statistical
## Software_, *55*(8), 1-24. <URL:
## http://dx.doi.org/10.18637/jss.v055.i08>.


## R Core Team (2021). _R: A Language and Environment for
## Statistical Computing_. R Foundation for Statistical
## Computing, Vienna, Austria. <URL: https://www.R-project.org/>.


## Makowski D, Lüdecke D, Patil I, Thériault R, Ben-Shachar M,
## Wiernik B (2023). "Automated Results Reporting as a Practical
## Tool to Improve Reproducibility and Methodological Best
## Practices Adoption." _CRAN_. <URL:
## https://easystats.github.io/report/>.


## Textor J, van der Zander B, Gilthorpe MS, Liskiewicz M, ##
Ellison GT (2016). "Robust causal inference using directed ##
acyclic graphs: the R package 'dagitty'." _International ## Journal
of Epidemiology_, *45*(6), 1887-1894. doi: ## 10.1093/ije/dyw341
(URL: https://doi.org/10.1093/ije/dyw341).


## Therneau T (2022). _A Package for Survival Analysis in R_. R
## package version 3.3-1, <URL:
## https://CRAN.R-project.org/package=survival>.
##
## Terry M. Therneau, Patricia M. Grambsch (2000). _Modeling
## Survival Data: Extending the Cox Model_. Springer, New York.
## ISBN 0-387-98784-3.


## Wickham H, Averick M, Bryan J, Chang W, McGowan LD, François
## R, Grolemund G, Hayes A, Henry L, Hester J, Kuhn M, Pedersen
## TL, Miller E, Bache SM, Müller K, Ooms J, Robinson D, Seidel
## DP, Spinu V, Takahashi K, Vaughan D, Wilke C, Woo K, Yutani H
## (2019). "Welcome to the tidyverse." _Journal of Open Source
## Software_, *4*(43), 1686. doi: 10.21105/joss.01686 (URL:
## https://doi.org/10.21105/joss.01686).


## Xie Y (2022). _knitr: A General-Purpose Package for Dynamic
## Report Generation in R_. R package version 1.41, <URL:
## https://yihui.org/knitr/>.
```

```
## Xie Y (2023). _formatR: Format R Code Automatically_. R
## package version 1.14, <URL:
## https://CRAN.R-project.org/package=formatR>.
```

References

Acemoglu, Daron, Simon Johnson, James A. Robinson, and Pierre Yared. 2008. Income and Democracy. *American Economic Review* 98 (3): 808–842.

Angrist, Joshua D., and Jörn.-steffen Pischke. 2015. *Mastering 'Metrics*. Princeton, Oxford: Princeton University Press. with french flaps edition edition.

Ashenfelter, Orley, and Alan Krueger. 1999. Estimates of the Economic Return to Schooling from a New Sample of Twins. *The American Economic Review* 84(5): 1157–1173, . American Economic Association.

Ashenfelter, Orley, and Cecilia Rouse. 1998. Income, Schooling, and Ability: Evidence from a New Sample of Identical Twins*. *The Quarterly Journal of Economics* 113 (1): 253–284.

Imai, Kosuke, and In Song Kim. 2019. When Should We Use Unit Fixed Effects Regression Models for Causal Inference with Longitudinal Data? *American Journal of Political Science* 63(2): 467–490. _eprint: https://onlinelibrary.wiley.com/doi/pdf/10.1111/ajps.12417

Stock James, H., and W. Watson Mark. 2017. *Introduction to Econometrics By Pearson*, 3rd edn. Pearson Education.

Ruhm, Christopher J. 1996. Alcohol Policies and Highway Vehicle Fatalities. *Journal of Health Economics* 15 (4): 435–454.

Difference-in-Differences

11.1 Introduction

In the Spring of 2023, the swift collapse of Silicon Valley Bank, the second-largest bank failure in the United States, sparked concerns of a global banking crisis. As the ripple effects of the risk spread across the world, banking stocks plummeted, instilling fears in the financial system. Haunted by the aftermath of the 2008 financial crisis, where about 500 banks collapsed, President Biden reassured American investors and depositors within hours of the Silicon Valley Bank failure, stating, "Let me repeat that: No losses will be borne by the taxpayers" (NYT, 14th March).[1] The bailouts under President Bush and Obama may have softened the global Great Recession in 2008, but they also ignited a widespread backlash, such as Occupy Wall Street movement in the United States, which arguably fueled populist politics.

President Biden's prompt response likely drew upon lessons learned from the 2008 crisis and the Great Depression of the 1930s, which tested policymakers' ability to manage banking panics. Regardless of the structural similarities or differences in the origins of the crisis, the policy response aimed to stem financial collapse and restore depositor confidence. The groundwork had already been laid in the 1930s for enthusiasts of causal inference to examine whether the Bagehot rule, advocating swift liquidity support and confidence building measures, or a policy of nonintervention would effectively stabilize banks and restore trust among depositors and investors.

Crises, such as pandemics, economic depressions, and political upheavals, often throw curveballs at experts, policymakers, and politicians, putting their data collection, inference, and knowledge to the test. In this chapter, we begin by exploring one such challenge: the Great Depression of the 1930s. The devastating event led to a sharp decline in depositor confidence and compelled policymakers to implement

---

[1] https://www.nytimes.com/2023/03/14/us/politics/bailout-biden-financial-crisis.html.

© The Author(s), under exclusive license to Springer Nature Singapore Pte Ltd. 2023
V. Dayal and A. Murugesan, *Demystifying Causal Inference*,
https://doi.org/10.1007/978-981-99-3905-3_11

policies to halt the downward spiral. We discuss gleanings from a comparative case study from this time, by deploying the difference-in-differences (DID) method to analyze the variation in policy responses between two banking districts within the same state.

To understand the origins of the DID approach, we briefly journey back to John Snow's analysis of cholera in the nineteenth-century England. From there, we'll delve into the central assumption of the DID method: parallel trends between the treated and control groups. We will also explore how policy analysts can relax this assumption and still offer valuable recommendations, using Manski and Pepper's (2018) study on the effect of Right-To-Carry gun laws in the United States as an example. Manski advocates moving away from 'incredible certitudes' of point estimates and instead embracing a more honest portrayal of our knowledge through informative bounds, which can lead to effective policymaking.

Furthermore, we will introduce the Synthetic Control Method, a tool that researchers can employ to conduct quantitative comparative studies. We'll examine its application in studying the economic consequences of German reunification on West Germany. However, before diving into these captivating examples, we'll start with a simple case of a policy change in a two-period, two-group setting to elucidate the basic DID framework for making causal inferences.

11.2 Concepts and Examples

11.2.1 Worker Injury Benefits and Time Out of Work

The effect of incentives on work and leisure choices has been extensively researched by scholars, particularly in the context of unemployment insurance and welfare programs. One area of focus has been the relationship between unemployment benefits and the length of unemployment among individuals, a topic that has sparked both research inquiry and public debate. On one side of the spectrum, there are arguments suggesting that generous benefits incentivize people to be 'lazy', discouraging them from actively seeking employment and fostering a culture of dependence on taxpayer money. On the other side, proponents argue that welfare programs are essential for social fairness in civil society and may have unintended positive effects, such as enhancing job matching efficiency. For policymakers, the challenge lies in comprehending the overall impact of these benefits on individuals' decisions regarding work and making informed policies based on that understanding.

11.2.1.1 A Benefits Policy Change in Kentucky

Meyer et al. (1995) (henceforth, MVD) studied the impact of higher worker injury benefits on the duration of work absence. Their study aimed to address the question of how incentives, such as increased benefits, might influence workers to prolong their time away from work following an injury. In July 1980, the state of Kentucky in the US raised the maximum benefit from 131 to 217 dollars per week, a whopping

66% increase. This increased cap benefited high-income workers, as it only applied to workers earning above a specific threshold wage. Workers injured on or before June 30, 1980, would receive a compensation of let's say C dollars per week if their wages exceeded the threshold at the time of his injury. In contrast, workers with the same wage who happened to get injured at least a day later, by chance, starting from July 1, 1980, would receive a higher amount of C + X dollars. Here, X was a sizeable 66% increase over C for the treated group of high-wage workers. On the other hand, the policy change had no effect on lower wage workers, who serve as the control group in the study.

MVD conducted their analysis by examining a random sample of indemnity claims both before and after the policy change in 1980. Their objective was to determine if the increase in benefits led to longer periods of work absence among the treated group of high-income workers. To achieve this, the authors employed a simple difference-in-differences approach. They compared the change in claims between the treatment group, composed of high-income workers in Kentucky affected by the policy change on July 1, 1980, to the change in claims observed in the control group, consisting of low-income workers unaffected by the policy change.

The results of their study indicated that the policy change led to a 19% increase in the average duration of compensation after an injury for high-income workers. In contrast, the change in claims among low-income earners was close to zero, as predicted, since the policy should not have affected them. In the next section, we will bring out the fundamental features of the differences-in-differences design to isolate the causal effect of policy changes in this simple setting.

11.2.1.2 Illustrating the Basic Intuition of DID

The DID method compares the changes in outcomes between two groups: the 'treated' group that experiences the policy change (e.g., higher benefits for high-wage workers) and the 'control' group that does not. The basic idea behind DID is that if both groups exhibit the same trend in their outcomes before the policy change, any difference in the trend after the policy change can be attributed to the policy intervention. In other words, we assume that the trends for the two groups would have remained identical or parallel if it weren't for the policy change.

To illustrate this idea, Fig. 11.1 provides a visual representation. It depicts the mean outcome of the treated group (shown in green) and the control group (shown in brown) over time. The outcome is represented on the y-axis, while we depict time on the x-axis, with time = 0 indicating the period before the policy change, t = 1 representing the activation of the policy (1 July 1980), and time = 2 representing the period after the policy change.

The crucial assumption of the DID method is that the trend in the outcome of the control group will be parallel to that of the treated group in the absence of the policy change. This means that the slope of the line connecting the means of the control and treated groups should be the same before the policy change, as shown by the brown and green lines in Fig. 11.1.

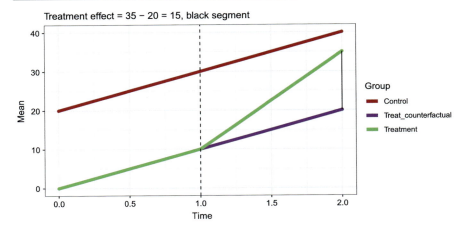

Fig. 11.1 Basic intuition of DID, hypothetical example

After the policy change, we expect the trend in the outcome of the treated group to deviate from that of the control group if the policy change (at $t = 1$) has an effect. This deviation, or the treatment effect, is represented by the (solid) black vertical segment in Fig. 11.1, which equals $35 - 20 = 15$.

Let's take a closer look at the calculation of the DID estimate. During the period from time $= 1$ and time $= 2$, the mean outcome for the control group increases by 10, while the mean outcome for the treatment group increases by 25. If we were to compare only the outcomes at time $= 2$, the difference between the control and treatment groups would be 5 (equals $40 - 35$). However, to obtain the treatment effect, we need to subtract the counterfactual outcome at time $= 2$ from the treatment group's actual outcome at that time.

Based on our assumption of parallel trends between the treatment and control groups, we estimate our counterfactual outcome by considering the trend or change in outcome of the control group. The counterfactual outcome of the treatment group represents the outcome that the treatment group would have experienced if there had been no policy intervention. The treatment effect can be calculated as the difference between the actual outcome and the counterfactual outcome. In the example depicted in Fig. 11.1, the treatment effect amounts to 15, obtained by subtracting the counterfactual outcome of 20 (estimated for the treated group) from the actual outcome of 35 (for the treated group), thanks to the parallel trend assumption.

11.2.1.3 DID Estimation of Treatment Effect

Returning to the MVD paper, Fig. 11.2 displays the mean log of duration out of work before and after the benefits policy change in July 1980. MVD employ a regression framework to estimate the treatment effect, using three dummy variables: one for the policy change period, one for the high-income earners, and one for the interaction of policy change and high-income earners. The treatment effect is obtained from the coefficient on the interaction term, as explained in the R section.

11.2 Concepts and Examples

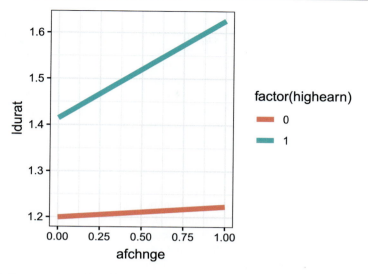

Fig. 11.2 Outcomes (mean log of duration out of work) of high and low earners, before and after the policy change

MVD also conduct additional regressions that control for various covariates such as gender, marital status, age, and type of injury. In our matching chapter (Chap. 7), we took a different approach using the same dataset. Instead of controlling for these covariates in the regression framework, we explicitly match individuals to compare apples-to-apples. In Rosenbaum's (2017) matching approach, he compared the change for the treated group and the change for the matched comparison group without using a DID.

In the MVD regression approach, controlling for these covariates does not affect the treatment effect, which is a good sign as this is similar to what is expected when estimating treatment effects in ideal randomized experiments. As discussed in the chapter on experiments (Chap. 6), randomized treatment assignments are ideal as they sever the link between the treatment variable and other variables. MVD's study provides evidence for the intensive margin, indicating that individuals respond to the policy by choosing to stay out of work for longer durations with the increased injury compensation program.

To deepen our understanding of the DID approach, let us discuss the case of historical banking crisis during the Great Depression. Unfortunately, such crises are recurring problems and, therefore highly policy-relevant.

11.2.2 Great Depression Policies to Avoid Banking Collapse

During the Great Depression, the severe economic contraction that began in 1929 led to stock markets crashing, fueling widespread fear of an impending economic collapse across the US. As a result, there was a sharp increase in deposit withdrawals from banks, placing immense strain on their liquidity, pushing several banks toward crisis and collapse. The Federal Reserve (Fed) faced a crucial decision on how to alleviate this crisis and prevent a complete collapse of the banking system. The pressing question at hand was whether to provide struggling banks with additional credit or adopt a more conservative approach, perceiving the situation as a structural problem stemming from poor bank loan portfolios. To shed light on this issue, we turn to Richardson and Troost's (2009) quantitative case study, which examines how Mississippi managed its banking crisis during the Great Depression.

Conducting randomized controlled trials in such scenarios is typically infeasible due to the ethical and financial constraints. However, Richardson and Troost discovered a viable alternative—a *natural experiment* in Mississippi—to examine the effects of two contrasting policies: easy credit compared to conservative policy, on the risk of banking collapse. They focused on the operations of two Federal Reserve Districts operating in Mississippi: Atlanta Fed, or District 6, and the St. Louis Fed Reserve, or District 8. By analyzing the divergent responses of these two districts, they investigated the variation in the number of banks that survived the crisis.

District 6 adopted the Bagehot rule, which meant aggressive intervention as a lender of last resort to stabilize the banking situation. They readily extended credit to distressed banks to alleviate liquidity challenges. In contrast, District 8 adopted the Real Bills doctrine of nonintervention, conservatively withholding credit during economic downturns and limiting interventions during banking panics. In sum, District 6 pursued aggressive intervention, while District 8 did not.

According to Richardson and Troost, this variation in policies within Mississippi enables us to consider District 6 as the 'treated' group, with the policy of increased lending, and District 8 as the 'control' group. The fact that we are comparing regions within the same state should provide some reassurance regarding the similarity of culture, language, and other characteristics. However, we need to consider whether this truly brings us an apples-to-apples comparison. Despite being in the same state, there may be differences in economic activity and other factors between the two districts that could raise concerns about the validity of the comparison.

The DID design offers a solution to address these differences by comparing the changes in outcomes over time within the treated and control groups. This design effectively controls for time-invariant differences between the groups, under the assumption that they follow a parallel trend before the treatment and would continue to do so if not for the treatment. Angrist et al. (2015) provide a simplified analysis of Richardson and Troost (2009), which we have replicated. Their insightful discussion sheds light on the key features of the Richardson and Troost analysis and helps us grasp the fundamentals of the DID method.

In Fig. 11.3, we can clearly observe that the changes in the number of banks in business for both Districts between 1929 and 1930, prior to the crisis, exhibit an almost identical (downward) trend. This observation is crucial as it demonstrates the presence of a **parallel trend**, which is a key requirement to satisfy for a valid estimate from the DID method. The parallel trend assumption means that, in the absence of the policy, the treated and control groups would have experienced the same trajectory of outcomes over time. It is important to emphasize that even if

11.2 Concepts and Examples

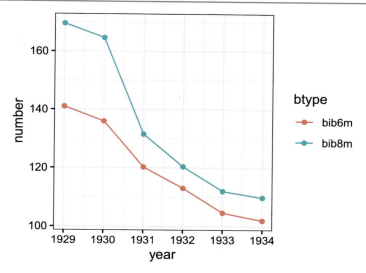

Fig. 11.3 Number of banks

the initial (pre-treatment) levels of the two groups differ, the DID method can still estimate the causal impacts as long as they have identical trends (i.e., the same slope on the trend line).

To evaluate the impact of District 6's policy of lending easily during the crisis, we need to compare it with a counterfactual scenario in which the policy was not implemented. We can use the control group of District 8 to estimate what would have transpired in District 6 in the absence of the policy. If District 6 had not implemented the policy of easy lending during the crisis, we would have expected to observe an abrupt change in the number of banks in business, similar to what we observe for District 8 in Fig. 11.3. District 8 experienced a sharp decrease in the number of banks between 1930 and 1931.

By examining the difference in the first difference of the number of banks in business at the end of 1930 between the two groups, and subsequent (second) difference at the end of 1931, we can determine the **treatment effect** of the policy adopted by District 6 between 1930 and 1931.

It is important to recognize that the parallel trend assumption, which lies at the core of the DID identification strategy, should not be taken for granted. Blindly accepting this assumption without critical consideration and empirical validation is not advisable.

To assess the validity of the parallel trend assumption, we examine historical data before the collapse in Mississippi. The data supports the parallel trend assumption as we observe similar trends between 1929 and 1930 in both districts. However, the trends diverged between 1930 and 1931. Interestingly, they became similar again after 1931 when District 8 also adopted an easy lending policy, aligning with District

6.² Jalil (2014) conducted a study using finer county-level data on banks in District 6 (Atlanta Fed) and compared them to banks in contiguous counties within 50 miles in other Districts to arrive at similar results.³

Gleaning such lessons from history is critical in improving policymakers' ability to handle such crises and formulate effective policies. While it is important to acknowledge the complexities of the current financial landscape, having reliable techniques for causal inference enables us to learn from the past and navigate future crises better. As highlighted by Reinhart and Rogoff (2011) who take a panoramic view of financial crises since the fourteenth century in their book, "This Time is Different", to reveal that such crises often follow similar patterns. They caution policymakers about the illusion created by the long intervals in recurrent crises, which can fade memories and past policy learning and fuel the illusion that "this time is different".

11.2.3 Snow's Prototype DID Design

The Mississippi case study serves as a notable example of a natural experiment as "some key elements of a randomized experiment occur on their own, even though the investigator neither creates nor assigns the treatments," in the words of Rosenbaum (2017, p. 101). As we detailed in Chap. 1, John Snow's classic study of London's cholera epidemic in the mid-nineteenth century included one such natural experiment, the "Grand Experiment".

In this experiment, Snow compared differences in cholera incidence between areas that were supplied water by two South London water companies: Lambeth and Southwark and Vauxhall (SVC). The DID design employed in Snow's study is considered a quasi-experimental design. The DID approach enables us to estimate causal effects by addressing unobserved confounders using data before and after the treatment (see related discussion in Chap. 10 on panel data).

Snow's study took advantage of the fact that Lambeth changed its water source upstream of the river Thames in 1852, resulting in cleaner water being supplied to areas served by the company, in contrast to SVC, which served as the control group.

Snow's study employed a two-period, two-group design, with both regions using a similar water source during the pre-treatment period in 1849. The treatment took place in 1852, when Lambeth changed its water sourcing upstream to a cleaner source. The post-treatment period where the incidence of cholera was observed, occurred in

---

² We also learn from historical records that District 8 contracted credit by 10%, while District 6 expanded by 40% during the liquidity crisis. This raises the question of how much of the treatment effect can be attributed to the policy intervention in District 6 and how much is influenced by the slight contraction in District 8.
³ The contiguous districts were District 5 (Richmond), District 4 (Cleveland), District 11 (Dallas), and District 8 (St. Louis, as the original study). Such robustness in results builds confidence in the quality of the estimated causal effect.

11.2 Concepts and Examples

Table 11.1 Cholera deaths

Group	Number of sub-districts	1849	1853	Difference	Percentage change
Control	12	2261	2458	197	9
Fully treated	4	162	37	−125	−77
DID				**−322**	

1854. The treatment group consisted of four sub-districts served by Lambeth, while the control group comprised 12 sub-districts served by SVC.

The DID design would estimate the treatment effect by calculating the difference in the two differences specified below

$$\delta_{DD} = (Y_{Lambeth,1854} - Y_{Lambeth,1849}) - (Y_{SVC,1854} - Y_{SVC,1849}). \quad (11.1)$$

Snow's design exemplifies how a quasi-experimental setting can help in identifying causal relationships between an intervention and an outcome.

Table 11.1 presents a comparison of cholera deaths in the 12 sub-districts served solely by the SVC (control group) and the 4 sub-districts served by Lambeth (treated group), in 1849 and 1854, as reported by Snow (1855). In the sub-districts exclusively served by SVC, there was a notable increase of 9% in cholera deaths between the two years, or 197 more deaths in 1854 compared to 1849. In contrast, in the 4 sub-districts served solely by Lambeth, the deaths recorded a staggering decrease of 77%, or 125 less deaths in 1854 compared to 1849. The difference-in-differences estimate equals −322 as seen in the last row.

While Snow did not explicitly validate the parallel trend assumption, he presented extensive evidence to support the comparability of the treated and control groups, ensuring an apples-to-apples comparison as discussed in Chap. 1. Snow's pioneering work on the DID design has led to one of the most widely used methods for causal inference. The DID method continues to be refined and enhanced by experts in the field.[4]

11.2.4 Assumptions and DID Validity

11.2.4.1 Critical Assumptions in DID

The validity of the DID treatment effect estimate relies on several key assumptions. Firstly, researchers need to empirically verify whether the parallel trend assumption holds true. This is typically done by examining the trends between the treated and control groups using pre-treatment data. Instead of relying solely on visual inspection

---

[4] DID is an active area of research during the writing of this book. Ongoing studies propose and refine methods to address the bias when estimating treatment effects when the treatments are staggered over time. See an excellent discussion by Huntington-Klein (2021).

of graphs, researchers can estimate the DID coefficients for the pre-treatment periods and should expect to find null treatment effects.

For instance, in the study of the pre-1929 banking crisis, researchers analyzed the trends between District 6 (treated) and District 8 (control) and observed that they were similar and almost parallel, indicating that the parallel trend assumption was satisfied pre-treatment. However, even if parallel trends are evident in the pre-treatment period, researchers must provide a sound rationale for expecting these trends to remain parallel in the absence of the treatment, in the post-treatment period. In other words, the counterfactual outcome should continue to follow the same trend as the treatment group. As this cannot be empirically tested, it relies on the researcher's arguments and reasoning that it holds in the context of the study.

Another crucial assumption for estimating accurate treatment effects using the DID method is that no other treatments or interventions occur concurrently with the treatment of interest. Researchers need to thoroughly document that no other changes or interventions occurred during that specific period. Additionally, researchers can examine outcomes that should not be affected by the treatment, known as placebo outcomes, to check if they show any significant change. If the placebo outcomes show significant changes, it is not a good sign and indicates that there may be confounding changes.

To illustrate the concept of placebo outcomes, let's consider a program in Argentina during the 1990s, a time marked by privatization in various parts of the continent. Galiani et al. (2005) study the impact of privatizing the drinking water supply on child mortality in Argentina using the DID method. The researchers provide evidence for the validity of the parallel trend assumption in the pre-treatment data. Their findings revealed that privatizing the water supply led to an 8% reduction in child mortality rates (and a 26% reduction in the poorest regions), specifically attributed to waterborne diseases.

Galiani et al. (2005) next ascertain whether the observed decrease in child mortality rates was primarily due to the privatization of the water supply or other potential confounding factors. They identified a significant decrease in child mortality related to waterborne diseases, emphasizing the role of improved water quality. Conversely, deaths caused by other factors, such as respiratory diseases, should remain unaffected if the only policy change was the privatization of the water supply. They considered several placebo outcomes, such as respiratory and cardiac diseases. Galiani et al. (2005) found no significant effect on these placebo outcomes. The authors argued that this asymmetry in the 'treatment effects' indicates the absence of other policy changes or treatments coinciding with the water supply privatization. If additional treatments, such as improved health facilities, were introduced simultaneously, they could potentially affect deaths caused by waterborne diseases as well as other diseases. Thus, the absence of treatment effects on placebo outcomes improved the reliability of causal effects Galiani et al. (2005) identified with the DID method.

11.2.5 Informative Bounds on the Effect of Right-to-Carry Gun Laws

To what extent can we draw reliable causal inferences using the DID design when the pre-trends are not strictly parallel? Is it possible to relax the assumptions and still make meaningful causal claims? In their work, Manski and Pepper (2018) use an alternative approach which can provide valuable insights even when the parallel trend assumption is not met.

Using the case of Virginia's Right to Carry laws, Manski and Pepper demonstrate the trade-offs between 'incredible certitude' of the point estimates achieved through strong assumptions, such as parallel trends, and informative bounds on treatment effects that can be obtained with weaker assumptions. By examining a range of assumptions, researchers can establish bounds on treatment effects, enabling them to offer policy-relevant information even when the strict parallel trend assumption is not satisfied.

Gun laws are a contentious topic in the US, with some studies suggesting that the right-to-carry a firearm improves the safety of people while others find that it is deadly dangerous. Proponents of gun ownership argue that individuals are less likely to engage in criminal activities if they believe their potential victims might be armed. However, opponents contend that easy access to guns can lead to more accidents and fatal confrontations, as well as an increase in criminal behavior. These conflicting perspectives underscore the need for rigorous causal analysis to provide informed policy recommendations.

In 1989, Virginia passed a right-to-carry law, allowing individuals to carry licensed guns. In contrast, neighboring Maryland did not enact any changes to its firearm legislation, serving as a control group. To examine the impact of right-to-carry laws, Manski and Pepper (2018) conducted a comparative analysis of crime rates in Virginia and Maryland. The study aimed to address the policy question of whether right-to-carry laws improve safety and reduce crime or have the opposite effect. Additionally, the researchers investigate which types of crimes are potentially influenced, either positively or negatively.

We now present Table 11.2 (reproduced from Manski and Pepper 2018). Can we deduce the effect of right-to-carry (RTC) laws from the table? If we consider right-to-carry laws (RTC) as a treatment and crime (Y) as the outcome, the effect of RTC on crime in Virginia (VA) can be expressed in terms of potential outcomes by

$$Y_{VA}(1) - Y_{VA}(0). \tag{11.2}$$

This equation captures the difference in potential crime rates between Virginia when the RTC law is in effect and when it is not.

Following the implementation of RTC law in Virginia in 1989, the murder rate in 1990 was recorded as 8.81, denoted as $Y_{VA}(1)$. However, due to the RTC implementation in Virginia, we cannot observe the counterfactual outcome of the murder rate $Y_{VA}(0)$ in the state if the law had not been implemented. The authors note that the neighboring state of Maryland did not implement the RTC law and can serve as the control group.

Table 11.2 Murder rates per 100,000 residents by year and state

Year	Maryland	Virginia
1988	9.63	7.75
1990	11.55	8.81

Let's consider three different types of invariance assumptions in analyzing the impact of the right-to-carry (RTC) law on murder rates in Virginia.

One assumption is the time invariance assumption. This assumes that if there had been no right-to-carry law, the murder rate in Virginia in 1990 would have been the same as in 1988. Under this assumption, we treat Virginia's murder rate in 1988 as the counterfactual, and the estimated treatment effect is calculated as $8.81 - 7.75 = 1.06$. This suggests an increase in murder rates after the implementation of the RTC laws.

The second assumption is the inter-state invariance assumption, which posits that, without the right-to-carry law, Virginia would have had the same murder rate as Maryland. Under this assumption, we consider Maryland's murder rate as the counterfactual for Virginia. The estimated treatment effect is then calculated as $11.55 - 8.81 = -2.74$. This indicates a decrease in murder rates of over 25% after the implementation of the RTC law.

The third invariance assumption is the parallel trends or the Difference-in-Differences (DID) invariance assumption. This assumption implies that, without the law, Virginia would have followed the same trend as Maryland. We arrive at the counterfactual by taking the base level in Virginia before treatment and adding the parallel trend or the change observed in Maryland, $7.75 + (11.55 - 9.63) = 9.67$. Using this assumption, the estimated treatment effect is calculated as $8.81 - 9.67 = -0.86$. This suggests that the right-to-carry law led to a decrease in the murder rate.

Each of these assumptions has its strengths and weaknesses, resulting in different counterfactuals and treatment effect estimates. Policymakers should be aware of the validity of these assumptions and their implications before drawing conclusions or making decisions based on the analysis.

☞ **Discussion.** Which of the three assumptions do you think would be the most reasonable in the context of this study?

The graph presented in Fig. 11.4 reveals that the parallel trend assumption does not hold for the analysis of murder rates in Virginia and Maryland. This contrasts with the earlier figure depicting the trends in banks in business, which provided evidence supporting the parallel trend assumption. In the light of this empirical reality, Manski and Pepper propose the use of less restrictive assumptions and suggest formalizing bounds on the treatment effect. For instance, they propose relaxing the invariance assumptions so we can arrive at an upper and lower bound of the treatment effect, rather than just a point estimate of the treatment effect.

11.2 Concepts and Examples

Fig. 11.4 Murder rates in Virginia (blue line) and Maryland (red line). Virginia enacted a right-to-carry statute in 1989 (vertical dotted line)

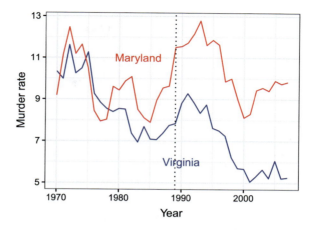

Fig. 11.5 Treatment effect using Maryland crime rates $+1$ (upper bound) and Maryland crime rate -2.7 (lower bound) as counterfactuals

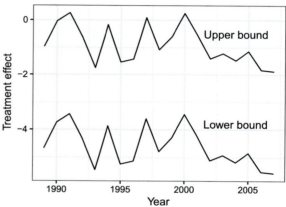

Figure 11.4 illustrates the murder rates over time for Virginia (blue line) and Maryland (red line). Both states display similar overall movement in terms of their trends. They experienced a spike in the murder rates during the early 1970s, followed by a sharp decline in the latter half of the 1970s. However, this decline continued gradually into the 1980s for Virginia, with a few fluctuations along the way. In contrast, Maryland experienced a steeper decline. The disparity continued in the early 1990s, where Maryland's murder rate spiked sharply and was followed by a rapid decrease, contrasting with Virginia's gradual pattern.

While Virginia's and Maryland's murder rates generally exhibit similar trends, there are notable fluctuations within each state. At certain times, Virginia experiences higher levels of murders than Maryland, despite typically having lower rates. In short, the trends are not parallel, and therefore it is important to consider these variations when estimating the treatment effect and ensure that our assumptions align with empirical reality.

The study covers the period from 1970 to 2007. During the years 1970–1989, we observe $Y_{VA}(0)$, and from 1990 to 2007, we observe $Y_{VA}(1)$, the potential outcome with the treatment. In contrast, for Maryland (MD), we only observe $Y_{MD}(0)$ throughout the entire study period.

Manski and Pepper (2018) approach examine a variety of assumptions to estimate the bounds of the effect. We consider just one such assumption on the difference in murder rates between Virginia and Maryland.

Let us define

$$Y_{VA}(0) - Y_{MD}(0) = \delta. \tag{11.3}$$

The value of δ is observed for each year from 1970 to 1989. One assumption is that from 1990 to 2007, δ falls between the values of max(δ from 1970 to 1989) and min(δ from 1970 to 1989), meaning $-2.7 < \delta < 1$. Since $Y_{VA}(0) = Y_{MD}(0) + \delta$, this assumption implies bounds on $Y_{VA}(0)$ and therefore, bounds on the treatment effect, $Y_{VA}(1) - Y_{VA}(0)$.

Figure 11.5 illustrates the upper and lower bounds of the treatment effect for the right-to-carry laws. The upper bound ranges from 0.26 to -1.88, and the lower bound ranges from -3.44 to -5.58.

Using the context of a knotty gun law issue in the US, which exemplifies many intricate policy problems, Manski and Pepper (2018) emphasize that while the use of bounds may not provide a simple and definitive conclusion, they are informative for policymakers as grounded in more realistic assumptions. Policymakers would be better served by relying on informative bounds rather than seeking 'incredible certitudes'.

☞ **Discussion.** Read the Manski and Pepper (2018) paper and reason why previous studies have found contradicting results (sometimes using the same data).

11.2.6 The Synthetic Control Method

11.2.6.1 Economic Costs of German Reunification

Comparative case studies are a cornerstone of empirical research in the field of political science. They involve meticulous examination of a few carefully selected cases to derive insightful inferences about the differences in characteristics and outcomes of the compared groups. However, qualitative methods can be limited by small sample sizes and are not amenable to statistical analysis. On the other hand, larger sample sizes or quantitative data can complement comparative methods by enabling statistical inference. Nonetheless, relying solely on statistical methods present challenges in making causal inferences. This is where the Synthetic Control Method (SCM) comes into play (Abadie et al. 2015).

The SCM has been hailed as a research design that bridges the gap between qualitative and quantitative approaches when investigating cause-and-effect questions in the social sciences. It offers empirical researchers the ability to carefully select comparison units, akin to qualitative methods, in order to reduce biases while still harnessing some of the advantages offered by statistical inference. Abadie et al. (2015) provide a comprehensive overview of the SCM by applying it to study the economic impact of East and West German unification on the regions that constituted West Germany prior to reunification.

The SCM enables researchers to use a systematic and quantitative approach in selecting comparison units, even when working with a few aggregate entities such as states or countries, instead of thousands of individual observations. The selection of comparison units is a critical step in comparative case study research, as it requires making meaningful apples-to-apples comparisons by carefully considering the characteristics of the units being compared. SCM provides a rigorous methodology for choosing comparison units by combining the characteristics of multiple units to create a comparable synthetic unit as a counterfactual to the treated unit.

To illustrate, let's consider estimating the impact of the 1990 German unification on West Germany's economy. Constructing a counterfactual scenario for West Germany involves determining what would have happened to it's economy if the unification had not occurred. However, finding a single country with identical characteristics to preunification West Germany is challenging, making it difficult to establish a valid comparison group. This is a typical problem for many comparative studies.

Here, the SCM comes to the rescue by leveraging the characteristics of multiple countries to create a *Synthetic* West Germany that closely resembles preunification West Germany. Abadie et al. (2015) employed the SCM to construct Synthetic West Germany using a weighted average of several OECD countries, such as Austria, the US, Japan, Switzerland, and the Netherlands. This Synthetic West Germany serves as a reliable counterfactual that enables researchers to estimate the causal impact of German unification on the economy of West Germany.

11.2.6.2 SCM: Under the Hood

Let's take a quick look under the hood to gather the basic intuition of the SCM. We begin with a sample of J+1 units such as countries, where the unit of interest, denoted by j = 1, is the treated unit, and the remaining are the donor pool of control units. Taking the example from the empirical case discussed by the Abadie et al. (2015), West Germany serves as the treated unit, while sixteen OECD countries (including the previously mentioned five) constitute the potential control units. We assume a balanced panel where the units are observed at different points represented as t = 1,..., T. Additionally, there should be an adequate number of preintervention periods, denoted as T_0 as well as an adequate number of postintervention periods, denoted as T_1, resulting in a total of $T = T_0 + T_1$.

To construct a synthetic control, we calculate a weighted average of the donor pool, where the weights ($W = w_1, \ldots, w_{j+1}$) should be equal to or between 0 and 1 ($0 \leq w_j \leq 1, j = 2, \ldots, J$) and they should add up to 1 ($w_2 + \cdots + w_{j+1} = 1$).

Figure 11.7, reproduced from Abadie et al. (2015), shows that applying the SCM estimated weights for OECD countries generated a Synthetic West Germany that closely matches the real West Germany GDP data before the treatment (reunification) in 1990. The graph visually demonstrates that the Synthetic West Germany

Fig. 11.6 Pre- and postunification difference in per capita GDP between West Germany and Synthetic West Germany

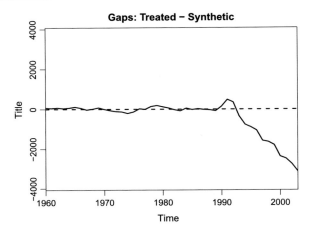

Fig. 11.7 Trends in per Capita GDP

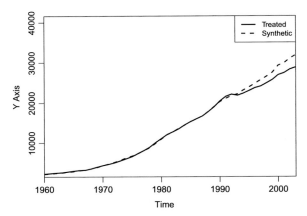

(represented by the dashed line) overlapped with the treated West Germany (represented by the bold line).

Figure 11.6 captures the key elements of the Synthetic Control Method and demonstrates its ability to estimate causal impacts. The figure reveals that by appropriately weighting the donor pool countries, a Synthetic West Germany can be constructed, exhibiting a close match to real West Germany per capita GDP before 1990 (the gap between real and synthetic is nearly zero before the reunification in 1990).

The counterfactual Synthetic West Germany serves as a projection of what the outcome for West Germany would have been without reunification, and it surpassed the actual GDP for West Germany. In the first two years following treatment, the estimated effect is close to zero or even slightly positive, as depicted by the small hill in Fig. 11.6 after 1990. However, over the subsequent decade, the negative impacts of reunification on West Germany become more pronounced, leading to a gap that emerges between the treated West Germany and the Synthetic counterpart. This is evident in the sharp increase in the gap, as illustrated in Fig. 11.6.

11.3 R Code

Figure 11.7 further emphasizes this disparity, with the Synthetic West Germany represented by dashed lines and the actual West Germany depicted in bold, clearly indicating that the actual GDP of West Germany falls below the synthetic values.

☞ **Discussion.** Read the Abadie et al. (2015) paper and explain how the authors conduct placebo studies with SCM.

The authors demonstrate that their main results are robust to changes, such as reduction in the number of donor pool countries. They conclude by emphasizing that the power of the SCM is in its ability to combine certain strengths of quantitative and qualitative approaches and to bridge the gap between them.

11.3 R Code

11.3.1 Worker Injury Benefits and Time Out of Work

Here, we replicate Wooldridge's (2014) presentation of the Meyer, Viscusi, and Durbin paper.

The key variables are

- `afchnge`, which is 1 after the change in worker compensation laws
- `ldurat` which is the log of the duration that a worker is out of work following injury
- `highearn` high earning workers.

We load packages. The data is in the wooldridge package:

```
library(wooldridge)
library(tidyverse)
library(texreg)
data(injury)
```

We first plot boxplots:

```
ggplot(injury, aes(y = factor(afchnge), x = ldurat)) +
    geom_boxplot() + facet_wrap(~highearn)
```

We now plot lines joining the means of the two groups, before and after (Fig. 11.8):

```
ggplot(injury, aes(x = afchnge, y = ldurat,
    col = factor(highearn))) + geom_smooth(method = "lm",
    se = F, linewidth = 2) + theme_bw()
```

We now estimate the DID with regression (Table 11.3):

Fig. 11.8 Boxplots of log of duration before and after change, faceted by low and high earners

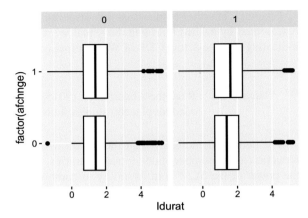

```
mod1 <- lm(ldurat ~ afchnge + highearn +
    I(afchnge * highearn), data = injury)
texreg(list(mod1))
```

11.3.2 Great Depression Policies to Avoid Banking Collapse

In their book Mastering Metrics, Angrist and Pischke simplified the analysis in the original Richardson and Troost, to bring out the key feature of a DID analysis.[5] We will examine the banks in business (outcome variable) and how it is affected by easy lending versus restrictive lending (treatment variable). The easy lending was in the sixth district and restrictive lending was in the eighth district of the Atlanta Fed.

We load the packages and the data. The lubridate package helps us work with date data. The data is in the masteringmetrics package:

```
library(tidyverse)
library(lubridate)
library(masteringmetrics)
data("banks")
glimpse(banks)
## Rows: 1,878
## Columns: 5
## $ date <date> 1929-07-01, 1929-07-02, ~
## $ bib6 <int> 141, 141, 141, 141, 141, ~
## $ bio6 <int> 141, 141, 141, 141, 141, ~
## $ bib8 <int> 169, 169, 169, 169, 169, ~
## $ bio8 <int> 169, 169, 169, 169, 169, ~
```

---

[5] Richardson and Troost work with daily data, and their's is a very detailed analysis. Angrist and Pischke aggregate the data or rather find the means over years, and then proceed, so that it helps simplify, but the essence of the analysis comes through.

11.3 R Code

In the banks data, we have the date and the banks in business in the sixth (`bib6`) and the eighth district (`bib8`). We create a year variable with the mutate function:

```
banks2 <- banks %>%
    mutate(year = year(date))
head(banks2)
## # A tibble: 6 x 6
##   date         bib6  bio6  bib8  bio8
##   <date>      <int> <int> <int> <int>
## 1 1929-07-01   141   141   169   169
## 2 1929-07-02   141   141   169   169
## 3 1929-07-03   141   141   169   169
## 4 1929-07-04   141   141   169   169
## 5 1929-07-05   141   141   169   169
## 6 1929-07-06   141   141   169   169
## # ... with 1 more variable: year <dbl>
```

Now that we have created the head variable, we will use the summarize function to create the mean number of banks in business each year in the sixth and eighth districts:

```
bankag <- banks2 %>%
    group_by(year) %>%
    summarize(bib6m = mean(bib6), bib8m = mean(bib8))
head(bankag)
## # A tibble: 6 x 3
##    year bib6m bib8m
##   <dbl> <dbl> <dbl>
## 1  1929   141  170.
## 2  1930   136.  165.
## 3  1931   120.  132.
## 4  1932   113.  120.
## 5  1933   105.  112.
## 6  1934   102   110.
```

We now 'gather' the banks in business into one column:

```
bankag2 <- gather(bankag, "btype", "number",
    2:3)
head(bankag2)
## # A tibble: 6 x 3
##    year btype  number
##   <dbl> <chr>   <dbl>
## 1  1929 bib6m    141
## 2  1930 bib6m    136.
## 3  1931 bib6m    120.
## 4  1932 bib6m    113.
## 5  1933 bib6m    105.
## 6  1934 bib6m    102
```

We filter the data for the years 1930 and 1931, which are our 'before' and 'after' years:

```
bankag2 %>%
    filter(year == 1930 | year == 1931)
## # A tibble: 4 x 3
##    year  btype number
##    <dbl> <chr>  <dbl>
## 1  1930  bib6m   136.
## 2  1931  bib6m   120.
## 3  1930  bib8m   165.
## 4  1931  bib8m   132.
```

Our DID estimate can be calculated from the output: $(120 - 136) - (132 - 165) = 17$ (see p. 183 mastering metrics).

We visually inspect the data to see whether the parallel trend assumption appears to hold (see p. 185, Mastering Metrics):

```
ggplot(bankag2, aes(x = year, y = number,
    col = btype)) + geom_point() + geom_line() +
    theme_bw()
```

The lines before 1930 and after 1931 are parallel, with a distinct dip in the eighth district relative to the sixth district between 1930 and 1931.

11.3.3 Informative Bounds on the Effect of Right-to-Carry Gun Laws

R code to produce plots

```
library(tidyverse)
Manski <- read_csv("Manski.csv")
```

The key variables are

- `V_mur`: the murder rate in Virginia.
- `M_mur`: the murder rate in Maryland.
- `Year`: the year.

```
ggplot(Manski) + geom_line(aes(x = Year,
    y = V_mur), col = "blue") + geom_line(aes(x = Year,
    y = M_mur), col = "red") + geom_vline(xintercept = 1989,
    linetype = "dotted") + ylab("Murder rate") +
    theme_bw() + annotate("text", x = 1990,
    y = 6, label = "Virginia", col = "blue") +
```

11.3 R Code

```
annotate("text", x = 1983, y = 11, label = "Maryland",
    col = "red")
```

```
ggplot(Manski[20:38, ]) + geom_line(aes(x = Year,
    y = V_mur - M_mur - 1)) + geom_line(aes(x = Year,
    y = V_mur - M_mur + 2.7)) + ylab("Treatment effect") +
    theme_bw() + annotate("text", x = 2004,
    y = -0.5, label = "Upper bound") + annotate("text",
    x = 2004, y = -3.8, label = "Lower bound")
```

11.3.4 Economic Costs of German Reunification

We load packages. The journal webpage for Abadie et al. (2015) provides a link to the data:

```
rm(list = ls())
library(foreign)
library(Synth)
library(xtable)
library(tidyverse)
```

We read in the data. The Synth package performs the computations, and has been created by the authors:

```
d <- read.dta("repgermany.dta")
glimpse(d)
## Rows: 748
## Columns: 11
## $ index     <dbl> 1, 1, 1, 1, 1, 1, 1,~
## $ country   <chr> "USA", "USA", "USA",~
## $ year      <dbl> 1960, 1961, 1962, 19~
## $ gdp       <int> 2879, 2929, 3103, 32~
## $ infrate   <dbl> NA, 1.075182, 1.1160~
## $ trade     <dbl> 9.693181, 9.444654, ~
## $ schooling <dbl> 43.8, NA, NA, NA, NA~
## $ invest60  <dbl> NA, NA, NA, NA, NA, ~
## $ invest70  <dbl> NA, NA, NA, NA, NA, ~
## $ invest80  <dbl> NA, NA, NA, NA, NA, ~
## $ industry  <dbl> NA, NA, NA, NA, NA, ~
```

Here, we follow the paper on the synth package (Abadie et al. 2011). As a result, the results we get are slightly different from those in Abadie et al. (2015). We need to use the dataprep function to provide the data to the synth function.

The data is for different countries (16 OECD members) including Germany for the years 1960–2003. The outcome variable is real per capita GDP (Purchasing Power Parity, 2002 US Dollars):

```
dataprep.out <- dataprep(foo = d, predictors = c("gdp",
    "trade", "infrate"), dependent = "gdp",
    unit.variable = 1, time.variable = 3,
    special.predictors = list(list("industry",
        1981:1990, c("mean")), list("schooling",
        c(1980, 1985), c("mean")), list("invest80",
        1980, c("mean"))), treatment.identifier = 7,
    controls.identifier = unique(d$index)[-7],
    time.predictors.prior = 1981:1990, time.optimize.ssr = 1960:1989,
    unit.names.variable = 2, time.plot = 1960:2003)
##
## Missing data: treated unit; special predictor: special.industry.1981.1990 ;
for period: 1990
##  We ignore (na.rm = TRUE) all missing values for predictors.op.
# dataprep.out
```

We now fit the model to find the weights for the different candidate control countries:

```
synth.out <- synth(data.prep.obj = dataprep.out,
    method = "BFGS")
```

```
synth.tables <- synth.tab(dataprep.res = dataprep.out,
    synth.res = synth.out)
names(synth.tables)
## [1] "tab.pred" "tab.v"    "tab.w"
## [4] "tab.loss"
```

We now use the output to prepare a table that gives us the weights for the different control countries:

```
library(knitr)
library(kableExtra)
kbl(synth.tables$tab.w, booktabs = T, format = "latex",
    caption = "Synthetic weights for West Germany")
```

Table 11.4 shows that Austria, Switzerland, and the USA get the largest weights. Further, we can tabulate the predictions, as in Table 11.5:

```
kbl(synth.tables$tab.pred[, 1:2], booktabs = T,
    caption = "Germany and Predictions of synthetic Germany")
```

We can also tabulate the gaps over time, as in Table 11.6:

```
gaps <- dataprep.out$Y1plot - (dataprep.out$Y0plot %*%
    synth.out$solution.w)
```

11.3 R Code

Table 11.3 Statistical models

	Model 1
(Intercept)	1.20***
	(0.03)
afchnge	0.02
	(0.04)
highearn	0.22***
	(0.04)
afchnge * highearn	0.19**
	(0.06)
R^2	0.02
Adj. R^2	0.02
Num. obs.	7150

***$p < 0.001$; **$p < 0.01$; *$p < 0.05$

Table 11.4 Synthetic weights for West Germany

	w.weights	unit.names	unit.numbers
1	0.152	USA	1
2	0.051	UK	2
3	0.432	Austria	3
4	0.006	Belgium	4
5	0.006	Denmark	5
6	0.008	France	6
8	0.010	Italy	8
9	0.007	Netherlands	9
10	0.027	Norway	10
12	0.189	Switzerland	12
14	0.076	Japan	14
16	0.006	Greece	16
18	0.005	Portugal	18
19	0.007	Spain	19
20	0.010	Australia	20
21	0.008	New Zealand	21

```
kbl(data.frame(gap = gaps[21:44, 1]), booktabs = T,
    caption = "Gaps between Germany and synthetic Germany")
```

The gaps can be plotted as in Fig. 11.1. Figure 11.1 here corresponds to Fig. 11.3 in the paper. We see that prior to 1990 the gap between Germany and the synthetic controls is negligible, and afterwards the gap increases, with German unification resulting in a negative impact:

Table 11.5 Germany and predictions of Synthetic Germany

	Treated	Synthetic
gdp	15808.900	15807.087
trade	56.778	59.595
infrate	2.595	4.239
special.industry.1981.1990	34.538	34.435
special.schooling.1980.1985	55.500	54.116
special.invest80.1980	27.018	27.025

Table 11.6 Gaps between Germany and Synthetic Germany

	gap
1980	120.97579
1981	59.57323
1982	−29.05954
1983	−85.61341
1984	53.76256
1985	−18.37646
1986	22.05303
1987	−14.25173
1988	−31.88383
1989	−81.39593
1990	143.32262
1991	486.15077
1992	354.91962
1993	−353.54513
1994	−773.01810
1995	−899.40679
1996	−1067.36098
1997	−1580.19887
1998	−1639.64325
1999	−1796.52849
2000	−2372.75331
2001	−2483.31150
2002	−2754.86035
2003	−3134.11884

```
gaps.plot(synth.res = synth.out, dataprep.res = dataprep.out)
```

We can plot the evolution of the outcome as in Fig. 11.2. Figure 11.2 here corresponds to Fig. 11.4 in the paper:

```
path.plot(synth.res = synth.out, dataprep.res = dataprep.out)
```

For inference, the code requires a loop and running the estimation several times. Then, a distribution is generated. We refer the reader to the R code that accompanies the paper.

11.4 Resources

11.4.1 For Understanding Better

Chapter on DID in the book *The Effect: An Introduction to Research Design and Causality* by Huntington-Klein (2021).

11.4.2 For Going Further

Manski and Pepper's (2018) paper on Right-to-Carry Laws.

Packages Used in This Chapter

The citations for the packages used in this chapter are[6]

```
## Abadie A, Diamond A, Hainmueller J (2011). "Synth: An R
## Package for Synthetic Control Methods in Comparative Case
## Studies." _Journal of Statistical Software_, *42*(13), 1-17.
## <URL: https://www.jstatsoft.org/v42/i13/>.


## Arnold J (2022). _masteringmetrics: Datasets for Mastering
## 'Metrics_. R package version 0.1, <URL:
## https://github.com/jrnold/masteringmetrics>.


## Dahl D, Scott D, Roosen C, Magnusson A, Swinton J (2019).
## _xtable: Export Tables to LaTeX or HTML_. R package version
## 1.8-4, <URL: https://CRAN.R-project.org/package=xtable>.
```

---

[6] The tidyverse package itself contains several packages.

```
## Grolemund G, Wickham H (2011). "Dates and Times Made Easy with
## lubridate." _Journal of Statistical Software_, *40*(3), 1-25.
## <URL: https://www.jstatsoft.org/v40/i03/>.


## Leifeld P (2013). "texreg: Conversion of Statistical Model
## Output in R to LaTeX and HTML Tables." _Journal of Statistical
## Software_, *55*(8), 1-24. <URL:
## http://dx.doi.org/10.18637/jss.v055.i08>.


## Makowski D, Lüdecke D, Patil I, Thériault R, Ben-Shachar M,
## Wiernik B (2023). "Automated Results Reporting as a Practical
## Tool to Improve Reproducibility and Methodological Best
## Practices Adoption." _CRAN_. <URL:
## https://easystats.github.io/report/>.


## R Core Team (2021). _R: A Language and Environment for
## Statistical Computing_. R Foundation for Statistical
## Computing, Vienna, Austria. <URL: https://www.R-project.org/>.


## R Core Team (2022). _foreign: Read Data Stored by 'Minitab',
## 'S', 'SAS', 'SPSS', 'Stata', 'Systat', 'Weka', 'dBase', ..._.
## R package version 0.8-82, <URL:
## https://CRAN.R-project.org/package=foreign>.


## Spinu V (2022). _timechange: Efficient Manipulation of
## Date-Times_. R package version 0.1.1, <URL:
## https://CRAN.R-project.org/package=timechange>.


## Wickham H, Averick M, Bryan J, Chang W, McGowan LD, François
## R, Grolemund G, Hayes A, Henry L, Hester J, Kuhn M, Pedersen
## TL, Miller E, Bache SM, Müller K, Ooms J, Robinson D, Seidel
## DP, Spinu V, Takahashi K, Vaughan D, Wilke C, Woo K, Yutani H
## (2019). "Welcome to the tidyverse." _Journal of Open Source
## Software_, *4*(43), 1686. doi: 10.21105/joss.01686 (URL:
## https://doi.org/10.21105/joss.01686).


## Xie Y (2022). _knitr: A General-Purpose Package for Dynamic
## Report Generation in R_. R package version 1.41, <URL:
## https://yihui.org/knitr/>.
```

```
## Xie Y (2023). _formatR: Format R Code Automatically_. R
## package version 1.14, <URL:
## https://CRAN.R-project.org/package=formatR>.
```

References

Abadie, A., A. Diamond, and J. Hainmueller. 2011. Synth: An R Package for Synthetic Control Methods in Comparative Case Studies. *Journal of Statistical Software* 42: 1–17.

Abadie, A., A. Diamond, and J. Hainmueller. 2015. Comparative Politics and the Synthetic Control Method. *American Journal of Political Science* 59 (2): 495–510. https://onlinelibrary.wiley.com/doi/pdf/10.1111/ajps.12116

Angrist, J.D., J.-S. Pischke, and J.-S. Pischke. 2015. *Mastering 'Metrics*. Princeton; Oxford: Princeton University Press.

Galiani, S., P. Gertler, and E. Schargrodsky. 2005. Water for Life: The Impact of the Privatization of Water Services on Child Mortality. *Journal of Political Economy* 113 (1): 83–120.

Huntington-Klein, N. 2021. *The Effect: An Introduction to Research Design and Causality*, 1st ed. Boca Raton: Chapman and Hall/CRC.

Jalil, A.J. 2014. Monetary Intervention Really Did Mitigate Banking Panics During the Great Depression: Evidence Along the Atlanta Federal Reserve District Border. *The Journal of Economic History* 74 (1): 259–273. Publisher: [Economic History Association, Cambridge University Press].

Manski, C.F., and J.V. Pepper. 2018. How Do Right-to-Carry Laws Affect Crime Rates? Coping with Ambiguity Using Bounded-Variation Assumptions. *The Review of Economics and Statistics* 100 (2): 232–244.

Meyer, B.D., W.K. Viscusi, and D.L. Durbin. 1995. Workers' Compensation and Injury Duration: Evidence from a Natural Experiment. *The American Economic Review* 85 (3): 322–340.

Reinhart, C.M., and K.S. Rogoff. 2011. *This Time Is Different: Eight Centuries of Financial Folly*. Reprint. Princeton, NJ: Princeton University Press.

Richardson, G., and W. Troost. 2009. Monetary Intervention Mitigated Banking Panics during the Great Depression: Quasi-Experimental Evidence from a Federal Reserve District Border, 1929–1933. *Journal of Political Economy* 117 (6): 1031–1073. Publisher: The University of Chicago Press.

Rosenbaum, P. 2017. *Observation and Experiment: An Introduction to Causal Inference*. Cambridge, Massachusetts; London, England: Harvard University Press.

Snow, John. 1855. On the Mode of Communication of Cholera (J. Churchill, 2nd Ed, London), pp. 1–162.

Wooldridge, J.M. 2014. *Introductory Econometrics A Modern Approach*, 5th ed. Mason, Ohio: Cenage Learning.

Integrating and Generalizing Causal Estimates

12.1 Introduction

Researchers around the globe conduct a large number of policy-relevant studies. As a result, the work on integrating and generalizing studies has grown rapidly in recent years. This literature uses diverse approaches, and is published in technical form in journals. In Sect. 12.2, we provide a simplified non-technical overview. In Sect. 12.3, we provide R code for (1) simulation to get a feel for the concepts and (2) estimation with real data. We begin with meta-analysis, which is well-established and widely practiced. We then consider analyses guided by the potential outcomes framework and causal graphs.

In this chapter, we consider questions of the following sort:

- We have some studies that estimate effects. How do we sum them up? We can first examine the estimates (and confidence intervals) produced by the studies. Further, we can use a statistical model to summarize the distribution of the effects estimated in different studies.
- We have a specific target population in mind. For that target population, what are the possible effects of an intervention? We have some data related to the target population. Should we only choose experiments or also consider observational studies? How can we define internal and external validity, using the potential outcomes framework? How can we generalize an estimate from an experiment to a target population? How do causal graphs help us navigate these issues?

12.2 Concepts and Examples

12.2.1 Statistical Approach

Meta-analysis flowered in the 1990s. Meta-analysis generalizes effects, but is not limited to causal effects. Often, meta-analysis generalizes causal effects from clinical trials.

12.2.1.1 Meta-Analysis and the BCG Vaccine

Several books explain meta-analysis in an accessible manner (for example, Borenstein et al. 2021). We select studies carefully, and then use the effects from these studies. We display the effects and their confidence intervals in a 'forest plot'. We then use a statistical model to estimate an overall effect. We give more weight to studies with high precision and less to studies with low precision.[1]

COVID-19 drew attention to the importance of vaccines. The BCG vaccine was developed to tackle tuberculosis (TB), and has been used since 1921. In the United States, tuberculosis cases fell from 1953 to 1986. The downward trend reversed from 1986. Also, there was an increase in drug-resistant tuberculosis. Experts debated the effectiveness of the BCG vaccine. This motivated Colditz et al. (1994) to carry out a meta-analysis.

Colditz et al. (1994) meticulously detail the inclusion criteria, as well as the process they followed in selecting clinical trials examining the effectiveness of the BCG vaccine. A total of 1264 titles or abstracts were looked through to locate studies that might be included. They then selected case-control studies and clinical trials. Here, we concentrate on the meta-analysis based on selected clinical trials.

Figure 12.1 shows the forest plot of the different studies. In the first row in Fig. 12.1, we see that the Aronson study conducted in 1948 estimated the **risk ratio** as 0.41, with a 95% confidence interval of (0.13, 1.26). The risk ratio is a ratio of ratios. How was it calculated in the Aronson study? Among the 123 people who received the BCG vaccine 4 got TB, whereas among the 139 people who did not receive the BCG vaccine 11 got TB. The risk ratio, a ratio of ratios, equals 0.41 (4/123 divided by 11/129). The forest plot reports the risk ratio and the confidence interval in the right-most column. The center of the forest plot graphs the estimated risk ratios and confidence intervals. In the first row, the square in the center of the line shows the estimated risk ratio of 0.41. The line in the center spans the confidence interval. We can visually compare different studies by looking at the forest plot. We can see that most of the studies have effect sizes that are less than one with a few having effect sizes close to one.

The Comstock and Weber study conducted in 1969 had an effect size that was 1.56. We also notice that the TPT Madras study effect is on the line indicating

---

[1] Denoting individual studies by i, the observed effect sizes by y_i, and the latent effect sizes by δ_i, the y_i are assumed to be distributed as $N(\delta_i, \sigma_i^2)$. The δ_i are assumed to have a distribution with mean μ and variance τ^2: $N(\mu, \tau^2)$ (Williams et al. 2018).

12.2 Concepts and Examples

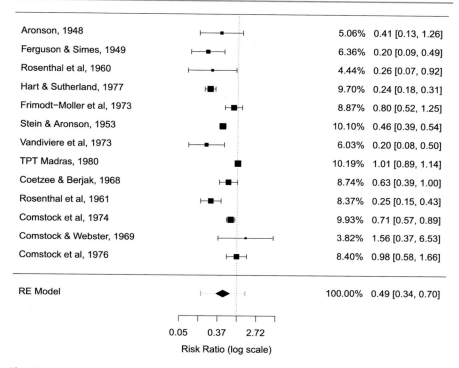

Fig. 12.1 Forest plot for BCG vaccine. Each row corresponds to a study. The first column on the left lists the studies. Estimated risk ratios and 95% confidence intervals are plotted next to that column. To the right of that, we have the weights given to each study. The last column on the right has the numbers corresponding to the estimated effects and the 95% confidence interval. The last row under the line going across has the Random Effects (RE) model estimates. See the text for how a risk ratio is calculated

a risk ratio of 1. Regarding the Madras study, Colditz et al. (1994, pp. 696–697) write, "Confidence in the efficacy of BCG vaccine was rocked by the results of the Madras trial in which BCG vaccine failed to show any benefit against pulmonary TB. Critics of the trial point out that follow-up was at 2.5 year intervals, case detection in children was based entirely on symptoms of cough followed by sputum examination, and peak incidence was not in the usual young age group but in older individuals." Such debates and observations had, as noted earlier, motivated the meta-analysis.

An overall effect size is reported from a 'random effects' model, and is graphically shown by a diamond. Because we think the studies in a meta-analysis are similar (but not exactly the same), we include them in the analysis. Each study incorporates a range of factors, such as the setting of the study, and characteristics of the sample. Hence, the effect sizes in various research studies may differ. We use a random effects model and get an estimated confidence interval for the overall effect (relative risk of 0.49, 95% CI, 0.34 to 0.70). The confidence interval for the overall effect is much narrower than for the original studies. The 95% prediction interval lies between 0.15

and 1.55, and this tells us about the range in which the effect in a future study may fall (Borenstein et al. 2021).

12.2.1.2 Bayesian Meta-Analysis and Beta Blocker

Another similar approach is Bayesian meta-analysis. Once again, the effects in different studies are viewed as neither totally distinct nor totally similar. Probability is seen as an uncertainty rather than a frequency in the Bayesian method. The mean effect size and the standard deviation of genuine effect size are not fixed numbers but have probability distributions.[2] Also, we assign prior probability distributions to the parameters. The analysis creates a posterior probability distribution by combining the prior distribution with the data. Gelman et al. (2013) observe that Bayesian methods are being used increasingly, since we can interpret the results in a common-sense manner.

Gelman et al. (2013) illustrate Bayesian meta-analysis using the data from a study by Yusuf et al. (1985). The original study by Yusuf et al. (1985) was a meta-analysis of 22 clinical trials examining the effects of beta blockers after heart attacks.

The R package baggr was used with the data in Yusuf et al. (1985) to carry out the Bayesian meta-analysis as reported by Gelman et al. (2013). Most of the studies showed a modest reduction in mortality from the use of beta blockers (Fig. 12.2). The posterior distribution for possible treatment effects is displayed in Fig. 12.3. We get a median predicted effect of -0.25, with a 2.5 percentile value of -0.58 and a 97.5 percentile value of 0.11.

12.2.2 Analyses Guided by the Potential Outcomes Framework

Several researchers have contributed to a literature that examines the issue of extending causal estimates to a target population, using a potential outcomes approach. We begin with Manski (2020), who has used the potential outcomes framework along with partial identification to suggest ways to conduct meta-analysis.

12.2.2.1 Manski Bounds and Blood Pressure

Manski (2020) suggests that patients, not studies, should be the units of analysis in meta-analysis.[3] He also raises the issue of internal and external validity. Manski illustrates with the example of the effects of medication on blood pressure in the American population. The National Health and Nutrition Examination Survey (NHANES) is an ongoing survey assessing the health status of people in America. The NHANES data has information on blood pressure and medication. However,

---

[2] The setup is as in the random effects model, but, in addition, (μ, and τ^2) have prior distributions, and $\tau^2 > 0$ (Williams et al. 2018).
[3] According to him, the clinician may want to know $E(y(t)|x_0)$, where t is one of the treatments, y(t) is the potential outcome, and x_0 represents the clinically observed covariates of the patient '0'.

12.2 Concepts and Examples

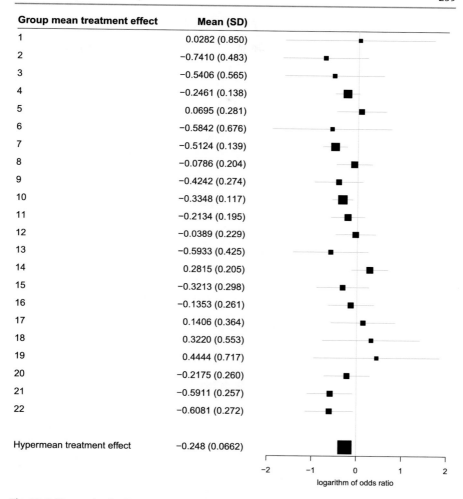

Fig. 12.2 Forest plot for Bayesian meta-analysis of beta blocker

this data poses the issue of non-random assignment of treatment effects, so a simple difference of means will not be an internally valid estimate.

Manski focused on people older than 60 years of age, using data from 2007 to 2016. Manski calculated the lower and upper bounds of medication's effect on blood pressure without making any assumptions about the treatment selection process.[4] He obtained the following bounds for mean systolic blood pressure with and without treatment: [133.4, 138.2] and [103.2, 179.6]. Given that no assumptions are made about the treatment selection process, the bound with treatment is quite narrow (Fig. 12.4).

---

[4] We discussed an example using Manski bounds in the potential outcomes chapter.

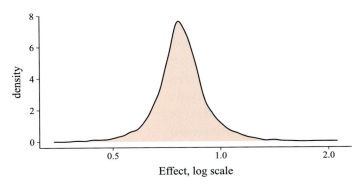

Fig. 12.3 Bayesian meta-analysis of beta blocker

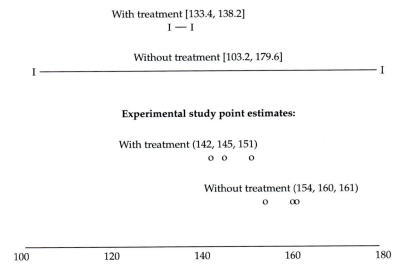

Fig. 12.4 Effect of medication on systolic blood pressure. Survey data bounds (above), and experimental study point estimates (below)

Manski criticizes the expert group that developed high blood pressure management guidelines. The expert group, the Eighth Joint National Committee (JNC 8), highlighted three trials. The point estimates of these trials are displayed in Fig. 12.4. Although these trials may have strong internal validity, they have imperfect external validity. Many aspects such as age and country of the subjects in these experiments were different from those of the American population. Hence the external validity for the American population is limited.

12.2.2.2 Target Validity: Internal and External Validity

Causal inference today is marked by a great deal of concern about validity, internal and external. These terms suggest validity within and external to a study, and are intuitive. It is useful to be specific about them. Westreich et al. (2019) use the potential outcomes framework to clarify these two types of validity.

Westreich et al. (2019, p. 438) write that a result is internally valid "when the effect *estimated* in the study sample is unbiased for the *true effect* in the sample." (Emphasis in original). According to them, a result is externally valid "if the true effect in the study sample is unbiased for the true effect in the target population." They suggest a combined metric for internal and external validity, which they call 'target validity'.

Validity is reduced when we have bias. We consider a case where our target population is the population from which the sample is drawn. Target validity bias = internal validity bias + external validity bias.

According to Westreich et al. (2019), internal validity bias = true causal effect in the sample − estimated causal effect in the sample. In potential outcomes notation, we can express this as $BIAS_I = [E(Y(1)|S = 1) - E(Y(0)|S = 1)] - [\hat{E}(Y|A = 1, S = 1) - \hat{E}(Y|A = 0, S = 1)]$. Y(1) and Y(0) are potential outcomes, and A is treatment. Here S = 1 indicates that the unit is in the sample.

External validity bias = true causal effect in the target population − true causal effect in the study population. In potential outcomes notation, the equation above can be expressed as $BIAS_E = [E(Y(1)) - E(Y(0))] - [E(Y(1)|S = 1) - E(Y(0)|S = 1)]$.

Internal and external validity are related to random sampling and random treatment assignment. If a study uses random treatment assignment, then it is expected to have high internal validity. If a study uses random sampling, then it is expected to have high external validity. A study could have both high internal validity bias and high external validity bias. From a policy point of view, we need low target validity bias.

12.2.2.3 Generalizing Experiments and Surgery

Westreich (2020) offers a straightforward illustration of generalizability. In a randomized experiment, suppose there are 75% men and 25% women participants. We get an overall risk difference in the randomized experiment of −12.5% if the risk difference is −15% for males and −5% for women. However, a risk difference estimate of −10% is obtained if the proportion of males and women in our target group is equal. We reweight the risk difference for men and women. The randomized experiment gives us a good estimate of the sample average treatment effect (SATE). We need to reweight the estimate to get the target population average treatment estimate (TPATE).

Following Devaux and Egami (2022), the SATE is

$$SATE = E[Y_i(1) - Y_i(0); \text{sample}]. \tag{12.1}$$

The TPATE is

$$\text{TPATE} = E[Y_i(1) - Y_i(0); \text{target population}]. \quad (12.2)$$

Devaux and Egami (2022) highlight two conditions for the identification of the TPATE.
The first is ignorability of sampling and treatment effect heterogeneity:

$$E[Y_i(1) - Y_i(0)|X_i = x; \text{sample}] = E[Y_i(1) - Y_i(0)|X_i = x; \text{population}] \quad (12.3)$$

where X represents the pre-treatment covariates.

The second is overlap. For any X that is in the population, its probability of being in the sample is positive.

In practice, we can use different methods to conduct such a generalization of an experiment. An application is the generalization of the coronary artery surgery study by Dahabreh et al. (2019). For those with chronic arterial disease, coronary artery bypass surgery combined with medical therapy was compared to medical therapy alone in the study. For the randomized participants, the risk difference was -2.7%, with a 95% confidence interval (CI) of $(-8.5, 3.0)$. Using an outcome model, the risk difference for the target population was -1.5% with a 95% CI of $(-7.2, 4.2)$.

12.2.2.4 External Robustness of Experiments and Health Insurance

Although we have seen that we can estimate the average treatment impact for the target group, we may not always be able to. Even if we have a certain target audience in mind, we may not have statistics on that target population. Devaux and Egami (2022) developed a measure of external robustness. Their measure indicates how different a population would have to be from the sample to explain away the population treatment effect. If the estimated external robustness is high, unless the population we are generalizing to is very different, the estimated causal effect remains similar. Devaux and Egami's (2022) measure of external robustness lies between 0 and 1. Higher values indicate greater external robustness.

To connect external robustness to the Westreich (2020) example used above, think of a study sample in a randomized experiment where we have a certain proportion of men and women, and we estimate the risk difference. The risk difference is positive for men and negative for women, there are more men than women in the sample, and the overall risk difference is positive. Yet, if the population proportion of men and women is different, if we have more women than men, we may no longer have a positive risk difference. If even a small difference in the proportion of men and women in the sample and the population changes the sign of the result when we generalize from the sample to the population, we have low external robustness.

For example, in the case of health insurance, Devaux and Egami (2022) present an application of their approach to the study by Domurat et al. (2021). They investigated the impact of reminder letters on household health insurance enrollment. In the experimental study, the estimated mean difference was 1.3% points (95% CI = [0.8, 1.7]). The external robustness of the study by Domurat et al. (2021) was low,

12.2 Concepts and Examples

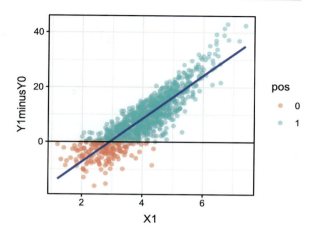

Fig. 12.5 External robustness. Simulated data for the variation of $Y(1) - Y(0)$ (difference in potential outcomes) (on the Y-axis) with a covariate X1 (on the X-axis). We see that for values of $X1 > 4$, there are far more positive values of $Y(1) - Y(0)$ than for $X1 < 4$

0.18. This means the generalizability of the study is low. Devaux and Egami (2022) explain their measure in detail; in a later section, we use simulation to get a feel for this approach to external robustness.

Figure 12.5 shows simulated data for the variation of $Y(1) - Y(0)$ (difference in potential outcomes) (on the Y-axis) with a covariate X1 (on the X-axis). We see that for values of $X1 > 4$, there are far more positive values of $Y(1) - Y(0)$ than for $X1 < 4$. $Y(1) - Y(0)$ also varies with another covariate X2. If the distribution of X1 and X2 is different in the population, the SATE and the TPATE will differ.

12.2.3 Analyses Guided by Causal Graphs

Bareinboim and Pearl (2016) present a unified conceptual approach to causal analysis. They address such issues as confounding, selection bias, generalizability, transportability, and data fusion.

A remarkable R package dosearch implements the unified causal approach to causal analysis presented in Bareinboim and Pearl (2016). The user needs to input a causal graph, indicate what data is available, and ask a query. The dosearch package helps us find the adjustment formula, for a variety of scenarios. In a later section, we present the R code to use dosearch.

12.2.3.1 Selection into Experiment

We will consider a simple example. We start with a causal graph (Fig. 12.6). We have a selection variable S that shows that the sample differs from the population in terms of the variable W.

We have (1) observed data on w, which provides information on the distribution of w in the population, p(w), and (2) we have an experimental dataset, with random assignment of x, and with w as a covariate, in which the selection variable s depends on w, which in symbols is $p(y, w|s, do(x))$. What is $do(x)$? In an experiment, we actively intervene and are not passively observing but *doing*, and we express this in

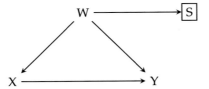

Fig. 12.6 Selection into experiment. We are interested in the effect of X on Y in the target population. We have a selection variable S that shows that the sample differs from the population from which it is drawn in terms of the variable W

Fig. 12.7 Selection into experiment, but with intermediate variable W affecting selection S. We are interested in the effect of X on Y in the target population

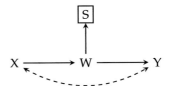

symbols as do(x), where x is the treatment. We are interested in $p(y|do(x))$ which is the effect of x on y in the population. After receiving the required inputs from us, the dosearch package provides the relevant adjustment formula:

$$p(y|do(x)) = \sum_w (p(w)p(y|do(x), w, s)). \qquad (12.4)$$

Equation 12.4 is the nonparametric adjustment formula. We need to reweight our experimental results to take into account the differing distribution of w in the population. This adjustment formula is widely used when generalizing an experimental study to its population. Pearl (2015, p. 263) writes "the re-calibration formula goes back to eighteenth century demographers facing the task of predicting overall mortality (across populations) from age-specific data."

Let us consider a different scenario. Now the selection into the experiment is based on a variable that lies on the causal path between treatment and response (Fig. 12.7).

After receiving the required inputs from us, the dosearch package provides the relevant adjustment formula:

$$p(y|do(x)) = \sum_w (p(w|x)p(y|do(x), w, s)). \qquad (12.5)$$

The adjustment formula is different in the scenario represented by Fig. 12.7 compared to the scenario represent by Fig. 12.6. Compare Eqs. 12.4 and 12.5. Thus, what the causal graphs literature shows is that in different scenarios we would have to use a different adjustment formula. We cannot always use the well-known and often-used adjustment formula in Eq. (12.4) and moreover, in some scenarios, we may not achieve identification.

12.2 Concepts and Examples

12.2.3.2 Causal Graphs and Data Fusion for Salt and Blood Pressure

We may at times have different studies that provide separate information on two parts: (1) the effect of X on Z and (2) the effect of Z on Y. How do we get the effect of an intervention of X on Y? This is the task of data fusion (Bareinboim and Pearl 2016). Further, what if the effect of X on Z is available from a survey and the effect of Z on Y is available from experiments? Karvanen et al. (2021) looked at the effect of salt-adding behavior on blood pressure by combining estimates of (1) the effect of salt-adding behavior on salt in the body from survey data and (2) the effect of salt in the body on blood pressure from a meta-analysis of experimental studies (Fig. 12.8). Karvanen et al. (2020, p. 11) found that "a regular salt user (salt score 6) with hypertension could reduce his or her sodium intake by 7.9 mmol (0.46 g, equals 1.2 g of salt) and systolic blood pressure by 3.0 mmHg on average by discontinuing the use of salt in preparation and at table."

12.2.3.3 Causal Graphs and Implementation Issues in HIV Management

A study may investigate the causal effects of a program. If the program is now implemented in a different population, the program effects will depend on the context, but in what ways? Mehrotra et al. (2019) have examined this issue in the case of setting up community adherence groups (CAGs) for HIV management. In the case of HIV treatment, CAGs aim to reduce congestion and improve retention in care. Whether CAGs work or not depends on context, and context will always vary. How transportable is our knowledge of such interventions?

Mehrotra et al. (2019) take the case of community interventions for HIV where those infected get support to stay on in therapy. They consider a detailed causal graph that shows different variables that lie on the path between treatment and outcome, from CAG to Mortality. They indicate differences between the variables in the experiment and the population within which it may be implemented.

We simplify their causal graph. In Fig. 12.9, we are considering the effect of CAG on mortality. CAG affects mortality via retention in care. There are unobserved common causes of CAG and retention. A randomized trial gives us an estimate of the causal effect of CAG on mortality. Distance to clinic affects both CAG and retention in care. Socioeconomic status affects both retention in care and mortality.

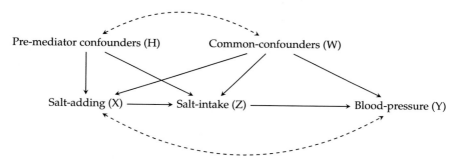

Fig. 12.8 Data fusion for salt and blood pressure. We are interested in the effect of X on Y, and have studies for the effect of X on Z, and Z on Y

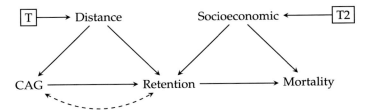

Fig. 12.9 Simplified selection diagram for HIV. A prior study has estimated the causal effect of community adherence groups (CAG) on mortality. Now CAG will be implemented in a different population. While transporting the results of the study, we have to see which variables will have different distributions in the study and the population. T and T2 point to Distance to clinics and Socioeconomic variables that are different in the population in which the intervention will be implemented

Variables like distance and socioeconomic status characterize 'context' and are likely to differ between the study sample and the population in which the intervention will be implemented. We use the square nodes T and T2 to show how the study sample and the intervention population may differ.

We would like to transport the estimates to a different population with different distance and socioeconomic variables. The adjustment formula for the scenario in Fig. 12.9 would be more intricate than for the simpler cases in Figs. 12.6 and 12.7. We have only presented a simplified version of the causal graph that they develop. In Mehrotra et al.'s (2019) paper, the causal graph is far more detailed, with more context brought in. Using a causal graph gives us a qualitative sense of possible issues in implementation. It is a useful tool to help us think about how the effects of the program after implementation in a different population will possibly differ from those estimated in the study.

12.3 R Code

12.3.1 Statistical Approach

12.3.1.1 Simulation for Meta-Analysis

We first generate synthetic data and then conduct a meta-analysis to get an intuitive feel for meta-analysis.

We use the metafor package. The metafor package has very detailed and comprehensive documentation:

```
library(metafor)
library(tidyverse)
```

We generate synthetic data for several studies, A to H. Each study has two groups, 1 (treatment) and 2 (control); the groups have the same size within each study, but the size varies between each study.

12.3 R Code

We assume that the true effect of each study comes from a distribution of true effects. The distribution of true effects is assumed to be normally distributed with mean = 0.5 and standard deviation = 0.3. We draw 10 random numbers from such a distribution to get the true effects for the studies:

```
set.seed(123)
numstudies <- 8
True_effects <- rnorm(numstudies, mean = 0.5, sd = 0.3)
True_effects
## [1] 0.3318573 0.4309468 0.9676125 0.5211525
## [5] 0.5387863 1.0145195 0.6382749 0.1204816
```

The studies vary in sample size:

```
minss <- 30
maxss <- 100
Study_sizes <- sample(20:60, numstudies, replace = F)
Study_sizes
## [1] 24 46 47 28 48 54 27 45
```

The observations in the treatment group are drawn from a normal distribution with mean = true effect for that study, and standard deviation = 1:

```
#Study A
True_effect_A <- True_effects[1]
True_effect_A
## [1] 0.3318573
#Group 1 (Treatment)
nA1 <- Study_sizes[1] # size of group
# mean below is True_effect_A
xA1 <- rnorm(nA1, mean = True_effect_A, sd = 1)
mA1 <- mean(xA1)
sdA1 <- sd(xA1)
```

The observations in the control group are drawn from a normal distribution with mean = 0, and standard deviation = 1:

```
# Group 2 (Control)
nA2 <- Study_sizes[1]
xA2 <- rnorm(nA2, mean = 0, sd = 1)
mA2 <- mean(xA2)
sdA2 <- sd(xA2)
```

The difference in means for the treatment and control group in study 1 is given by

```
mA1 - mA2
## [1] 0.2623395
```

We use similar code to generate data for more studies, using the previously randomly drawn true effect sizes and study sizes.

The metafor package has a handy `escalc` function to calculate different effect size or outcome measures. Here, the measure we use is 'MD' for the mean difference, and we provide the related information for each study required to calculate the mean difference:

```
effect <- escalc(measure = "MD",
    # sample size in group 1 for study i
    n1i = c(nA1, nB1, nC1, nD1, nE1, nF1,
            nG1, nH1),
    # observed mean in group 1 for study i
    m1i = c(mA1, mB1, mC1, mD1, mE1, mF1,
            mG1, mH1),
    # observed standard deviation in group 1
    sd1i = c(sdA1,sdB1,sdC1,sdD1, sdE1, sdF1,
            sdG1, sdH1),
    n2i = c(nA2,nB2, nC2, nD2, nE2, nF2,
            nG2, nH2),
    m2i = c(mA2, mB2, mC2, mD2, mE2, mF2,
            mG2, mH2),
    sd2i = c(sdA2, sdB2, sdC2, sdD2,
            sdE2, sdF2, sdG2, sdH2))
```

We can view the output of the `escalc()` function; we see the yi, the observed effect sizes or outcomes, and the vi, the corresponding variances:

```
effect
##        yi      vi
## 1  0.2623  0.0714
## 2  0.6059  0.0416
## 3  1.0890  0.0385
## 4  0.4694  0.0650
## 5  0.6499  0.0459
## 6  0.9126  0.0376
## 7  0.6061  0.0534
## 8  0.1934  0.0467
write.csv(effect, "simeffect.csv")
```

We can fit a random effects model with the `rma()` function, by providing the output of the `escalc()` function as an input:

12.3 R Code

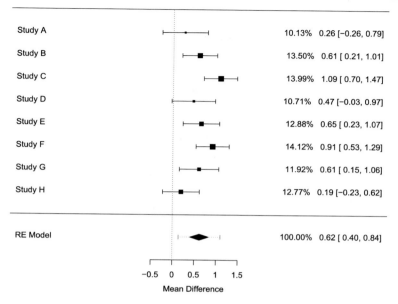

Fig. 12.10 Forest plot, random effects model, and simulated data

```
meta_res <- rma(yi, vi, data = effect)
```

We use the forest function to get the forest plot (Fig. 12.10). We used the showweights option, so the weights given to each study are displayed. For example study A got a weight of 10.13%. The addpred option adds a prediction interval to the figure. The width of the diamond tells us that in 95% of the cases, the mean effect size falls inside the width of the diamond. In 95% of cases, the true effect in a new study will be within the prediction interval:

```
forest(meta_res, showweights = T,
       addpred = T,
       slab = paste(c("Study A", "Study B",
                      "Study C", "Study D",
                      "Study E", "Study F",
                      "Study G", "Study H")))
```

We can use predict to get the numbers relating to the overall effect, the confidence interval for the overall effect, and the prediction interval for the effect in a new study. We can compare this with the distribution of the true effects used to generate the synthetic data: N(mean = 0.5, sd = 0.3):

```
predict(meta_res)
##
##     pred      se  ci.lb  ci.ub  pi.lb  pi.ub
##   0.6204  0.1100 0.4048 0.8360 0.1398 1.1010
```

☞ **Your turn** Modify the code above to generate your own data, and then do your own meta-analysis with the generated data.

12.3.1.2 Bayesian Meta-Analysis with the Simulated Data

We can also use the simulated data to see Bayesian meta-analysis in action. We use the baggr package. We use the same simulated data, but now have to customize the input the way baggr requires it:

```
library(baggr)
simeffect <- read_csv("simeffect.csv")
group <- c("A", "B", "C", "D", "E", "F", "G", "H")
tau <- simeffect$yi
tau
## [1] 0.2623395 0.6058631 1.0889757 0.4693711
## [5] 0.6498504 0.9126343 0.6060708 0.1933976
max(abs(tau))
## [1] 1.088976
sd(tau)
## [1] 0.3013734
se <- simeffect$vi^0.5
simsdat <- data.frame(group, tau, se)
```

We now use the baggr function to see the implications of the prior (Fig. 12.11):

```
baggr_sims <- baggr(simsdat, model = "rubin",
                    pooling = "partial", ppd = TRUE)
baggr_sims


effect_plot(baggr_sims)
```

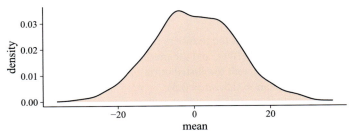

Fig. 12.11 Prior distribution and treatment effects

12.3 R Code

In baggr, the priors are weakly informative, and based on data. The prior is set for the hypermean using 10 times the max effect: hypermean is normal (mean = 0, sd = 10 times the max effect). The hyper-SD prior is set using 10 times the naive SD across sites: hypersd is uniform (min = 0, max = 3).

We confirm with the code below

```
plot(main = "", density(rnorm(1000,
        mean = rnorm(1000, 0, 10*max(abs(tau))),
        sd = runif(1000,0,10*sd(tau)))))
```

Figures 12.12 and 12.11 are very similar. It is possible to put in one's own priors and to test the sensitivity of the results to the priors. We now fit the model:

```
baggr_sims <- baggr(simsdat, model = "rubin",
                    pooling = "partial", ppd = FALSE)
baggr_sims
```

We can get a forest plot (Fig. 12.13):

```
forest_plot(baggr_sims)
```

We can get a plot of posterior predictions (Fig. 12.14):

Fig. 12.12 Prior distribution and treatment effects

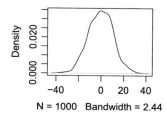

Group mean treatment effect	Mean (SD)
A	0.262 (0.267)
B	0.606 (0.204)
C	1.089 (0.196)
D	0.469 (0.255)
E	0.650 (0.214)
F	0.913 (0.194)
G	0.606 (0.231)
H	0.193 (0.216)
Hypermean treatment effect	0.622 (0.141)

Fig. 12.13 Forest plot

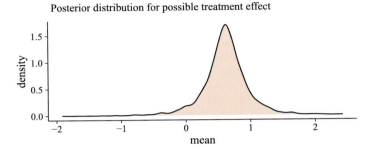

Fig. 12.14 Prior distribution and treatment effects

```
effect_plot(baggr_sims)

effect_draw(baggr_sims, summary = TRUE ,
            interval = 0.95)
##         2.5%        mean       97.5%      median
## -0.09395734  0.62462482  1.31831927  0.62801694
##           sd
##   0.34867505
```

The mean of the posterior distribution is very similar to the estimate of the overall effect using the random effects model.

12.3.1.3 Colditz et al. (1994) BCG Vaccine Study

This section covers the R code for results presented in Sect. 12.2.1.1. As we saw previously in this chapter, Colditz et al. (1994) carried out a meta-analysis for the efficacy of the BCG vaccine against TB.

We have to load the metafor package and the data which comes with the package:

```
library("metafor")
data("dat.bcg", package = "metafor")


library(tidyverse)
library(knitr)
```

We now calculate effect measures, here the relative risk (RR), using the `escalc()` function. Our measure here is 'RR' and we input the needed information:

```
dat <- escalc(measure = "RR", ai = tpos, bi = tneg, ci = cpos,
              di = cneg, data = dat.bcg, append = TRUE)
```

We use the `rma()` function to fit a random effects model:

12.3 R Code

```
res <- rma(yi, vi, data = dat)
```

We produce a forest plot, displayed earlier in the chapter (Fig. 12.1).

The forest plot shows us the estimated effects and confidence intervals for different studies. The forest plot also shows us an estimate from a random effects model, with the confidence interval (width of diamond) and the prediction interval (dashed line). We use `atransf` to transform the output so that we get risk ratio rather than the log of risk ratio.

We can use `predict` to get the numbers relating to the overall effect, the confidence interval for the overall effect, and the prediction interval for the effect in a new study:

```
predict(res, transf = exp)
##
##     pred  ci.lb  ci.ub  pi.lb  pi.ub
##   0.4894 0.3441 0.6962 0.1546 1.5490
```

12.3.1.4 Bayesian Meta-Analysis of Beta Blockers

The baggr package has been written to make it easy to use Bayesian meta-analysis. We load the baggr package:

```
library(baggr)
```

We are replicating the reanalysis of the Yusuf et al. (1985) study of the effect of beta blockers on mortality after a heart attack by Gelman et al. (2013) with the baggr package (see Sect. 12.2.1.2). We input the results of each of 22 primary studies below, with the `read.table` function. For example, in study 1, 3 out of 39 people died in the control group, whereas 3 out of 38 people in the treatment group died:

```
df_beta <- read.table(text = "
  trial c n2i a n1i
  1 3 39 3 38
  2 14 116 7 114
  3 11 93 5 69
  4 127 1520 102 1533
  5 27 365 28 355
  6 6 52 4 59
  7 152 939 98 945
  8 48 471 60 632
  9 37 282 25 278
  10 188 1921 138 1916
  11 52 583 64 873
  12 47 266 45 263
  13 16 293 9 291
  14 45 883 57 858
```

274   12   Integrating and Generalizing Causal Estimates

```
15 31 147 25 154
16 38 213 33 207
17 12 122 28 251
18  6 154  8 151
19  3 134  6 174
20 40 218 32 209
21 43 364 27 391
22 39 674 22 680
", header = TRUE)
```

We estimate the effect sizes with the `prepare_ma` function. Here our effect is `logOR`, the log of the odds ratio. We can use the relative risk which is easier to interpret. Statisticians often work with the log of the odds ratio, because of convenient statistical properties. The relative risk and the log of the odds ratio do not differ much for low values:

```
df_ma <- prepare_ma(df_beta, group = "trial",
                    effect = "logOR")
max(abs(df_ma$tau))
## [1] 0.7410032
#hypermean is N(0, ten times above)
sd(df_ma$tau)
## [1] 0.3386134
# hypersd is uniform(0, above)
```

We can fit a Bayesian aggregate treatment effects model with the `baggr` function. By default, it uses weakly informative priors that are scaled to the data, and the priors used are printed in the console. We can get a sense of the priors by seeing the predicted treatment effects if we only use the priors and fit the model, using the `ppd = TRUE` option. When `ppd = TRUE`, the model will sample from the prior distributions and ignore data in inference:

```
bg_model_agg <- baggr(df_ma, effect = "logarithm of odds ratio",
                      ppd = TRUE)
```

We get the prediction from the prior in Fig. 12.15, with the `effect_plot` function:

```
effect_plot(bg_model_agg)
```

As we can see in Fig. 12.15, the priors effectively allow for a very wide range of possible treatment effects, and the distribution is centered on zero in terms of the logarithm of odds ratio. The package user is free to input a prior, and it is possible to see the sensitivity of the results to priors. However, here we go with the default priors that the package provides. We proceed now to fit the model using the data:

12.3 R Code

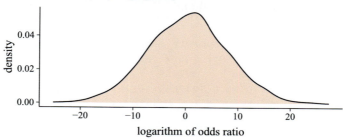

Fig. 12.15 Prior distribution

```
bg_model_agg <- baggr(df_ma,
  effect = "logarithm of odds ratio",
  ppd = FALSE)
```

We get our results below

```
bg_model_agg
## Model type: Rubin model with aggregate data
## Pooling of effects: partial
##
## Aggregate treatment effect (on logarithm of odds ratio):
## Hypermean (tau) =    -0.25 with 95% interval -0.38 to -0.11
## Hyper-SD (sigma_tau) = 0.1300 with 95% interval 0.0065 to 0.3121
## Total pooling (1 - I^2) = 0.89 with 95% interval 0.63 to 1.00
##
## Group effects omitted, as number of groups is > 20.
## Use print.baggr() with group = TRUE to print them.
```

The median of the posterior distribution of the overall mean of the treatment effects (log-odds) is −0.25, while the median of the posterior distribution of the standard deviation of the study effects is 0.13.

We can get a forest plot (Fig. 12.2, displayed earlier in the chapter) using the `forest_plot` function.

Gelman et al. (2013) claim that the overall mean effect is overemphasized by analysts. Instead of focusing just on the overall mean effect, they ought to attempt to quantify the uncertainty for a new study. The authors write (p. 227), "in particular, with the beta-blocker data, there is just over 10% posterior probability that the true effect … in a new study would be positive (corresponding to the treatment increasing the probability of death in that study)."

We get a plot of the posterior distribution (Fig. 12.3, displayed earlier in the chapter) for possible treatment effect by using the `effect_plot` function.

We can get a summary of the posterior predicted effect, in terms of log odds ratio:

```
effect_draw(bg_model_agg, summary = TRUE ,
            interval = 0.95)
##        2.5%        mean       97.5%      median
## -0.5870938  -0.2467955   0.1077653  -0.2521284
##          sd
##   0.1681070
```

We can use the transformation option to get a summary of the posterior predicted effect in terms of the odds ratio:

```
effect_draw(bg_model_agg, summary = TRUE, transform = exp,
            interval = 0.95)
##       2.5%       mean      97.5%     median         sd
## 0.5531396  0.7933453  1.1277654  0.7772527  0.1371460


effects <- effect_draw(bg_model_agg, summary = FALSE)
```

12.3.2 Analyses Guided by the Potential Outcomes Framework

12.3.2.1 Simulation for Generalizing Experiments

In Sect. 12.2.2.3, we mentioned the generalization of a coronary artery study by Dahabreh et al. (2019). We use simulation to look into generalizing results, and to get some intuition. We generate data along the lines of the numerical example in Lesko et al. (2017). We then use the code for the outcome model provided by Dahabreh et al. (2019).

We first generate data for a population of size 50000. The covariates w1 and w2 are binary:

```
library(tidyverse)
set.seed(333)
n <- 50000
w1 <- rbinom(n, 1, 0.15); #w1 is a covariate
w2 <- rbinom(n, 1, 0.2); #w2 is a covariate
mean(w1)
## [1] 0.14896
mean(w2)
## [1] 0.20178
```

The treatment A is binary, and has a probability of 0.5 of being 1:

12.3 R Code

```
A <- rbinom(n, 1, 0.5)
mean(A)
## [1] 0.50108
```

The outcome is binary. We generate the potential outcomes (y1 and y0), with probability of potential outcome with and without the treatment being equal to 1 (py1 and py0) depending on the covariates (w1 and w2):

```
py1 <- 0.10703 - 0.05 + 0.20*w1 + 0.20*w2 - 0.15*w1*w2
mean(py1)
## [1] 0.122807
py0 <- 0.10703 + 0.20*w1 + 0.20*w2
mean(py0)
## [1] 0.177178
y1 <- rbinom(n, 1, py1)
mean(y1)
## [1] 0.124
y0 <- rbinom(n, 1, py0)
mean(y0)
## [1] 0.17662
```

The observed outcome (Y) is given by

```
Y <- y0*(1 - A) + y1*(A)
```

Note that the average treatment effect is

```
mean(y1) - mean(y0)
## [1] -0.05262
```

We pull the generated variables together in a dataframe called datapop:

```
datapop <- data.frame(Y, y0, y1, py1, py0, A, w1, w2)
head(datapop)
##     Y y0 y1      py1     py0 A w1 w2
## 1   0  0  0  0.05703 0.10703 0  0  0
## 2   0  1  0  0.05703 0.10703 1  0  0
## 3   0  0  0  0.25703 0.30703 0  1  0
## 4   1  1  1  0.25703 0.30703 0  0  1
## 5   0  0  0  0.05703 0.10703 0  0  0
## 6   0  0  0  0.05703 0.10703 0  0  0
```

The sample used in the study is different in terms of distribution of w1 and w2 compared to the population. S denotes whether the row in the dataframe is in the sample or not:

```
datapop1 <- datapop %>%
  filter(w1 == 0, w2 == 0)

datapop1$S = 0
datapop1$S[1:320] = 1

datapop2 <- datapop %>%
  filter(w1 == 1, w2 == 0)

datapop2$S = 0
datapop2$S[1:480] = 1

datapop3 <- datapop %>%
  filter(w1 == 0, w2 == 1)

datapop3$S = 0
datapop3$S[1:480] = 1

datapop4 <- datapop %>%
  filter(w1 == 1, w2 == 1)

datapop4$S = 0
datapop4$S[1:720] = 1

datastack <- rbind(datapop1, datapop2, datapop3, datapop4)
head(datastack)
##    Y y0 y1     py1     py0 A w1 w2 S
## 1  0  0  0 0.05703 0.10703 0  0  0 1
## 2  0  1  0 0.05703 0.10703 1  0  0 1
## 3  0  0  0 0.05703 0.10703 0  0  0 1
## 4  0  0  0 0.05703 0.10703 0  0  0 1
## 5  1  1  0 0.05703 0.10703 0  0  0 1
## 6  0  0  0 0.05703 0.10703 0  0  0 1
tail(datastack)
##          Y y0 y1     py1     py0 A w1 w2 S
## 49995  1   1  0 0.30703 0.50703 0  1  1 0
## 49996  0   0  0 0.30703 0.50703 0  1  1 0
## 49997  1   0  1 0.30703 0.50703 1  1  1 0
## 49998  0   0  0 0.30703 0.50703 0  1  1 0
## 49999  0   1  0 0.30703 0.50703 1  1  1 0
## 50000  1   0  1 0.30703 0.50703 1  1  1 0
```

Now we have a dataset called datastack, in which $S = 1$ indicates that the data is in the study sample, and $S = 0$ that the data is not in the study sample:

12.3 R Code

```
datastack %>%
  group_by(S) %>%
  summarize(meanw1 = mean(w1),
            meanw2 = mean(w2))
## # A tibble: 2 x 3
##       S meanw1 meanw2
##   <dbl>  <dbl>  <dbl>
## 1     0  0.130  0.185
## 2     1  0.6    0.6
```

We now use an outcome model estimator proposed and used from the paper by Dahabreh et al. (2019). We run a model for the outcome for the treatment group and the control group in the sample separately. We then predict the values of the outcome for each unit using all the data in the sample given the treatment and control models. Finally, we get the estimated sample average treatment effect in the population:

```
# Running glm model on data in sample for treated.
S1data_A1<-subset(datastack, S == 1 & A == 1)
  OR1mod<- glm(formula=Y~w1 + w2 + w1*w2,
               family="binomial", data = S1data_A1)

# Predicting response.
p1<- predict(OR1mod,newdata=S1data_A1, type="response")
  mean(p1)
## [1] 0.2487153

# Running glm model on data in sample for treated.
S1data_A0<-subset(datastack, S==1 & A==0)
  OR0mod<- glm(formula = Y ~ w1 + w2 + w1*w2,
               family="binomial", data=S1data_A0)

# Predicting response.
p0<- predict(OR0mod,newdata=S1data_A0, type="response")
  mean(p0)
## [1] 0.3349562
```

Our estimate of the SATE is

```
  diff<-mean(p1)-mean(p0)
  diff
## [1] -0.08624087
```

```
# code from Dahabreh et al. 2019 c in Colnet
# Dahabreh, Robertson, Tchetgen, Stuart, Hernan
# Generalizing causal inferences from individuals
# in randomized trials to all trial-eligible indiv
# Biometrics
OM_est<-function(data){
  S1data_A1<-subset(data, S==1 & A==1)
  OR1mod<- glm(formula=Y~w1 + w2 + w1*w2,
        family="binomial", data=S1data_A1)
  p1<- predict(OR1mod,newdata=data, type="response")
  data$p1<-p1
  S1data_A0<-subset(data, S==1 & A==0)
  OR0mod<- glm(formula=Y~w1 + w2 + w1*w2,
            family="binomial", data=S1data_A0)
  p0<- predict(OR0mod,newdata=data, type="response")
  data$p0<-p0
  diff<-mean(data$p1)-mean(data$p0)
  list<-list(mu1=mean(data$p1), mu0=mean(data$p0), diff=diff,
          p1=p1, p0=p0, OR1mod=OR1mod, OR0mod=OR0mod)
  return(list)
}

OM <- OM_est(datastack)
list
## function (...)  .Primitive("list")
```

The estimated mean for the treatment group, the control group, and the population average treatment effect can be extracted via the code below

```
OM$mu1
## [1] 0.1228346
OM$mu0
## [1] 0.16525
OM$diff
## [1] -0.0424154
```

We can now use bootstrapping to get the confidence intervals. We suppress the output.

```
OM_est_b2 <-function(data, ids){
  dat <- data[ids, ]
  S1data_A1<-subset(dat, S==1 & A==1)
  OR1mod<- glm(formula = Y ~ w1 + w2 + w1*w2,family="binomial", data=S1data_A1)
  p1<- predict(OR1mod,newdata=dat, type="response")
  dat$p1<-p1
  S1data_A0<-subset(dat, S==1 & A==0)
  OR0mod<- glm(formula = Y ~ w1 + w2 + w1*w2,family="binomial", data=S1data_A0)
  p0<- predict(OR0mod,newdata=dat, type="response")
```

12.3 R Code

```
dat$p0<-p0
diff<-mean(dat$p1)-mean(dat$p0)
#list<-list(mu1=mean(data$p1), mu0=mean(data$p0), diff=diff,
         #p1=p1, p0=p0, OR1mod=OR1mod, OR0mod=OR0mod)
return(diff)
}

library(boot)
# note that R should be much higher
# kept low for speed
boot.out <- boot(data = datastack,
              statistic = OM_est_b2,
           R = 100)

boot.ci(boot.out, type ="perc")
```

12.3.2.2 Simulation to Illustrate External Robustness

In Sect. 12.2.2.4, we saw that Devaux and Egami (2022) had proposed a way of assessing the robustness to external validity of an experiment. This is useful because we may not have much information besides the result in the experiment itself. The measure of external robustness lies between 0 and 1, with higher values indicating greater external robustness. Devaux and Egami (2022) have the details of this measure; we use simulation to get a feel.

The exr package helps us estimate external robustness. The package harnesses machine learning techniques to predict conditional average treatment effects, and then estimates the external robustness, and provides a plot of the results. We use a simulation to provide an intuitive feel for the estimation of external robustness.

Base Case

The size of the study sample is given by n. The treatment assignment variable is D, and the probability of treatment $= 0.5$. X1 and X2 are covariates from a normal distribution with mean $= 4$ and sd $= 1$. We generate data:

```
set.seed(123)
n <- 1000
D <- rbinom(n, 1, 0.5)
X1 <- rnorm(n, 4, 1)
X2 <- rnorm(n, 4, 1)
```

Y0 and Y1 are the potential outcomes, and depend on the covariates, X1 and X2, and are generated by

```
Y0 <- rnorm(n, X1^2 - 0.5*X2^2, 1)
Y1 <- Y0 + X1^2 - 0.5*X2^2 + rnorm(n)
```

The difference in the average of the potential outcomes is

```
mean(Y1) - mean(Y0)
## [1] 8.602537
```

The observed outcome Y is

```
Y <- Y0*(1 - D) + Y1*D
```

We put the variables in a dataframe:

```
datY <- data.frame(Y1, Y0, Y, D, X1, X2)

head(round(datY, 2))
##         Y1     Y0      Y D   X1   X2
## 1    13.79   5.82   5.82 0 3.40 3.18
## 2     3.61   2.79   3.61 1 3.01 3.69
## 3    38.35  19.77  19.77 0 5.03 3.10
## 4    22.92  11.33  22.92 1 4.75 4.63
## 5   -12.60  -6.13 -12.60 1 2.49 5.12
## 6    -7.65  -4.00  -4.00 0 3.90 6.13
library(tidyverse)
```

We create a variable Y1 − Y0, i.e., the difference in the potential outcomes. A reminder: both potential outcomes cannot be observed for the same unit in real data. However, this is simulated data, and it is useful for this reason:

```
datY <- datY %>%
  mutate(Y1minusY0 = Y1 - Y0)


datY <- datY %>%
  mutate(pos = ifelse(Y1minusY0 > 0, 1, 0),
         pos = factor(pos))
```

We plot Y1 − Y0 versus X1 in Fig. 12.16. There is clear heterogeneity of effects. Y1 − Y0 is positive for higher values of X1 and negative for lower values of X1:

12.3 R Code

Fig. 12.16 Base case, Y1 − Y0 against X1

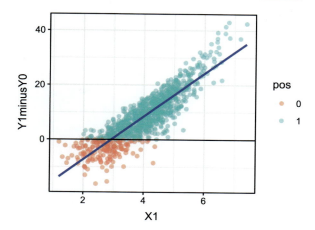

```
ggplot(datY) +
  geom_point(aes(y = Y1minusY0,
                 x = X1,
                 col = pos), alpha = 0.5) +
  geom_smooth(aes(y = Y1minusY0,
                  x = X1), se = F, method = "lm") +
  geom_hline(yintercept = 0) +
  theme_bw()
```

```
## 'geom_smooth()' using formula = 'y ~ x'
```

We plot Y1 − Y0 against X2 in Fig. 12.17. Again we see some effect heterogeneity:

```
ggplot(datY) +
  geom_point(aes(y = Y1minusY0,
                 x = X2,
                 col = pos), alpha = 0.5) +
  geom_smooth(aes(y = Y1minusY0,
                  x = X2), se = F, method = "lm") +
  geom_hline(yintercept = 0) +
  theme_bw()
```

```
## 'geom_smooth()' using formula = 'y ~ x'
```

We install and load the exr package:

```
#library(devtools)
#install_github("naoki-egami/exr", dependencies = TRUE)
library(exr)
```

We run the relevant code using the exr package:

Fig. 12.17 Base case, Y1 − Y0 against X2

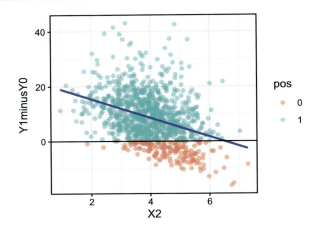

Fig. 12.18 External robustness for base case

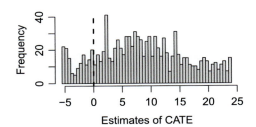

```
covariates <- c("X1","X2")
sate_est <- summary(lm(Y ~ D + X1 + X2, data = datY))$coef["D",c(1,2)]
sate_est
##   Estimate Std. Error
## 8.4006492  0.3202792
exr_out <- exr(outcome = "Y",
               treatment = "D",
               covariates = c("X1", "X2"),
               data = datY,
               sate_estimate = sate_est)
## Estimating CATE with grf...
## Estimating External Robustness...
plot(exr_out)
```

Figure 12.18 shows the plot of the output of estimated robustness for the base case. The measure of external robustness is 0.52, and the conditional average treatment effect varies from −5 to 25.

We now consider, in turn,

- the case of increased heterogeneity. We get a lower external robustness of 0.21.
- the case of increased effect size. We get a higher external robustness of 1.

12.3 R Code

Fig. 12.19 Increased heterogeneity, Y1 − Y0 versus X1

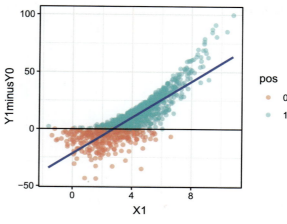

Fig. 12.20 Increased heterogeneity, Y1 − Y0 versus X2

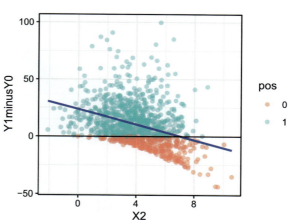

Increased Heterogeneity

We increase the heterogeneity by increasing the standard deviation of X1 and X2 twofold compared to the base case. We suppress the code here. We can compare Figs. 12.19, 12.20, and 12.21 with Figs. 12.16, 12.17, and 12.18.

The mean of Y1 − Y0 is

```
mean(Y1) - mean(Y0)
## [1] 10.26179
```

We can plot the output.

Increased Effect Size

In the generating equation for Y1, we add 10 relative to the base case, thus increasing the effect. We once again suppress the code. We can compare Figs. 12.22, 12.23, and 12.24 with Figs. 12.16, 12.17, and 12.18.

The mean of Y1 − Y0 is

286   12 Integrating and Generalizing Causal Estimates

Fig. 12.21 Increased heterogeneity

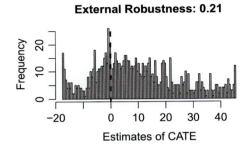

Fig. 12.22 Increased effect size, Y1 − Y0 versus X1

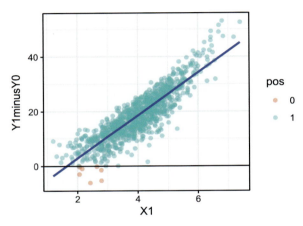

Fig. 12.23 Increased effect size, Y1 − Y0 versus X2

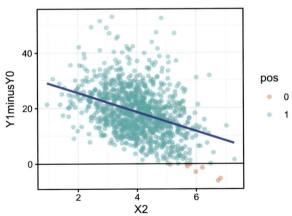

12.3 R Code

Fig. 12.24 Increased effect size

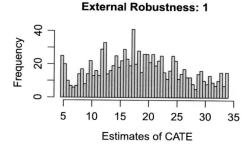

Fig. 12.25 Simple confounding case

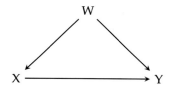

```
mean(Y1) - mean(Y0)
## [1] 18.60254
```

12.3.3 Analyses Guided by Causal Graphs

In an earlier section, we had provided an overview of analyses guided by causal graphs. The dosearch package helps us find the adjustment formula, for a variety of scenarios. We now see how we can use this remarkable package:

```
#install.packages("dosearch")
library(dosearch)
```

12.3.3.1 Simple Confounding

We will consider a simple example. We start with a causal graph (Fig. 12.25).

We are interested in a scenario as represented by the causal graph in Fig. 12.25, and want to know the effect of an intervention on X in order to affect Y, i.e., $P(Y|do(X))$. Note that $do(X)$ is the symbol used by Pearl to denote that we are doing and not only seeing, we are setting the variable X to a value, and we are intervening and not only observing.

We first input the component variables and arrows of the causal graph (Fig. 12.25):

```
graph <- "
x -> y
w -> y
w -> x
"
```

Fig. 12.26 Selection into experiment

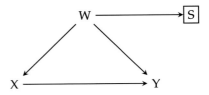

We tell the package that we have observed data on the variables y, x, and w:

```
data <- "
p(y,x,w)
"
```

Our query is: how do we estimate the causal effect of x on y, or $P(Y|do(X))$?

```
query <- "p(y|do(x))"
```

And now the package does a search to find an identification solution for the data, query and graph:

```
dosearch(data, query, graph)
## \sum_{w}\left(p(w)p(y|x,w)\right)
```

$$p(y|do(x)) = \sum_{w}(p(w)p(y|x,w)) \qquad (12.6)$$

Equation 12.6 is the basic nonparametric adjustment formula. Given this adjustment formula, or identification result, we can proceed to estimation—we can use regression or matching. If we use regression, then we would regress y on x and w. If we do not adjust for w, then we will not be able to identify the causal effect.

12.3.3.2 Selection into Experiment

We will consider a simple example (see Sect. 12.2.3.1). We start with a causal graph. We have a selection variable S that shows that the sample differs from the population in terms of the variable W (Fig. 12.26).

Now we input the graph:

```
graph <- "
x -> y
w -> y
w -> x
w -> s
"
```

We have (1) observed data on w, p(w), and we have an experimental dataset, with random assignment of x, and with w as a covariate, in which the selection variable s depends on w, which in symbols is $p(y, w|s, do(x))$:

12.3 R Code

Fig. 12.27 Selection into experiment, but with intermediate variable affecting selection

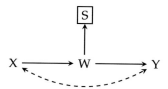

```
data <- "
p(w)
p(y, w|s, do(x))
"
```

Our query is: how do we estimate the causal effect of x on y?

```
query <- "p(y|do(x))"
```

In the input to the dosearch function, we include the selection bias input; we indicate that it is 's':

```
dosearch(data, query, graph, selection_bias = "s" )
## \sum_{w}\left(p(w)p(y|do(x),w,s)\right)
```

$$p(y|do(x)) = \sum_{w} (p(w)p(y|do(x), w, s)). \qquad (12.7)$$

Equation 12.7 is the nonparametric adjustment formula; we need to reweight our experimental results to take into account the differing distribution of w in the population. This is generally the adjustment formula used when generalizing an experimental study to its corresponding population, and which we have discussed in earlier sections.

Now we consider a different scenario, one where the selection into the experiment happens in such a way that the difference in distribution between the study sample and the population is in a variable that lies on the causal path between treatment and response (Fig. 12.27).

```
graph <- "
x <-> y
w -> y
x -> w
w -> s
"
```

We provide the data that is available to us:

```
data <- "
p(w, x)
p(y, w|s, do(x))
"
```

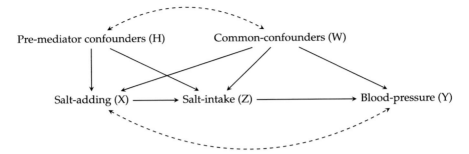

Fig. 12.28 Salt and blood pressure

Our query is: how do we estimate the causal effect of x on y?

```
query <- "p(y|do(x))"
```

```
dosearch(data, query, graph, selection_bias = "s" )
## \sum_{w}\left(p(w|x)p(y|do(x),w,s)\right)
```

$$p(y|do(x)) = \sum_{w}(p(w|x)p(y|do(x), w, s)). \qquad (12.8)$$

The adjustment formula is different in the scenario represented by Fig. 12.27 compared to the scenario represent by Fig. 12.26; compare Eqs. 12.8 and 12.7. Thus, in different scenarios we would have to adjust differently; and moreover, in some of these, we may not achieve identification.

12.3.3.3 Data Fusion

Karvanen et al. (2021) use the package to study data fusion (see Sect. 12.2.3.2). Given different datasets, how can we combine the information to estimate a causal effect?

We input the graph (Fig. 12.28) in the format required by the package:

```
graph3 <- "
X -> Z
Z -> Y
W -> X
W -> Z
W -> Y
H -> X
H -> Z
X <-> Y
H <-> C
"
```

12.4 Resources

Karvanen et al. (2021) have data from a survey and from an experiment:

```
datasources3 <- c(
  "P(X,Z,H,W)
  P(Y|do(Z),W)"
)
```

The query is: what is the causal effect of salt-adding (X) on blood pressure (Y)?

```
query3 <- "P(Y|do(X))"

result3 <- dosearch(datasources3, query3,
                    graph3)
result3
## \sum_{Z,W,H}\left(p(Y|do(Z),W)\left(p(W,H)p(Z|X,W,H)\right)\right)
```

The adjustment formula obtained is somewhat complicated:

$$p(y|do(x)) = \sum_{Z,W,H} \left(p(Y|do(Z), W) \left(p(W, H) p(Z|X, W, H) \right) \right). \quad (12.9)$$

Karvanen et al. (2021) use this adjustment formula.

12.4 Resources

12.4.1 For Better Understanding

1. Borenstein et al.'s (2021) book *Introduction to Meta-Analysis*.
2. Westreich (2020) book *Epidemiology by Design: A Causal Approach to the Health Sciences*.

12.4.2 For Going Further

1. Paper by Bareinboim and Pearl (2016), on *Causal Inference and the Data Fusion Problem*.
2. Paper by Westreich (2020) on *Target Validity and the Hierarchy of Study Designs*.

Packages Used in This Chapter

The citations for the packages[5] used in this chapter are

---

[5] The tidyverse package itself contains several packages.

```
## Bates D, Maechler M, Jagan M (2022). _Matrix: Sparse and Dense
## Matrix Classes and Methods_. R package version 1.5-1, <URL:
## https://CRAN.R-project.org/package=Matrix>.


## Eddelbuettel D, François R (2011). "Rcpp: Seamless R and C++
## Integration." _Journal of Statistical Software_, *40*(8),
## 1-18. doi: 10.18637/jss.v040.i08 (URL:
## https://doi.org/10.18637/jss.v040.i08).
##
## Eddelbuettel D (2013). _Seamless R and C++ Integration with
## Rcpp_. Springer, New York. doi: 10.1007/978-1-4614-6868-4
## (URL: https://doi.org/10.1007/978-1-4614-6868-4), ISBN
## 978-1-4614-6867-7.
##
## Eddelbuettel D, Balamuta JJ (2018). "Extending extitR with
## extitC++: A Brief Introduction to extitRcpp." _The American
## Statistician_, *72*(1), 28-36. doi:
## 10.1080/00031305.2017.1375990 (URL:
## https://doi.org/10.1080/00031305.2017.1375990).


## Egami N, Devaux M (2022). _exr: Quantifying Robustness to
## External Validity Bias_. R package version 0.1.0.


## Makowski D, Lüdecke D, Patil I, Thériault R, Ben-Shachar M,
## Wiernik B (2023). "Automated Results Reporting as a Practical
## Tool to Improve Reproducibility and Methodological Best
## Practices Adoption." _CRAN_. <URL:
## https://easystats.github.io/report/>.


## R Core Team (2021). _R: A Language and Environment for
## Statistical Computing_. R Foundation for Statistical
## Computing, Vienna, Austria. <URL: https://www.R-project.org/>.


## Tikka S, Hyttinen A, Karvanen J (2021). "Causal Effect
## Identification from Multiple Incomplete Data Sources: A
## General Search-Based Approach." _Journal of Statistical
## Software_, *99*(5), 1-40. doi: 10.18637/jss.v099.i05 (URL:
## https://doi.org/10.18637/jss.v099.i05).


## Viechtbauer W (2010). "Conducting meta-analyses in R with the
## metafor package." _Journal of Statistical Software_, *36*(3),
## 1-48. <URL: https://doi.org/10.18637/jss.v036.i03>.
```

```
## Wickham H, Averick M, Bryan J, Chang W, McGowan LD, François
## R, Grolemund G, Hayes A, Henry L, Hester J, Kuhn M, Pedersen
## TL, Miller E, Bache SM, Müller K, Ooms J, Robinson D, Seidel
## DP, Spinu V, Takahashi K, Vaughan D, Wilke C, Woo K, Yutani H
## (2019). "Welcome to the tidyverse." _Journal of Open Source
## Software_, *4*(43), 1686. doi: 10.21105/joss.01686 (URL:
## https://doi.org/10.21105/joss.01686).


## Xie Y (2022). _knitr: A General-Purpose Package for Dynamic
## Report Generation in R_. R package version 1.41, <URL:
## https://yihui.org/knitr/>.


## Xie Y (2023). _formatR: Format R Code Automatically_. R
## package version 1.14, <URL:
## https://CRAN.R-project.org/package=formatR>.
```

References

Bareinboim, Elias, and Judea Pearl. 2016. Causal Inference and the Data-fusion Problem. *Proceedings of the National Academy of Sciences* 113 (27): 7345–7352.

Borenstein, Michael, Larry V. Hedges, Julian Higgins, and Hannah R. Rothstein. 2021. *Introduction to Meta-Analysis*, 2nd ed. Hoboken: Wiley.

Colditz, Graham A., Timothy F. Brewer, Catherine S. Berkey, Mary E. Wilson, Elisabeth Burdick, Harvey V. Fineberg, and Frederick Mosteller. 1994. Efficacy of BCG Vaccine in the Prevention of Tuberculosis: Meta-analysis of the Published Literature. *JAMA* 271 (9): 698–702.

Dahabreh, Issa J., Sarah E. Robertson, Eric J. Tchetgen, Elizabeth A. Stuart, and Miguel A. Hernán. 2019. Generalizing Causal Inferences from Individuals in Randomized Trials to all Trial-eligible Individuals. *Biometrics* 75 (2): 685–694.

Devaux, Martin, and Naoki Egami. 2022. Quantifying Robustness to External Validity Bias. *SSRN Electronic Journal*.

Domurat, Richard, Isaac Menashe, and Wesley Yin. 2021. The Role of Behavioral Frictions in Health Insurance Marketplace Enrollment and Risk: Evidence from a Field Experiment. *American Economic Review* 111 (5): 1549–1574.

Gelman, Andrew, John B. Carlin, Hal S. Stern, David B. Dunson, Aki Vehtari, and Donald B. Rubin. 2013. *Bayesian Data Analysis*, 3rd ed. Boca Raton: Chapman and Hall/CRC.

Karvanen, Juha, Santtu Tikka, and Antti Hyttinen. 2020. Do-search - A Tool for Causal Inference and Study Design with Multiple Data Sources. arXiv:2007.08189 [stat].

Karvanen, Juha, Santtu Tikka, and Antti Hyttinen. 2021. Do-search: A Tool for Causal Inference and Study Design with Multiple Data Sources. *Epidemiology* 32 (1): 111–119 January.

Lesko, Catherine R., Ashley L. Buchanan, Daniel Westreich, Jessie K. Edwards, Michael G. Hudgens, and Stephen R. Cole. 2017. Generalizing Study Results: A Potential Outcomes Perspective. *Epidemiology (Cambridge, Mass.)* 28 (4): 553–561.

Charles, F. 2020. Manski. Toward Credible Patient-centered Meta-analysis. *Epidemiology* 31 (3): 345–352.

Mehrotra, Megha L., Maya L. Petersen, and Elvin H. Geng. 2019. Understanding HIV Program Effects: A Structural Approach to Context Using the Transportability Framework. *JAIDS Journal of Acquired Immune Deficiency Syndromes* 82 (3): S199–S205.

Pearl, Judea. 2015. Generalizing Experimental Findings. *Journal of Causal Inference* 3 (2): 259–266. Publisher: De Gruyter.

Westreich, Daniel. 2020. *Epidemiology by Design: A Causal Approach to the Health Sciences*. New York, NY: Oxford University Press.

Westreich, Daniel, Jessie K. Edwards, Catherine R. Lesko, Stephen R. Cole, and Elizabeth A. Stuart. 2019. Target Validity and the Hierarchy of Study Designs. *American Journal of Epidemiology* 188 (2): 438–443.

Williams, Donald Ray, Philippe Rast, and Paul Christian Bürkner. 2018. Bayesian Meta-Analysis with Weakly Informative Prior Distributions. PsyArXiv.

Yusuf, Salim, Richard Peto, John Lewis, Rory Collins, and Peter Sleight. 1985. Beta Blockade During and After Myocardial Infarction: An Overview of the Randomized Trials. *Progress in Cardiovascular Diseases* 27 (5): 335–371.